ILLUSTRATED COURSE GUIDES

Problem Solving and Decision Making

THIRD EDITION

Jeff Butterfield

CENGAGE

Australia • Brazil • Mexico • Singapore • United Kingdom • United States

CENGAGE

***Problem Solving and Decision Making,* 3rd Edition: Illustrated Course Guides**
Jeff Butterfield

Product Director: Kathleen McMahon

Associate Product Manager: Reed Curry

Associate Content Developer: Maria Garguilo

Marketing Director: Michele McTighe

Marketing Manager: Jeff Tousignant

Marketing Coordinator: Cassie Cloutier

Contributing Author: Lisa Ruffolo

Developmental Editor: Lisa Ruffolo

Content Project Manager: Jen Feltri-George

IP Analyst: Amber Hill

Senior IP Project Manager: Kathy Kucharek

Proofreader: Brandy Lilly

Indexer: Elizabeth Cunningham

Print Buyer: Fola Orekoya

Composition: Lumina Datamatics Inc.

Art Director: Diana Graham

Cover Template Designer: Lisa Kuhn, Curio Press, LLC www.curiopress.com

Text Designer: GEX Publishing Services

Library of Congress Control Number: 2016938485

ISBN-13: 978-1-337-11925-2
ISBN-10: 1-337-11925-3

Cengage
20 Channel Street
Boston, MA 02210
USA

Cengage is a leading provider of customized learning solutions with employees residing in nearly 40 different countries and sales in more than 125 countries around the world. Find your local representative at: **www.cengage.com.**

Cengage products are represented in Canada by Nelson Education, Ltd.

To learn more about Cengage platforms and services, register or access your online learning solution, or purchase materials for your course, visit **www.cengage.com.**

Printed at CLDPC, USA, 09-25

About the Series

Students work hard to earn certificates and degrees to prepare for a particular career—but do they have the soft skills necessary to succeed in today's digital workplace? Can they communicate effectively? Present themselves professionally? Work in a team? Industry leaders agree there is a growing need for these essential soft skills; in fact, they are critical to a student's success in the workplace. Without them, students will struggle and even fail. However, students entering the workforce who can demonstrate strong soft skills have a huge competitive advantage.

The *Illustrated Course Guides—Soft Skills for a Digital Workplace* series is designed to help you teach these important skills, better preparing your students to enter a competitive marketplace. Here are some of the key elements you will find in each book in the series:

- **Focused content allows for flexibility:** Each book in the series is short and focused, covering only the most essential skills related to the topic. You can use the modular content in standalone courses or workshops or you can integrate it into existing courses.
- **Visual design keeps students engaged:** Our unique pedagogical design presents each skill on two facing pages, with key concepts and instructions on the left and illustrations on the right. This keeps students of all levels on track.
- **Varied activities put skills to the test:** Each book includes hands-on activities, team exercises, critical thinking questions, and scenario-based activities to allow students to put their skills to work and demonstrate their retention of the material.

Read the Preface for more details on the key pedagogical elements and features of this book. We hope the books in this series help your students gain the critical soft skills they need to succeed in whatever career they choose.

Advisory Board

We thank our Advisory Board who gave us their opinions and guided our decisions for the third editions. They are as follows:

Paulette Gannett – SUNY – Broome Community College
Sherry Sparrowk – Peninsula College
Audrey Styer – Morton College
Charlene West – Durham Technical Community College

Preface

Welcome to *Problem Solving and Decision Making, Second Edition: Illustrated Course Guides*. If this is your first experience with the Illustrated Course Guides, you'll see that this book has a unique design: each skill is presented on two facing pages, with Essential Elements on the left and illustrations and examples pictured on the right. The layout makes it easy to learn a skill without having to read a lot of text and flip pages to see an illustration. The design also makes this a great reference after the course is over! See the illustration on the right to learn more about the pedagogical and design elements of a typical chapter.

Focused on the Essentials

Each two-page lesson presents only the most important information about the featured skill. The left page of the lesson presents about five key Essential Elements, which are the most important guidelines that a student needs to know about the skill. Absorbing and retaining a limited number of key ideas makes it more likely that students will retain and apply the skill in a real-life situation.

Hands-On Activities

Every Essential Elements lesson contains a You Try It exercise, where students demonstrate their understanding of the lesson skill by completing a task that relates to it. The steps in the You Try It exercises are often general, requiring that students use critical thinking to complete the task.

Real World Advice and Examples

To help put lesson skills in context, many lessons contain yellow shaded boxes that present real-world stories pulled from today's workplace. Some lessons also contain Do's and Don'ts tables, featuring key guidelines on what to do and not do in certain workplace situations relating to the lesson skill. The Technology @ Work lesson at the end of every part covers Web 2.0 tools and other technologies relating to the part.

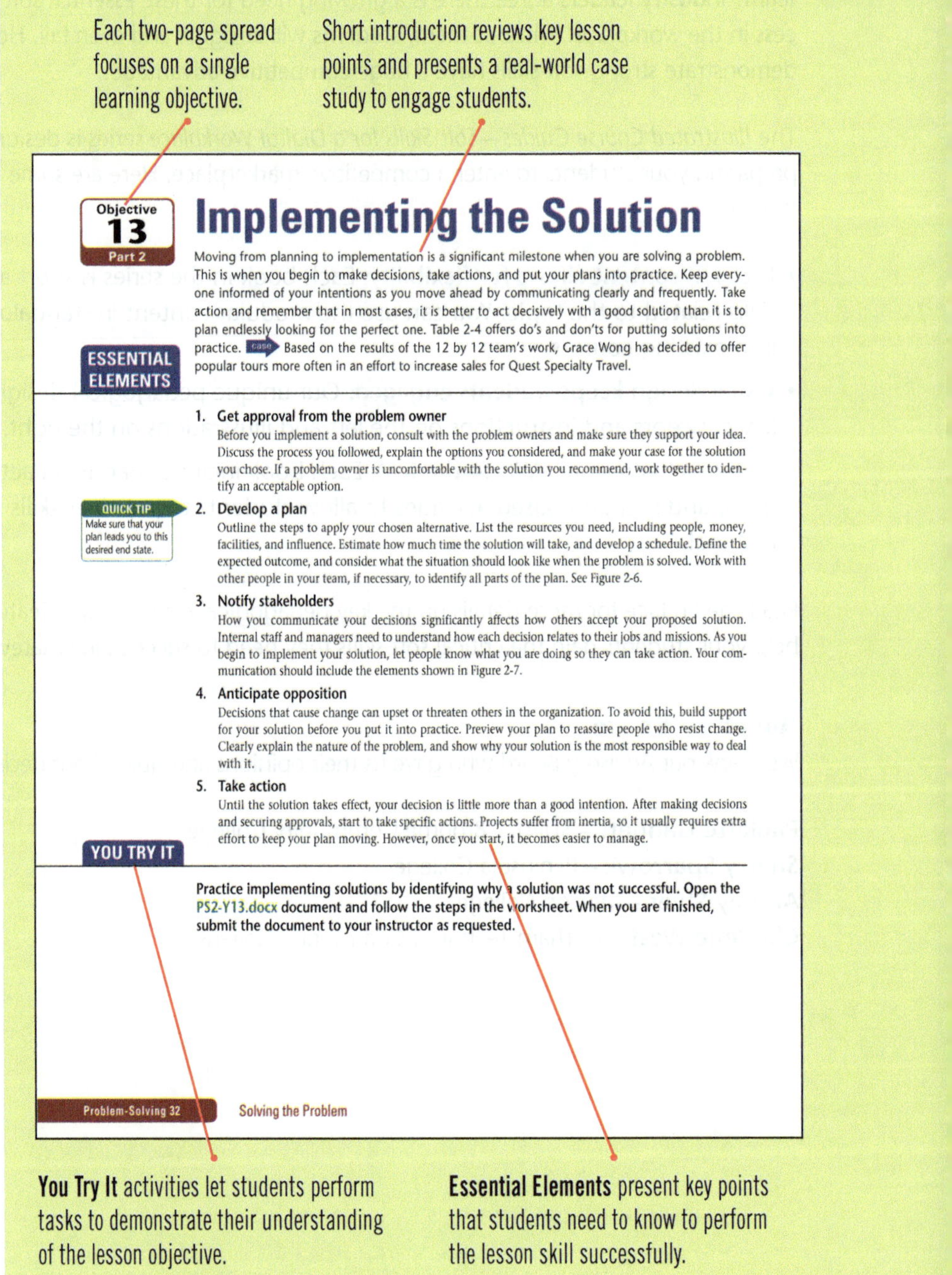

Every lesson features large illustrations of examples discussed in the lesson.

FIGURE 2-6: Develop a plan

FIGURE 2-7: Communicate with stakeholders

Topics to discuss with stakeholders:
What the decision is
How the solution will be put into place
How it will be monitored and evaluated
How changes will be decided on and made

TABLE 2-4: Implementing the solution do's and don'ts

guidelines	do	don't
Communicate with others	• Involve the problem owner in the decision • Describe the steps you followed to make a decision • Communicate clearly and frequently • Notify staff and managers	• **Don't** go forward with the solution if the problem owner is uncomfortable • **Don't** withhold information in the hopes of having everyone agree
Develop a plan	• Outline the steps to take to put the solution into place • Identify the resources you need • Draft a realistic schedule • Reconsider your goals	• **Don't** underestimate the amount of time you need to complete each step of the plan • **Don't** move forward if your plan doesn't meet your goals
Anticipate opposition	• Build support for your solution • Continue to communicate about your plans and progress	• **Don't** ignore the opposition • **Don't** block out opposing points of view, but don't abandon the solution either
Take action	Start following your plan soon after making a decision	**Don't** let inaction end your efforts to solve the problem

Unintended consequences: when solving one problem spurs new ones

Anyone with an e-mail account has been frustrated by spam—junk e-mail sent out in bulk to clog your inbox with advertisements for often phony or fraudulent products. Recently, the flood of spam slowed to a trickle when a group of servers in San Jose, California, were disconnected from the Internet. These servers were considered the source of 40 percent of the world's spam. Shortly after that, the antivirus developer McAfee reported that botnets had taken control of about 12 million new IP addresses, or Internet accounts. A *botnet* refers to a collection of software robots, or bots, that run independently on computers without revealing themselves to the owner. They take advantage of computing resources and often gather e-mail addresses for spamming. What triggered the dramatic increase in bots? McAfee researchers concluded they were a response to the server shutdown in San Jose. The new bots were patrolling for new e-mail addresses, which will eventually lead to new floods of spam. "The question is not whether spam will return to previous levels," the McAfee report said, "but rather when it will return."

This is an example of the law of unintended consequences, a truism maintaining that any purposeful activity produces some unintended consequences. The classic example is of a road bypass built to relieve traffic congestion but results in two busy streets instead of one. As you consider solutions, keep in mind that at least one of them is likely to produce an unintended side effect.

Source: Freakonomics, "The Unintended Consequences of Attacking Spam," *The New York Times*, May 6, 2009.

Problem-Solving and Decision Making

Solving the Problem   Problem-Solving 33

Do's & Don'ts tables present key tips for what to do and not do.

News to Use boxes provide real-world stories related to the lesson topic.

Lessons and Exercises

This book is divided into five parts, with each part containing about eight 2-page lessons, or learning objectives. The lessons use Quest Specialty Travel, a fictional adventure travel company, as the case study. The assignments on the peach pages at the end of each part increase in difficulty. Data files and case studies provide a variety of interesting and relevant business applications. Assignments include:

- **Soft Skills Reviews** provide multiple choice questions that test students' understanding of the part material.
- **Critical Thinking Questions** pose topics for discussion that require analysis and evaluation. Many also challenge students to consider and react to realistic critical thinking and application of the part skills.
- **Independent Challenges** are case projects requiring critical thinking and application of the part skills.
- **Real Life Independent Challenges** are practical exercises where students can apply the skills they learned in an activity that will help their own lives. For instance, they might create a resume, write a letter to a potential employer, or role play for a job interview for their dream position.
- **Team Challenges** are practical projects that require working together in a team to solve a problem.
- **Be the Critic Exercises** are activities that require students to evaluate a flawed example and provide ideas for improving it.

Contents

Preface iv

Problem Solving and Decision Making

Part 1: Identifying and Defining Problems .... Problem-Solving 1

1: Understanding Problem Solving .... Problem-Solving 2
2: Analyzing Problems .... Problem-Solving 4
3: Working with Problem Owners and Stakeholders .... Problem-Solving 6
4: Developing Effective Problem Statements .... Problem-Solving 8
5: Determining Causes .... Problem-Solving 10
6: Simplifying Complex Problems .... Problem-Solving 12
Innovative ways to solve problems: open source science
7: Identifying and Managing Risks .... Problem-Solving 14
Crisis management
8: Avoiding Problem-Solving Traps .... Problem-Solving 16
Technology @ Work: Crowdsourcing .... Problem-Solving 18
Practice .... Problem-Solving 20

Part 2: Solving the Problem .... Problem-Solving 25

9: Gathering and Analyzing Data .... Problem-Solving 26
10: Developing Alternatives .... Problem-Solving 28
11: Evaluating Options .... Problem-Solving 30
12: Implementing the Solution .... Problem-Solving 32
Unintended consequences: when solving one problem spurs new ones
13: Monitoring and Managing the Solution .... Problem-Solving 34
14: Verifying the Solution .... Problem-Solving 36
15: Using Adaptive Techniques .... Problem-Solving 38
Solving problems in a blink
16: Developing Ethical Solutions .... Problem-Solving 40
Technology @ Work: Mashups .... Problem-Solving 42
Practice .... Problem-Solving 44

Part 3: Thinking Critically .... Problem-Solving 49

17: Understanding Critical Thinking .... Problem-Solving 50
18: Identifying Arguments .... Problem-Solving 52
19: Assessing the Credibility of an Argument .... Problem-Solving 54
20: Exploring Weaknesses in an Argument .... Problem-Solving 56
21: Overcoming Obstacles to Critical Thinking .... Problem-Solving 58
Critical thinking and feeling
22: Avoiding Deductive Reasoning Fallacies .... Problem-Solving 60

23: Avoiding Inductive Reasoning Fallacies ....Problem-Solving 62
24: Becoming a Critical Thinker ....Problem-Solving 64
Guesstimating is critical thinking
Technology @ Work: Electronic Books....................Problem-Solving 66
Practice ....Problem-Solving 68

Part 4: Group Decision Making and Problem Solving ....Problem-Solving 73
25: Understanding Group Dynamics....................Problem-Solving 74
Star power or team effectiveness?
26: Evolving from a Group to a Team....................Problem-Solving 76
Consensus decisions and groupthink
27: Using Divergent Thinking ....Problem-Solving 78
Mind mapping software
28: Using Convergent Thinking ....Problem-Solving 80
29: Reaching Closure....................Problem-Solving 82
30: Avoiding Common Group Traps ....Problem-Solving 84
31: Working with Large Groups....................Problem-Solving 86
32: Building Sustainable Agreements....................Problem-Solving 88
Technology @ Work: Online Scheduling Tools....................Problem-Solving 90
Practice ....Problem-Solving 92

Part 5: Decision Support Tools ....Problem-Solving 97
33: Understanding Decision Support Systems....................Problem-Solving 98
34: Modeling Decisions Quantitatively ....Problem-Solving 100
35: Describing Data Objectively ....Problem-Solving 102
36: Working with Formulas and Functions ....Problem-Solving 104
37: Performing What-If Analyses....................Problem-Solving 106
38: Weighing Factors....................Problem-Solving 108
39: Creating Decision Trees ....Problem-Solving 110
The art of information graphics
40: Using Graphics to Display Data....................Problem-Solving 112
Technology @ Work: Spreadsheet Tools....................Problem-Solving 114
Practice ....Problem-Solving 116

Glossary....................1

Index 3

Instructor Resources

The Instructor Resources provide instructors with a wide range of tools that enhance teaching and learning. These resources and more can be accessed from the instructor companion site. Log in at www.cengage.com/SSO.

- **Instructor's Manual**—The Instructor's Manual is a valuable teaching tool for your course. It includes detailed lecture topics with teaching tips for each part.

- **Sample Syllabus**—Prepare and customize your course easily using this sample course outline.

- **PowerPoint Presentations**—Each part has a corresponding PowerPoint presentation that you can use in lecture, distribute to your students, or customize to suit your course.

- **Figure Files**—The figures in the text are provided on the Instructor companion site to help you illustrate key topics or concepts. You can create traditional overhead transparencies by printing the figure files. Or you can create electronic slide shows by using the figures in a presentation program such as PowerPoint.

- **Solutions to Exercises**—Solutions to Exercises contains every file students are asked to create or modify in the lessons and end-of-part material. This section also includes a solutions to the Soft Skills Reviews and Independent Challenges.

- **Data Files for Students**—To complete most of the exercises in this book, your students will need Data Files. You can post the Data Files on a file server for students to copy. The Data Files can be downloaded from www.cengage.com/SSO.

- **Test Banks**—Cengage Learning Testing powered by Cognero is a flexible, online system that allows instructors to author, edit, and manage test bank content from multiple Cengage Learning solutions and to create multiple versions. It works on any operating system or browser with no special installs or downloads needed, so tests can be created from anywhere with Internet access.

Part 1

Identifying and Defining Problems

Files You Will Need:

- PS1-Y2.docx
- PS1-Y3.docx
- PS1-Y4.docx
- PS1-Y5.docx
- PS1-Y6.docx
- PS1-Y7.docx
- PS1-Y8.docx
- PS1-TechWork.docx
- PS1-IC1.docx
- PS1-IC2.docx

Whether you are working in a large or small company, training to rejoin the workforce, or preparing to start a career, you spend most of your productive hours solving problems. Although problems can cause frustration and substantial difficulties, creative thinkers and successful professionals learn to view them as opportunities for improving a business, service, or task because they compel you to recognize and confirm your goals. This part outlines the process of solving problems, discusses how to analyze problems and their causes, and identifies common problem-solving pitfalls. case You are working at Quest Specialty Travel as an assistant to Grace Wong, the vice president of finance. Tour sales at Quest have not increased in many months, even during the height of the summer travel season. Grace is in charge of a new project at Quest called 12 by 12 that is looking for a solution to this problem. The goals of the project are to increase sales by 12 percent. As an assistant, you are helping her identify problems customers have with Quest tours and with traveling overall. Grace asks you to learn more about creative thinking and problem solving to contribute productively to the 12 by 12 project.

OBJECTIVES

1. Understand problem solving
2. Analyze problems
3. Work with problem owners and stakeholders
4. Develop effective problem statements
5. Determine causes
6. Simplify complex problems
7. Identify and manage risks
8. Avoid problem-solving traps

Objective 1 Part 1

Understanding Problem Solving

A professional in any occupation is, or should be, a problem solver. Not everyone begins a career as an effective problem solver, but you can learn and develop the skill of solving problems over time. People who can identify, define, and solve problems are valued members of an organization. Developing this ability will contribute to the success of your career as you seek positions with greater responsibility. Table 1-1 compares the do's and don'ts of effective problem solving. case To prepare for an upcoming 12 by 12 project meeting to discuss goals and assign tasks, Grace asks you to develop a list of problem-solving guidelines.

DETAILS

Consider the following guidelines as you begin solving problems:

- **Identify yourself as a problem solver**
  Whether you are a professional who works as a member of staff or management, much of what you do every day is solve problems and make decisions. In fact, the role of problem solver is one that distinguishes the professional from the line worker. Recent college graduates and others who are new to the workforce often solve problems by reacting to them. However, you are more effective if you learn and use an organized approach to problem solving.

QUICK TIP
Variations on problems include dilemmas, paradoxes, and difficulties, such as trouble performing tasks.

- **Recognize problems**
  Learn to recognize problems so that you see them developing and can act quickly to solve them. A dictionary defines a problem as an unsettled question or the source of distress or difficulty. In an organization, a **problem** is an obstacle that stands in the way of achieving a desired goal. In short, a problem is the difference between the current state and where you want to be. For example, if you expect to sell 100 tours each month, but are only selling 50, then you have a problem. See Figure 1-1.

QUICK TIP
No single or simple set of steps solves every type of problem. Most solutions involve creative thinking and logical exploration.

- **Select an intuitive approach for solving problems**
  People usually solve problems in one of two ways: intuitively or systematically. **Intuition** is your knowledge of something without having to discover or learn it, and it is typically your first reaction to a problem or question. When you solve a problem intuitively, you react immediately and instinctively, without following a particular procedure. This reactive approach is well suited to situations where you need to make a quick decision or solve a routine problem. In those cases, you can often use your common sense to decide on a solution. For example, if the problem is that customers often have to wait to receive brochures for the popular Hawaiian tour, you can solve the problem by printing additional brochures.

- **Select a systematic approach for solving problems**
  When you are **systematic**, you solve a problem in a methodical and organized manner. Systematic problem solving takes a reasoned, rational approach and is appropriate for larger, more complicated problems or situations that involve a lot of risk. One systematic problem-solving method is to adapt a solution from a prior problem and apply it to your current situation. For example, one way to begin solving the problem of declining sales at Quest Specialty Travel is to examine advertising campaigns that increased sales in the past. Figure 1-2 lists the basic problem-solving steps.

- **Make decisions**
  A major part of problem solving involves making effective decisions. **Decisions** are choices you make when faced with a set of options or alternatives. You can also think of decisions as tiny problems you need to solve, and then apply problem-solving techniques to guide your choices. As you improve your problem-solving skills, you will naturally develop your decision-making ability as well.

FIGURE 1-1: Defining a problem

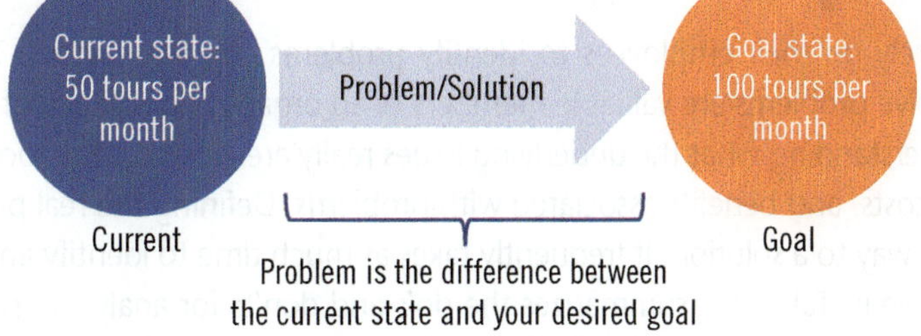

FIGURE 1-2: Basic problem-solving steps

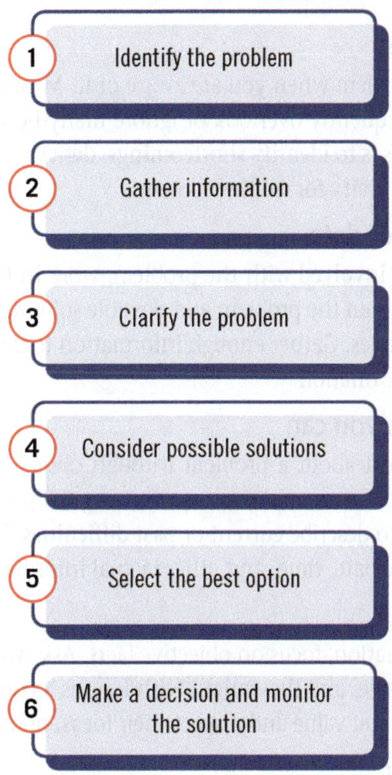

TABLE 1-1: Problem solving do's and don'ts

guideline	do	don't
Identify yourself as a problem solver	• Feel confident you can solve the problem	• Don't give up easily if one idea does not work
Recognize problems	• Consider problems as opportunities to find innovative solutions • Define and then redefine the problem	• Don't ignore problems until they are too big to solve easily • Don't stick to your original conception of the problem if you are having trouble finding a solution
Select an approach	• Use your intuition for simple problems • Follow a systematic process for complex problems • Review and reconsider the problem, your goals, and possible solutions • Consider the problem from different perspectives	• Don't create a detailed procedure that is difficult to complete or duplicate • Don't jump to conclusions
Make decisions	• Consider all the alternatives before selecting one • Trust your intuition, but make sure the facts support your decision	• Don't make rash decisions • Don't second guess yourself if you feel you made the right choice

Objective 2
Part 1

Analyzing Problems

Companies rely on their employees to identify problems and solve them. That is why people who can effectively solve problems are valuable members of an organization. Much of the effort in problem solving involves understanding what the underlying issues really are. Look for the root causes, related information, ideas, risks, costs, and benefits associated with problems. Defining the real problem is the first major milestone on the way to a solution. It frequently takes as much time to identify and understand the problem as it does to solve it. Table 1-2 summarizes the do's and don'ts for analyzing problems. case Grace Wong asks you to determine whether the decline in Quest sales is part of a trend for the entire travel industry or if it is unique to Quest Specialty Travel.

ESSENTIAL ELEMENTS

QUICK TIP
Inertia means not acting, being so familiar with a problem that it doesn't occur to you to solve it.

1. **Look for deficiencies**

   A problem is only a problem when you are aware of it. Most organizations have a constant stream of difficulties, though they frequently overlook or ignore many because of time and inertia. The first step in the problem-solving process is to identify shortcomings, deficiencies, or dissatisfactions. Be observant, ask questions, and develop sensitivity for subtle problems.

2. **Interview and gather data**

   Talk to people who are involved with the problem, work in the area, or may be affected by your solution. Learn all that you can about the problem and possible solutions. The best insights often come from the least obvious people and sources. Gather enough information to develop a representative sample. Figure 1-3 outlines ways to gather information.

QUICK TIP
As you observe and discover information, you might have to redefine the problem.

3. **Observe as much as you can**

   You often learn the most about a problem through observation. You can observe a problem directly by watching an interaction, for example, or experiencing the problem yourself. You can also rely on the direct observations of others to describe current or past difficulties. When you use observed data, be sure to document details such as the date, time, and other factual information about the observation and the problem.

4. **Ask what, not who**

   When gathering information, focus on objective facts. Ask "what?" not "who?". Investigating problems can make people apprehensive, and they might withdraw as a consequence. Assure everyone that you are seeking their help and that you value and respect their ideas, opinions, and suggestions.

5. **Have a reality check**

   When you identify a suspected problem, ask yourself if it makes sense in light of the data you've collected. Trust your instinct and wait to start solving the problem until you are comfortable with your conclusion. If you are not satisfied, take more time to redefine the problem. Ask other people for opinions and advice.

YOU TRY IT

Practice analyzing problems by listing the steps you would take to analyze a problem. Open the PS1-Y2.docx document and follow the steps in the worksheet. When you are finished, submit the document to your instructor as requested.

FIGURE 1-3: Gathering information

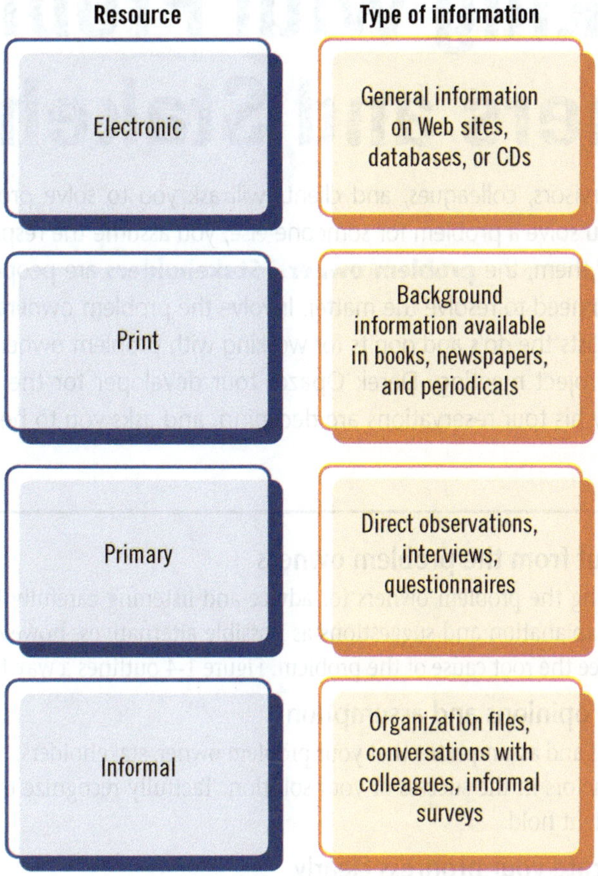

TABLE 1-2: Analyzing problems do's and don'ts

guideline	do	don't
Identification	• Look for possible deficiencies, shortcomings, and other types of problems • Ask questions of people involved to find out why goals are not met • Gather data from other sources	• Don't overlook or ignore possible problems • Don't limit yourself to a single type of information
Observation	• Observe where and how the problem occurs, if possible • Ask "what," not "who" • Assure people that you respect their ideas, opinions, and suggestions	• Don't intimidate people involved with the problem; ask for their cooperation • Don't threaten others so that they undermine the solution
Confirmation	• Review the data you gathered to confirm that you've correctly identified a problem	• Don't start solving the problem unless you are confident you identified it thoroughly

Objective 3 Part 1

Working with Problem Owners and Stakeholders

Managers, supervisors, colleagues, and clients will ask you to solve problems for them throughout your career. When you solve a problem for someone else, you assume the responsibility for developing a satisfactory solution for them, the **problem owners**. **Stakeholders** are people who are also affected or whose involvement you need to resolve the matter. Involve the problem owners and stakeholders as you begin to work. Table 1-3 lists the do's and don'ts for working with problem owners and stakeholders. case During the 12 by 12 project meeting, Derek Opazo, tour developer for the Americas, says that he does not understand why his tour reservations are declining, and asks you to help him find a way to increase the reservations.

ESSENTIAL ELEMENTS

> **QUICK TIP**
> Be sure to ask problem owners to suggest possible solutions.

1. **Solicit input from the problem owners**
   Start by asking the problem owners for advice and listening carefully to the explanation of the problem. Treat their explanation and suggestions as possible alternatives, however, because the problem owners do not always see the root cause of the problem. Figure 1-4 outlines a way to solve a problem for someone else.

2. **Recognize opinions and assumptions**
   The opinions and assumptions that your problem owner, stakeholders, and other important people hold are important factors in the success of your solution. Tactfully recognize the biases, agendas, and motivations that each might hold.

> **QUICK TIP**
> Document conversations with follow up e-mails to create a record of your communication.

3. **Communicate your progress clearly**
   Communicate regularly with problem owners and stakeholders. Use e-mail, memos, and other documents to create a log of your conversations, ideas, alternatives, and solutions. Frequent, though not overwhelming, communication avoids surprising a problem owner or stakeholder.

4. **Do your homework carefully**
   Establish the credibility of your work by pursuing each step systematically. Demonstrate that you have worked through the problem in a methodical and thorough manner. Be objective in your communication, both written and oral, and make sure the problem owner is confident about your approach.

5. **Provide choices**
   Selecting one choice from many increases a sense of ownership, so present problem owners with options and ask them to select one or two. Recommend the best solution along with one or two other alternatives. Explain the pros and cons for each and let the problem owner make a final decision.

> **QUICK TIP**
> Give the problem owner a final report to create a sense of closure.

6. **Promote your solution**
   After solving a problem effectively, promote your efforts and results to the problem owners and stakeholders with a persuasive report or powerful presentation. See Figure 1-5. The size and format will vary depending on the size and importance of the problem.

YOU TRY IT

Practice working with problem owners and stakeholders by reorganizing a conversation. Open the PS1-Y3.docx document and follow the steps in the worksheet. When you are finished, submit the document to your instructor as requested.

FIGURE 1-4: Solving a problem for someone else

1. Ask for advice
"Why do you think the reservations have declined, Derek?"

2. Recognize opinions
Opinion: "People are afraid to travel to Central America."
Fact: "Reservations for tours in Central America declined by 25% this year."

3. Communicate progress
"Derek, I created the attached chart to compare reservations for Central American tours in the last 12 months. Let's talk about this today."

4. Give choices
"One thing we could do is cancel the Yucatan trip and concentrate on the profitable Caribbean tours. What do you think?"

5. Do your homework
"I reviewed the customer surveys and found some interesting suggestions."

6. Promote your solution
"I summarized my solution to the problem in a presentation I'll give to the team this afternoon."

FIGURE 1-5: Promote your solution

mangostock/Photos.com

TABLE 1-3: Working with problem owners do's and don'ts

guideline	do	don't
Initial discussion	• Discuss the problem with the stakeholder • Ask questions to define the problem • Ask for suggested solutions • Make sure you include all the details • See the problem from the stakeholder's perspective • Separate opinions from facts	• **Don't** accept the stakeholder's solution as the only one • **Don't** confuse the stakeholder's opinion with substantiated facts
Progress	• Communicate the progress you make toward solving the problem • Use e-mail and memos to document your progress • Recommend an ideal solution and one or two alternatives • Demonstrate why you suggest one solution over another	• **Don't** overwhelm others with communication • **Don't** surprise the stakeholder by trying a solution without their participation or approval • **Don't** present only one possible solution • **Don't** fail to do your homework
Solution	• Promote effective solutions • Present the solution in a report or presentation	• **Don't** overpromote yourself, but don't let the credit for the solution go to someone else either

Objective 4 Part 1

Developing Effective Problem Statements

As you solve problems, communicate clearly and succinctly about what you are doing and the progress you are making. Start by providing a statement of the problem. A **problem statement** is a clear, concise description of the problem and the effect you expect from the solution. Its purpose is to describe a single problem objectively, not to find a cause, assign blame, or define the solution. Include the problem statement in your proposals, progress reports, and discussions with stakeholders. Table 1-4 outlines the do's and don'ts of developing a problem statement. case After gathering data about the problem of Quest's declining tour sales, you are ready to summarize your understanding of the problem in a problem statement you include in a progress report for Grace Wong.

ESSENTIAL ELEMENTS

1. **Describe the ideal situation**
   Frame the problem for your audience by starting with a brief description of the ideal situation. A problem represents a deviation from the norm. By describing the desired state, you help others understand the current situation. Use terms and comparisons that your audience considers important. See Figure 1-6.
2. **Briefly summarize the problem**
   Contrast the ideal situation with the current state. Identify the condition that is preventing the goal, outcome, or state from being achieved.

> **QUICK TIP**
> Describe objective symptoms of the problem that others can observe.

3. **Identify symptoms of the problem**
   Let your audience know where the problem is manifesting itself. Describe the symptoms of the problem that others can see or detect so they understand the problem you are working on.

> **QUICK TIP**
> Use numbers and other specific, concrete details to describe the problem.

4. **Describe the size and scope of the problem**
   Stakeholders and other interested people will try to assess how significant the problem is. Help them to do this by providing information about the size and scope of the matter. See Figure 1-7.
5. **Identify the consequences**
   Use specific detail to describe how the problem affects your audience and the organization. Identify any direct and indirect costs associated with the problem. Emphasize the benefits of your work by outlining the consequences of a solution.
6. **Explain any other research or investigation that you may pursue**
   Your problem statement is likely to be a work in process. If you are still collecting data, interviewing affected parties, or developing alternative solutions, let your audience know. Your understanding of the problem may change as new information becomes available.

YOU TRY IT

Practice developing effective problem statements by writing a problem statement. Open the PS1-Y4.docx document and follow the steps in the worksheet. When you are finished, submit the document to your instructor as requested.

FIGURE 1-6: Parts of a problem statement

Ideal situation:
Based on previous years, tour sales overall should be steady, with an increase in trips to adventure travel destinations.

Problem summary:
Customers report that fears about the economy, airline service, and security are preventing them from traveling.

Symptom:
Tour sales in all areas have decreased by 8 percent, with no increase in adventure travel.

Size and scope:
Even our most popular European tours show no increase in enrollment, despite heavy promotion.

Consequences:
Plans to add tours, develop our Web site, and expand staff are now on hold until we can solve this problem.

Research:
Fifty percent of travel companies reported significant loss of revenue last year.

FIGURE 1-7: Describe the size and scope of the problem

Marcus Clackson/Photos.com

TABLE 1-4: Problem statement do's and don'ts

guideline	do	don't
Purpose	• Describe a single problem • Use objective measures	• Don't address more than one problem • Don't identify causes • Don't assign blame • Don't describe the solution
Audience	• Provide the problem statement to the person who is supervising or approving your problem-solving activities • Involve others who are helping to solve the problem	• Don't give the problem statement to everyone in the organization
Content	• Identify the ideal situation from the point of view of your audience • Describe the condition that prevents the ideal situation • Identify symptoms • Describe the size and scope of the problem objectively • Identify consequences	• Don't list every condition or symptom; focus on the most important ones • Don't offer opinions about possible consequences

Objective 5 Part 1

Determining Causes

ESSENTIAL ELEMENTS

A common tendency is to overlook the root cause of problems and focus on the symptoms. Complex situations usually involve interrelated problems, each with a different cause. To link a problem to its cause, you must perform a **root-cause analysis**, a study that determines the real basis for the problem. Because many problems demand more than a one-time solution, root-cause analysis is often part of a continuous improvement effort. Table 1-5 lists the do's and don'ts for determining causes. case After defining the problem of declining sales at Quest Specialty Travel, you are ready to determine possible causes.

QUICK TIP
Because symptoms are usually easy to identify; it is tempting to pursue them instead of causes.

1. **Differentiate between symptoms and causes**

   A **symptom** is evidence of a change, such as a decrease in revenue. A **cause** is the reason for or the origin (root) of a change, such as customers being unable to afford travel vacations. You can usually determine if something is a symptom by asking whether it is being caused by, or due to something else. If the answer is "yes," then it is a symptom. A "no" means it is more likely to be a root cause.

2. **Look for more than one cause**

   Organizational problems rarely have a single cause. Many factors typically contribute to complicated issues, and some are easier to identify than others. Find the most significant causes of the problem and work on those first. For example, the most obvious cause of Quest's problems might be the rising cost of airfare and ground transportation. However, additional research might reveal that people are also concerned about weather issues after a series of well-publicized hurricanes. Identify the major issues so you can develop appropriate solutions.

QUICK TIP
Often, the minor factors become less trouble when the major causes are remedied.

3. **Consider the cost**

   Although you should identify the basis of a problem before solving it, attacking the root causes is not always the best approach. Sometimes the costs of fixing the problem are higher than treating the symptoms. For example, Quest developed a tour to Asia without local guides to reduce the price of the tour. Customer satisfaction on the tour is very low, and not including guides is the main cause of the problem. However, it is now prohibitively expensive to find, train, and hire local guides in Asia. In such cases, treating the symptom (reducing the tour cost even further to increase customer satisfaction might be the best solution.

4. **Use the 5 Whys technique**

   A popular approach used to uncover and define problems is called **5 Whys**. Popularized by Toyota in the 1970s, the 5 Whys involves looking at a problem and asking "why?" or "what was the cause of this situation?" at least five times. Challenge each answer with another "why" until you determine the root cause of the problem. Each answer should help further clarify the cause.

QUICK TIP
This is sometimes called a fishbone or Ishikawa diagram.

5. **Create a cause-and-effect diagram**

   Complicated problems typically grow out of many related issues. A popular way to visualize a complex problem is by creating a **cause-and-effect diagram**. See Figure 1-8. Write the main problem in a box, and then draw a horizontal line from the box across the page like the spine of a fish. Identify related factors that contribute to the problem by drawing lines from the spine and labeling each. Include as many factors as you can. Examine the drawing to determine the main causes of the problem.

YOU TRY IT

Practice determining causes by creating a list, table, or diagram. Open the PS1-Y5.docx document and follow the steps in the worksheet. When you are finished, submit the document to your instructor as requested.

FIGURE 1-8: Cause-and-effect diagram

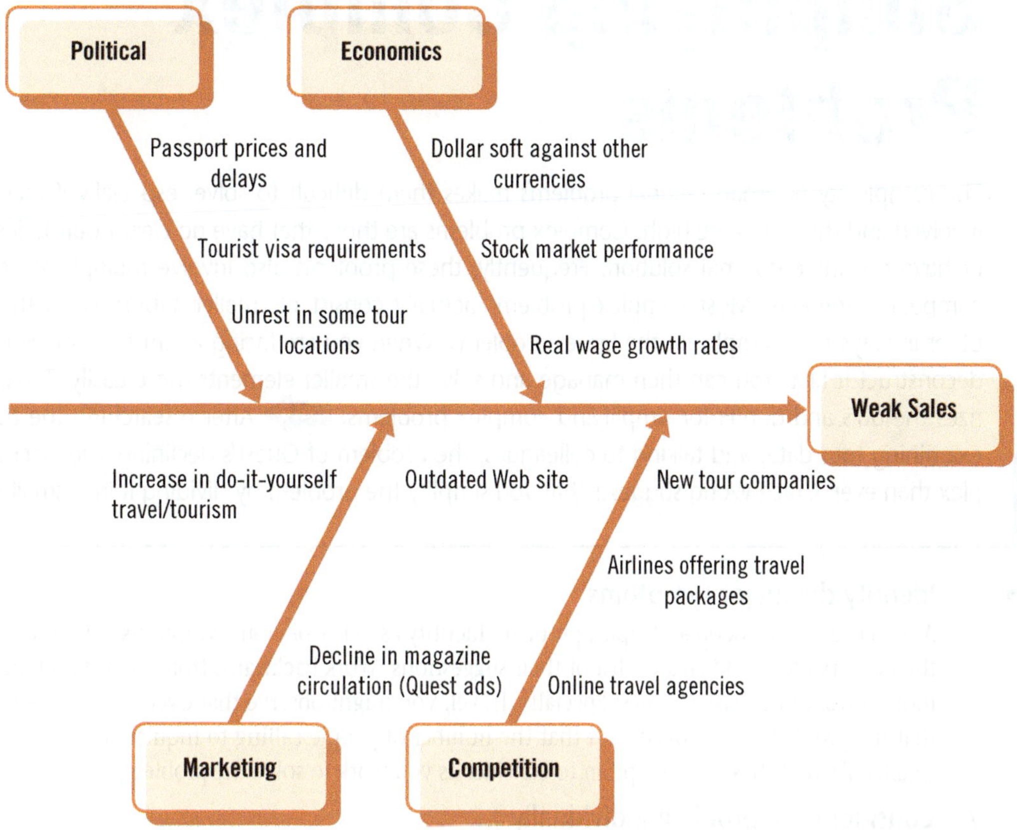

TABLE 1-5: Determining causes do's and don'ts

guideline	do	don't
Causes and symptoms	• Differentiate between causes and symptoms • Look for more than one cause • Find the most significant causes of the problem and work on those first	• Don't mistake evidence of a change (symptom) for the reason for the change (cause) • Don't limit yourself to one reason for the problem
Trade-offs	• Consider the pros and cons of attacking the root cause • Choose to treat the symptom if the trade-offs make that the best solution	• Don't try to solve every problem by addressing the root cause • Don't fix the problem if the costs are much higher than treating the symptoms
Techniques	• Use the 5 "Whys" approach to uncover and define problems • Create a cause-and-effect diagram to visualize a complex problem	• Don't be afraid to ask the same question more than once • Don't hesitate to redefine a problem • Don't discard a cause-and-effect diagram if it doesn't reveal the cause of a problem immediately

Objective 6 Part 1

Simplifying Complex Problems

The complexity of organizational problems makes them difficult to solve, especially if many people are involved and the stakes are high. Complex problems are those that have no clear boundaries, are unique, or have no single optimal solution. Frequently, these problems also involve multiple stakeholders with competing agendas. Most complex problems actually consist of smaller subproblems that affect each other in ways that complicate the larger problems. When you are facing an intricate or difficult problem, deconstruct it first. You can then manage and solve the smaller elements more easily. Table 1-6 summarizes the do's and don'ts for simplifying complex problems. case After researching the travel industry, examining tour data, and talking to colleagues, the problem of Quest's declining sales seems more complex than ever. Grace Wong suggests that you simplify the problem by dividing it into smaller parts.

ESSENTIAL ELEMENTS

QUICK TIP
In many cases, symptoms are the result of different problems.

1. **Identify the major symptoms**

   As you begin to work on a complex problem, identify as many obvious symptoms as you can. Ask others for their observations and create a list of their suggestions. Work backwards from each symptom to identify its root causes. In the case of Quest Specialty Travel, you might observe that overall bookings have decreased, that net profits have dropped, and that the number of people calling to inquire about future travel is also smaller. Each of these is a symptom to consider as you work to solve the problem.

2. **Consider each problem individually**

   Although they may be related, problems are often best resolved when considered independently. For each subproblem that you identify, find its root cause and apply a solution. However, don't disregard related subproblems. Determine how they are related and how changes to one might affect the others.

3. **Rank the subproblems**

   Consider how each subproblem contributes to the overall level of dissatisfaction. Ask yourself which is causing the most significant deviation from what you want or expect. Some subproblems might be perceived as more troublesome than others. Rank these from most to least important. Focus your efforts on solving the problems that will have the most effect. Figure 1-9 ranks the four subproblems for Quest Specialty Travel considering three criteria: tour value, whether changes can be made immediately, and customer satisfaction.

4. **Look for interdependencies**

   Subproblems are often tightly interrelated. Consider how the various issues affect one another, and look for interdependencies. Solving a seemingly small problem might also solve a larger one at the same time. Sometimes, the symptoms of one problem are the root cause of another.

QUICK TIP
Breaking down a large, complex problem into smaller, solvable problems is called divide and conquer.

5. **Delegate subproblems**

   You might not have the authority, ability, or resources to properly address each part of a complex problem, so identify others who can solve part of the problem for you. Delegating portions of the problem to people who can more effectively resolve them magnifies your efforts and contributes to your success.

YOU TRY IT

Practice simplifying complex problems by separating a problem into smaller parts. Open the PS1-Y6.docx document and follow the steps in the worksheet. When you are finished, submit the document to your instructor as requested.

FIGURE 1-9: Breaking a complex problem into smaller parts

Main problem: Decreasing tour sales

Criteria →	Tour Value	Immediate Improvement	Customer Satisfaction	Score
Price	0	2	1	3
Promotion	0	0	0	0
Quality	1	0	1	2
Frequency	2	1	2	5

Subproblems (rows: Price, Promotion, Quality, Frequency)

Ratings of how well each solution could solve the subproblem

Total of ratings for each subproblem

Offering tours more frequently makes the most difference in solving the main problem

TABLE 1-6: Complex problem do's and don'ts

guideline	do	don't
Symptoms	• Identify as many symptoms as possible	• **Don't** discard suggested symptoms from anyone
Main problems	• Break each large problem into smaller problems	• **Don't** disregard related problems and subproblems
Subproblems	• Rank the contributing problems • Focus on the problems that have the most effect • Discover how one problem is related to another • Divide tasks among a team	• **Don't** try to solve all the subproblems yourself • **Don't** overlook small problems—solving a small problem might solve a larger one at the same time

Innovative ways to solve problems: open source science

Imagine competing for substantial prizes by solving problems. That's what a 2008 report by the National Research Council recommended to the National Science Foundation (NSF), the federal agency overseeing physical science research. The report encourages the NSF to offer prizes of $200,000 to $2 million "to encourage more complex innovations" in problem solving. Taking this approach one step further is InnoCentive, a company that links organizations that have problems to people all over the world, who are called solvers. For example, InnoCentive circulated a problem the Oil Spill Recovery Institute of Cordova, Alaska, was having: how to keep oil in Alaska storage tanks from freezing. John Davis, a chemist in Bloomington, Illinois, applied his knowledge of concrete to oil—if you keep both vibrating, they stay in their liquid form—and received $20,000 for his solution. According to Dwayne Spradlin, president and chief executive, InnoCentive began as an in-house innovation "incubator" at the pharmaceutical company Eli Lilly. The company posted problems online that its employees could not solve. This problem-solving approach, often called open source science, has been successful from the start. "Most of our companies tell us they have a one-third or better solve rate on their problems and that is more cost-effective than anything they could have done internally," Spradlin said. Karim Lakhani, a professor at Harvard Business School who has studied InnoCentive, says much of the success is based on the idea that solutions can come from anywhere or anyone. Dr. Lakhani said, "The further the problem was from the solver's expertise, the more likely they were to solve it," often by applying knowledge or equipment developed for another purpose.

Source: Dean, Cornelia, "If You Have a Problem, Ask Everyone," *New York Times*, July 22, 2008.

Objective 7 Part 1

Identifying and Managing Risks

Any decision you make or solution you implement involves some **risk**, which is an exposure to a chance of loss or damage. Although the solution you develop might succeed or fail, you are risking time, money, and effort with each decision you make. Risk is an inevitable part of business, especially when you are introducing creative changes. With careful planning, you can often avoid many of these risks or reduce their drawbacks. If the potential risk is significant enough, you might need to take a different approach altogether (which is called risk avoidance). case One of the smaller problems you identified for Quest Specialty Travel involves tour frequency—customers would like to take popular tours more often. Grace Wong encourages you to identify the risks associated with this problem and solution before introducing it to managers at Quest.

ESSENTIAL ELEMENTS

1. Be aware of potential risks

As you consider alternatives and possible solutions, ask what might go wrong with each. What is the likelihood that a particular solution will succeed or fail? What would the costs be if a solution didn't work out? Would failure complicate the problem further, or could you easily try a different solution? Consider the answers to these questions when making decisions and assessing your options.

2. Assess your risk/reward ratio

While risks are a part of any decision you make, rewards are associated with successful problem solutions. Consider both outcomes. Avoid solutions that carry significant risk, but minimal reward. If your recommended solution does not solve the main problem, much of the cost will come at the expense of your credibility. Solutions that are low risk and high reward are ideal. See Figure 1-10.

3. Reduce your risk by testing

Testing a solution involves trying it on a small or limited basis. A well-designed test shows the strengths and weaknesses of an idea while limiting your exposure and expense. If the test is unsuccessful, you can try another alternative with minimal cost. When your tests are successful, they often give you insight into ways you can refine and improve your solution before you implement it on a wider scale. For example, Quest could reduce its tour costs by switching to a no-frills airline. However, your customers might react negatively to the change. You could test this solution by using a low-cost carrier for a few select tours and then carefully surveying your clients about their perceptions.

4. Develop a fall-back position or a backup plan

Sometimes even well-conceived ideas fail. What will you do in response? The point of failure is a poor time to begin considering alternatives. The greater the potential effect of your decision, the more important it is to have a backup plan in place.

5. Keep everyone informed

Being surprised by something going wrong is often worse than the drawback itself. Avoid surprising your supervisor, problem owner, and other stakeholders by something you do. Keep them informed and communicate your intentions and actions. See Figure 1-11. They can sometimes see a problem before it happens and provide you with an early warning. If something does go wrong, keeping them in the loop will help to reduce the damage.

QUICK TIP

Be sure to communicate your plans to others who may be affected or whose help you will need.

YOU TRY IT

Practice identifying and managing risks by ranking possible solutions to a problem. Open the PS1-Y7.docx document and follow the steps in the worksheet. When you are finished, submit the document to your instructor as requested.

FIGURE 1-10: Assessing risks and rewards

Option	Potential Reward	Potential Risk
A	High	High
B	Moderate	Low
C	Low	Moderate

Option A has the highest potential reward, but high risk

Option B might be the preferred alternative because of its risk/reward ratio

FIGURE 1-11: Keep everyone informed

Jacob Wackerhausen/Photos.com

TABLE 1-7: Problem risks do's and don'ts

element	do	don't
Risk	• Identify all risks before making a decision • Identify the costs of each risk • Recognize the potential rewards • Seek solutions that are low risk and high reward	• Don't disregard the consequences of taking a risk • Don't minimize the risk or the reward • Don't choose solutions that are high risk and low reward
Testing	• Try out a solution on a limited basis • Make sure a test reveals strengths and weaknesses • Communicate the results of the test to everyone involved	• Don't ignore unpopular or unwelcome test results • Don't forget to test your backup plan of a solution • Don't avoid communicating bad news

Crisis management

Some problems are bigger than others and can affect the well-being of an entire organization. These are true crises and demand thoughtful, ethical responses. The most famous example of successful crisis management is Johnson & Johnson, who in the 1980s responded swiftly and openly to an unprecedented crisis: seven people died after taking Tylenol, a Johnson & Johnson product, that had been deliberately contaminated with cyanide. In response, companies hired public-relations firms and installed crisis management teams to respond to events ranging from true crises to bad publicity. Responding only with spin, however, is not enough. According to Ian Mitroff, a crisis-management specialist at the University of Southern California, companies need to make formal crisis-management plans that identify a team of people who will respond to the crisis and provide an overall script. Although many organizations think crises are rare and unlikely to affect them, the Institute for Crisis Management found that only 25 percent of business crises are surprises. Most are "smoldering" problems that result from mistakes management makes. Decision makers ignore signs of trouble, especially in larger organizations, where it is easy to pass a problem on to someone else. Another factor is that events such as product tampering are unlikely to happen. Although the worst crises have a low probability, they usually have a high cost. Preparing for the worst can obviously help you avoid it.

Source: Surowiecki, James, "In Case of Emergency," *The New Yorker*, June 13, 2005.

Objective 8 Part 1

Avoiding Problem-Solving Traps

Solving problems demands both logical and creative thinking, a willingness to redefine goals, and an acceptance of solutions that manage rather than eliminate problems. If you are like most problem solvers, your ability to think clearly, logically, and rationally is sometimes clouded by habits, unacknowledged biases, and other common traps that people trip on when solving complicated problems. Table 1-8 lists the do's and don'ts of problem-solving traps. case You are ready to recommend a solution for Quest—that they increase the quality and range of their adventure travel tours. As you discuss your ideas with Grace Wong, she cautions you to avoid common problem-solving traps.

ESSENTIAL ELEMENTS

QUICK TIP
As a reality check, ask trusted coworkers for their opinions and compare them to your own.

1. **Avoid the positive outcome bias**

   Be aware of the symptoms of overconfidence: underestimating how long it will take to complete a task; overestimating the likelihood of something that you hope will occur; or being overly optimistic about your decisions and answers to questions. Figure 1-12 illustrates the positive outcome bias.

2. **Avoid "not invented here"**

   The tendency to develop a strong sense of ownership in your own ideas and opinions might lead you to overlook potential solutions from other sources. When you are looking for solutions to problems, be as open as possible to alternatives. Do not prejudge ideas or opinions. Instead, evaluate all available information with an open mind. Some of the best options will come from unlikely places.

3. **Avoid the need for quick closure**

   People feel uncomfortable with doubt, uncertainty, and the lack of ready answers. This discomfort can be magnified when the problem is especially large and important. To reduce the associated anxiety, you might try to accelerate the process and grasp at unlikely alternatives. Using simple time-management approaches and planning the solution process objectively will help you to overcome this common trap.

QUICK TIP
This is also referred to as the "herd effect."

4. **Avoid the bandwagon effect**

   Organizations develop a unique culture and set of values that favor certain actions and behaviors. When working in a company with a strong set of cultural norms, it is easy to adopt popular opinions and follow the expectations of others, which is called the **bandwagon effect**. This effect is particularly dangerous when solving problems. Frequently, cultural norms have contributed to the problem in the first place. Be sure you are not pressured to conform to a solution that doesn't make sense. See Figure 1-13.

QUICK TIP
Being consciously aware of the bias helps you to be more objective with your decisions.

5. **Avoid self-serving bias**

   Many common decision traps cause people to act against their best interests. A **self-serving bias** is anything that leads you to see the data as you most want it to appear. You might make decisions or pursue solutions that suit your personal preferences. When you start to work on a problem, ask yourself if a particular outcome, solution, or choice is especially appealing to you. If so, try to be aware of it as you proceed.

YOU TRY IT

Practice avoiding problem-solving traps by reacting to a problem-solving scenario. Open the PS1-Y8.docx document and follow the steps in the worksheet. When you are finished, submit the document to your instructor as requested.

FIGURE 1-12: Avoid the positive outcome bias

Icarus was a figure in Greek mythology who used a pair of wings made out of feathers and beeswax. When he flew too close to the sun, the beeswax melted and he fell from the sky. His over-confidence made him biased that he would succeed where others had failed.

Eduardo Leite/Photos.com

FIGURE 1-13: Avoid the bandwagon, or herd, effect

Hemera Technologies/Photos.com

TABLE 1-8: Problem-solving traps do's and don'ts

element	do	don't
Bias	• Be aware of the symptoms of overconfidence • Identify outcomes that are especially appealing to you	• **Don't** be overly optimistic about your decisions • **Don't** interpret information as you most want it to be
Other traps	• Evaluate all available information with an open mind • Use time-management approaches to plan time for decision making • Be aware of the opinions and expectations of others in your organization	• **Don't** overlook possible solutions from other sources • **Don't** prejudge ideas or opinions • **Don't** rush a decision • **Don't** give into pressure to conform to a solution that doesn't make sense

Technology @ Work: Crowdsourcing

Crowdsourcing is a term coined by Jeff Howe in *Wired* magazine to characterize a way of using groups to solve problems. The groups are usually online communities, such as members of a blog or visitors to a Web site, called a crowd. An organization broadcasts a problem to the crowd as an open call for solutions. The crowd submits solutions, and then sorts through them, finding the best ones. The organization selects and owns the ultimate solution, and sometimes rewards members of the crowd. On the Challenge.gov Web site, the U.S. government uses crowdsourcing to solve national problems. See Figure 1-14. The advantages of crowdsourcing to a company are that it can investigate problems at low cost and might produce innovative solutions from a wider range of amateurs and experts than it employs. The risks to the company are that it might waste time looking for a solution from the crowd, who is not committed to helping the company solve the problem. case Because Quest's problem is common to the travel industry, Grace Wong is considering working with other travel companies to solve the problem. She asks you to learn more about crowdsourcing to see if it would be a good technique for Quest.

ESSENTIAL ELEMENTS

QUICK TIP
Open-science problem solving is a form of crowdsourcing.

1. **Strength in numbers**

   Whether you are part of a company seeking to use the power of a crowd to solve a problem or you are a member of the crowd, the value of crowdsourcing comes from thousands or millions of people participating. Successful Web sites such as StumbleUpon (*www.stumbleupon.com*), Yelp (*www.yelp.com*), and Digg (*www.digg.com*) use crowdsourcing by inviting their visitors to vote on recommended Web sites, articles, restaurants, photos, or videos, for example, by submitting links or reviews.

2. **Collaboration matters**

   Crowdsourcing can provide valuable feedback for companies about their products. More than feedback, however, customers often want to collaborate. For example, t-shirt company Threadless invites customers and others to submit designs for t-shirts, and that crowd has developed into a loyal and enthusiastic customer base.

3. **Different, not necessarily better**

   Crowdsourcing is not designed for every business. As the crowd begins to make decisions, they start to determine the direction of a company or product. Crowdsourcing works well for businesses such as video Web sites, which are popular and draw enough numbers to provide a representative sample. Other products or businesses that have less appeal, such as household cleaners, are unlikely to attract enough of a crowd to solve problems.

4. **Good for the company, not for the crowd**

   In some cases, the company invites a crowd to solve a problem and profits substantially from it, while members of the crowd receive little compensation. That type of discouraging news can affect future crowdsourcing ventures, as crowd members wonder what the payoff is for them. The most successful examples of crowdsourcing involve volunteer efforts such as NASA's Stardust@Home, where the results are provided for the common good. See Figure 1-15.

YOU TRY IT

Learn more about crowdsourcing. Open the PS1-TechWork.docx document and follow the steps in the worksheet. When you are finished, submit the document to your instructor as requested.

FIGURE 1-14: Challenge.gov crowdsourcing site for government solutions

challenge.gov

FIGURE 1-15: NASA's Stardust@Home

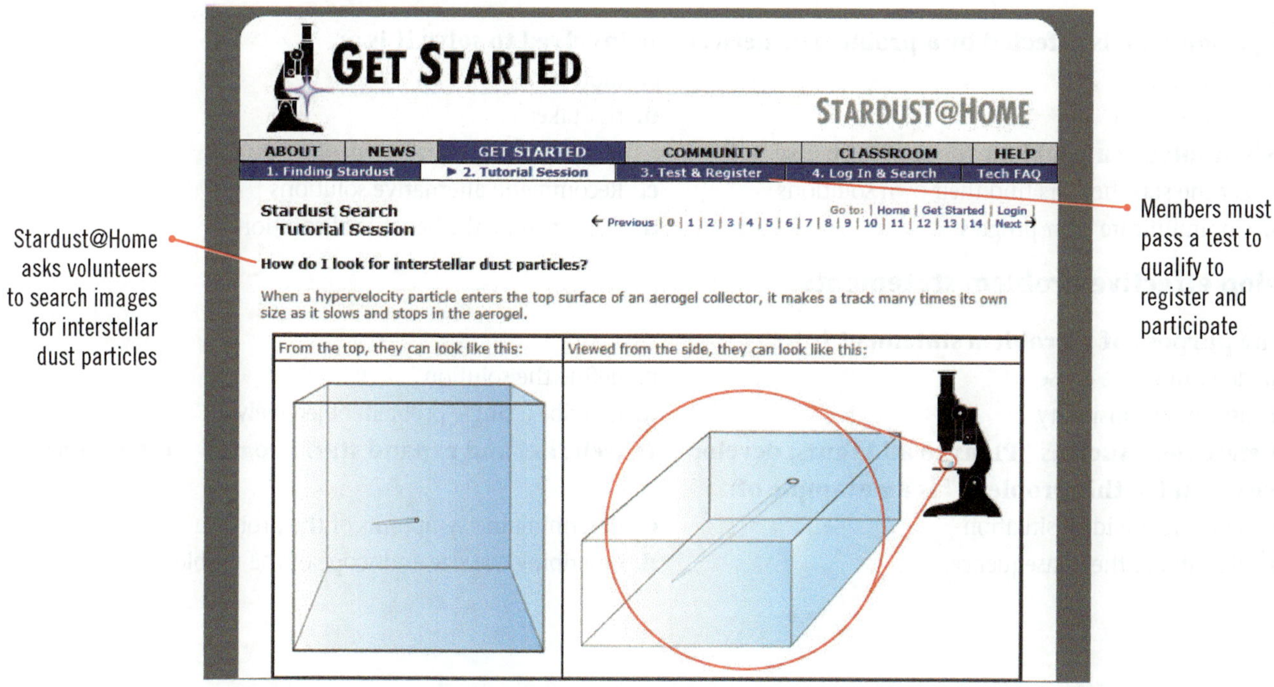

Courtesy of the Space Sciences Laboratory at UC Berkeley

Practice

Soft Skills Review

Understand problem solving.

1. **What is a problem for an organization?**
   a. Choice made when faced with a set of alternatives
   b. Difference between professional and line worker
   c. Set of objectives or goals
   d. Difference between current state and goal state
2. **Which of the following should you *not* do when solving problems?**
   a. Define the problem
   b. Accept the first solution
   c. Gather information
   d. Make a decision

Analyze problems.

1. **The first step in problem solving is to:**
   a. make a decision
   b. describe the problem-solving traps
   c. identify shortcomings
   d. communicate your progress
2. **Which of the following is a primary resource of information about a problem?**
   a. Observation
   b. Web site
   c. Magazine article
   d. Organization files

Work with problem owners and stakeholders.

1. **A person who is affected by a problem or needs to be involved to solve it is a:**
   a. stakeholder
   b. crowdsourcer
   c. motivator
   d. risk taker
2. **When solving a problem for someone else, which of the following should you *not* do?**
   a. Let the stakeholders find their own solutions
   b. Communicate your progress
   c. Recommend alternative solutions
   d. Demonstrate the benefits of solutions

Develop effective problem statements.

1. **The purpose of a problem statement is to:**
   a. determine the cause
   b. assign responsibility
   c. define the solution
   d. describe a single problem objectively
2. **A statement such as "Plans to add tours, develop our Web site, and expand staff are now on hold until we can solve this problem," is an example of:**
   a. defining the ideal situation
   b. identifying the consequences
   c. describing the symptoms of the problem
   d. describing the size and scope of the problem

Determine causes.

1. **What do you do when using the 5 Whys technique?**
   - **a.** Identify You, Yourself, Yours, Youth, and Yield
   - **b.** Draw a fishbone diagram
   - **c.** Ask why and challenge the answer with another "why" five times
   - **d.** Limit yourself to five questions
2. **What does a cause-and-effect diagram show?**
   - **a.** Who is causing a problem
   - **b.** Many solutions for a complicated problem
   - **c.** Many causes for a complicated problem
   - **d.** The root cause of a problem

Simplify complex problems.

1. **An effective way to deal with a complex problem is to:**
   - **a.** break it down into smaller problems
   - **b.** describe its size and scope
   - **c.** build your confidence for solving it
   - **d.** assign it to someone else
2. **After identifying subproblems, you should:**
   - **a.** sort or rank them
   - **b.** use the 5 Whys technique
   - **c.** brainstorm
   - **d.** focus on the main problem

Identify and manage risks.

1. **What is risk?**
   - **a.** A random form of success
   - **b.** Exposure to the possibility of loss or damage
   - **c.** A way to react to a problem
   - **d.** A way to solve a problem
2. **What type of solution should you seek when solving problems?**
   - **a.** One with low risk and high reward
   - **b.** One with low risk and low reward
   - **c.** One with high risk and high reward
   - **d.** One with high risk and low reward

Avoid problem-solving traps.

1. **Which of the following is a common problem-solving trap?**
   - **a.** Bandwagon effect
   - **b.** Not in my backyard syndrome
   - **c.** Office politics pitfall
   - **d.** Wild West mentality
2. **Which of the following is *not* a symptom of overconfidence?**
   - **a.** Underestimating the length of a task
   - **b.** Asking trusted coworkers for their opinions
   - **c.** Overestimating the chance that something you want will occur
   - **d.** Being overly optimistic about your decisions

Technology @ work: Crowdsourcing

1. **Crowdsourcing is a way to:**
   - **a.** use proven time-management techniques to solve problems
   - **b.** reduce risk and increase rewards
   - **c.** use many overseas workers to perform tasks
   - **d.** use groups to solve problems
2. **The most successful crowdsourcing examples involve:**
   - **a.** volunteer efforts where the results are provided for the common good
   - **b.** persuading customers to purchase services
   - **c.** products that have specific, limited appeal
   - **d.** high company profits with low crowd compensation

Critical Thinking Questions

1. **Successful teams—whether in sports or business—usually perform well because each member contributes talents and skills to the group effort. What contribution do problem-solving skills make to team efforts? Provide at least one example that illustrates your points.**
2. **You can take a problem-solving approach to resolving conflicts in an organization. Suppose you and your colleague are working together on a high-profile project to develop software for handling orders at your company. You want to adapt existing software and your colleague wants to develop new software. How would you apply the problem-solving steps shown in Figure 1-2 to resolve the conflict?**
3. **Describe a time when you solved a basic problem. Then describe a situation in which you solved a complex problem. What are the similarities and differences in the approaches and the solutions?**
4. **Samuel Johnson said, "Integrity without knowledge is weak and useless, and knowledge without integrity is dangerous and dreadful." What does this mean for solving problems in a contemporary business?**
5. **Based on the grids shown in Figures 1-9 and 1-10, list three typical business problems, such as flat sales, loss of loyal customers, and dissatisfied employees. Draw a grid showing how you would solve one of these problems.**

Independent Challenge 1

Lawrence Media in Nashville, Tennessee, specializes in promotional products for businesses, such as corporate apparel, executive gifts, and product giveaways. As an assistant to Ken Lawrence, the founder of the company, you participate in many meetings and projects. During a recent meeting with Ken and his project managers, he said Lawrence Media had a major problem retaining good salespeople. Figure 1-16 summarizes his statements. Ken asked you, the other assistants, and the project managers to help him solve the problem.

FIGURE 1-16

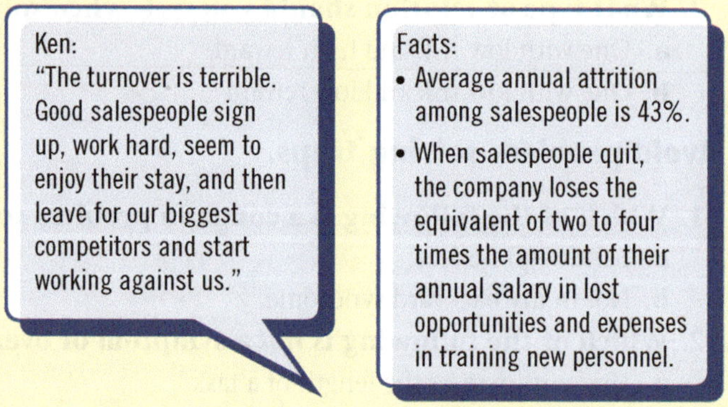

a. Open the **PS1-IC1.docx** document and follow the steps in the worksheet.
b. Proofread the document carefully to fix any grammar or formatting errors.
c. Submit the document to your instructor as requested.

Independent Challenge 2

You work with Carla Marcus, the owner of Sage Realty Services in Winnetka, Illinois. Her firm was one of the fastest growing companies in the area until recently. When the real estate market slowed nationwide, Sage Realty's sales dropped off significantly. Figure 1-17 illustrates Carla's problem. Carla asks you to help her analyze her problem and develop possible solutions.

FIGURE 1-17

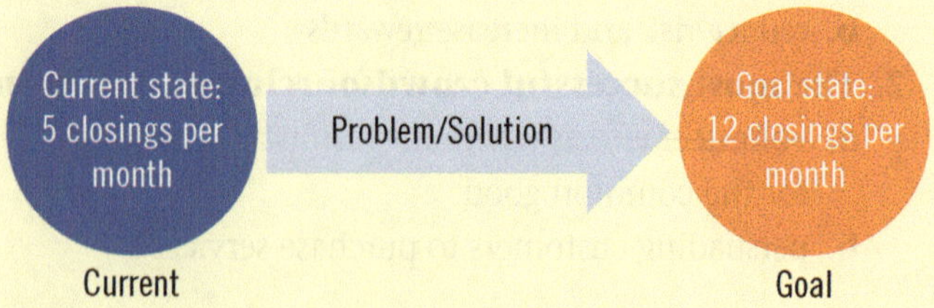

a. Open the **PS1-IC2.docx** document and follow the steps in the worksheet.
b. Proofread the document carefully to fix any grammar or formatting errors.
c. Submit the document to your instructor as requested.

Real Life Independent Challenge

You can apply the problem-solving techniques you learned in this part to challenges, difficulties, and other problems in other parts of your life. Start by selecting a problem you want to solve and then identify possible solutions.

a. In a document for personal use, list up to 10 problems you would like to solve, ranging from minor to major. Write these as statements in the form of complete sentences.

b. For each problem statement on your list, determine whether you or anyone you know can do anything about it. If not, move the problem to a new page with the heading "Out of Scope."

c. For each problem statement on the revised list, brainstorm possible solutions.

d. Select one problem and then organize the possible solutions into a table similar to that found in Figure 1-10. Which solution offers the best risk/reward ratio?

Team Challenge

You have just been hired by Colorado Green Builders, a company in Boulder, Colorado, specializing in sustainable building. The goals of your company are to design and build structures that use energy, resources, and materials efficiently. For your first project, you are assigned to a newly formed team that will communicate with clients and solve their problems. However, your new team itself is having problems: the team has only met once and one person dominated the discussion. Everyone else was silent or quietly responded to text messages. Your manager learned about the ineffective meeting and suggested that you start by creating a team charter, which spells out the rules for conduct for the team and its members.

a. Meet as a group to begin creating a team charter. Identify the goals of the Colorado Green Builders team. Discuss how often the team should meet, and what happens if a team member skips meetings or doesn't do their share of the work.

b. Identify the strengths of each member of the team. Discuss how to resolve conflicts and other team problems.

c. On your own, summarize the conclusions of your team. Be sure to include suggestions for resolving conflicts and handling team problems.

d. Meet again as a team and compile a single charter for your team.

Be the Critic

You are working for Athena Insurance, an insurance agency in Columbus, Ohio. Athena Insurance often contributes to local nonprofit organizations, and provides major support to one organization each year. You are a member of a committee that is selecting this year's organization. Figure 1-18 describes the meeting. Analyze the problem-solving discussion, noting its weaknesses, and send a list of the weaknesses to your instructor.

FIGURE 1-18

Alice (committee chair):
Let's support the food pantry.

Don:
That sounds like a good idea.

Sylvia:
I like any idea that helps people in need.

Frank:
I have to leave in 10 minutes.

Emily:
What about something else, such as the electronics recycling program?

Alice:
Electronics recycling doesn't seem as helpful as the food pantry.

Don:
I agree.

Frank:
So we've settled on the food pantry?

Part

2

Solving the Problem

Files You Will Need:

PS2-Y10.docx
PS2-Y11.docx
PS2-Y12.docx
PS2-Y13.docx
PS2-Y14.docx
PS2-Y15.docx
PS2-Y16.docx
PS2-TechWork.docx
PS2-IC1.docx
PS2-IC2.docx

After you identify a problem and explore its causes and related issues, it is time to develop a solution. The activities associated with solving a problem are different from the steps you have followed to this point. When you define a problem, you should be open-minded and flexible as you explore, research, and communicate with others. Developing and implementing a solution demands greater focus and deliberation. Planning tasks and managing your time become your most distinguishing skills. This part introduces you to solving problems methodically and then managing the solution to verify you made the right decision. case As an assistant to Grace Wong, the vice president of finance at Quest Specialty Travel, you have been working on a project called 12 by 12 that aims to increase sales by 12 percent. After identifying problems customers have with Quest tours and with traveling overall, Grace is ready to assemble all the data you and others have collected, discuss alternatives, and make decisions about the future of Quest. She asks you to work with her to solve the problem of declining tour sales at Quest Specialty Travel.

OBJECTIVES

9 Gather and analyze data
10 Develop alternatives
11 Evaluate options
12 Implement the solution
13 Monitor and manage the solution
14 Verify the solution
15 Use adaptive techniques
16 Develop ethical solutions

ster Close/Shutterstock

Objective 9
Part 2

Gathering and Analyzing Data

Before you solve a business problem, gather relevant data and then analyze it to find trends, indicators, and other useful information. Successful business decisions are based on sound information. Use the data you collect to prepare possible solutions and alternatives. To systematically gather and analyze the data related to your problem, start by identifying your goal and looking for information related to it. If you want to increase sales, for example, you should gather recent sales data. Then use tools to view that data in different ways, such as by product, region, or quarter, as shown in Figure 2-1. Keep one eye on your desired outcome to be sure the information you collect is helping you to reach your goals. Table 2-1 outlines the types of data you can collect. case Before you meet with Grace Wong to discuss solutions, she advises you to review the fundamentals of gathering and analyzing data.

DETAILS

Consider the following guidelines as you gather data:

- **Define your data needs**

  What information do you need to reach an informed decision? A thoughtful answer to this question helps guide your research. Make a list of important data and where you can find it. Consider the costs of acquiring this information (such as money and time), and plan to pursue the data that provides the best return on your efforts.

- **Do not overestimate what you know about the problem**

  The information you gather might contradict your assumptions. Be scientific and objective in your research. Let the data stand on its own and keep an open mind about interpreting it. Apply intellectual humility, and assume your research will reveal more than you already know about the problem.

QUICK TIP

Documenting your data and sources of information also supports your decision in case something goes wrong with your solution.

- **Document the data and its sources**

  As you talk with people, review documents, and make observations, take time to record basic information such as title, author, and location. Your records will be useful when you need to retrace your steps. As other people become involved, they might also need to review your work.

- **Examine existing information first**

  Acquiring information costs you and others time and effort. Before you start to collect new information through observations or studies, look for sources of existing information. Talk to others who already observed the problem and can quickly provide you with details. Company documents and records can reveal information with a quick search and review. Start to gather new data after you examine the available material.

- **Rely on people as your most important resource**

  Much of the information you need might be available only from other people in your organization. They often have insights or experience that is not available anywhere else. Even if they do not know about the problem directly or do not think they could contribute to the solution, identify and approach people who might be able to share data with you.

QUICK TIP

Use software tools such as spreadsheets, databases, and diagramming programs for flowcharts to help you see how one set of data relates to another.

- **Consider interrelationships**

  Most of the data you collect is interrelated because it is connected to the same problem. Examine all of the information together to see how it is connected. Does one factor or process show up repeatedly? Do you see a trend or pattern? What do the relationships tell you about the nature of the problem?

FIGURE 2-1: Viewing data in different ways

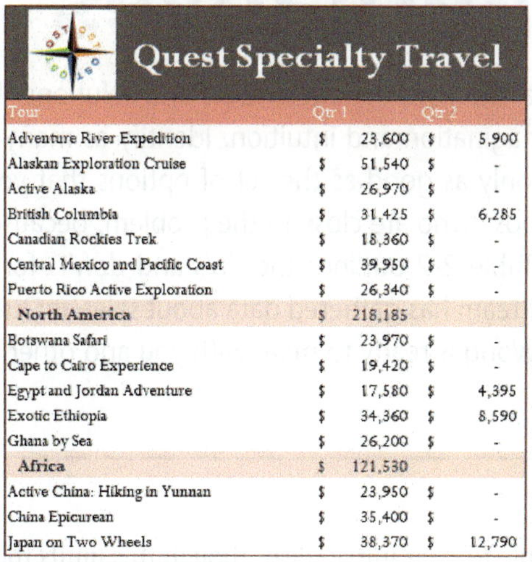

Quest Specialty Travel

Tour	Qtr 1	Qtr 2
Adventure River Expedition	$ 23,600	$ 5,900
Alaskan Exploration Cruise	$ 51,540	$ -
Active Alaska	$ 26,970	$ -
British Columbia	$ 31,425	$ 6,285
Canadian Rockies Trek	$ 18,360	$ -
Central Mexico and Pacific Coast	$ 39,950	$ -
Puerto Rico Active Exploration	$ 26,340	$ -
North America	$ 218,185	
Botswana Safari	$ 23,970	$ -
Cape to Cairo Experience	$ 19,420	$ -
Egypt and Jordan Adventure	$ 17,580	$ 4,395
Exotic Ethiopia	$ 34,360	$ 8,590
Ghana by Sea	$ 26,200	$ -
Africa	$ 121,530	
Active China: Hiking in Yunnan	$ 23,950	$ -
China Epicurean	$ 35,400	$ -
Japan on Two Wheels	$ 38,370	$ 12,790

Spreadsheet of sales data

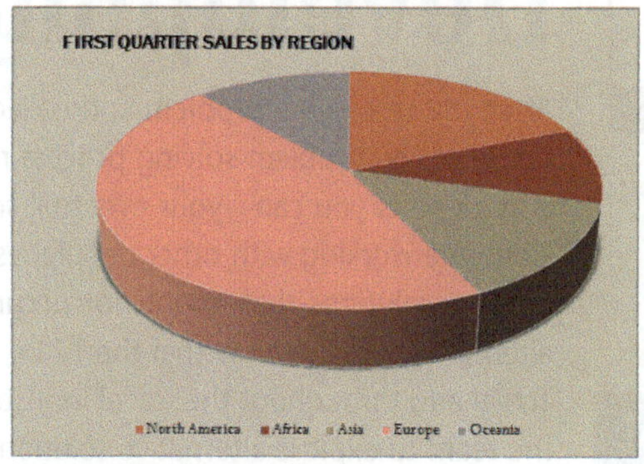

Chart showing sales by region

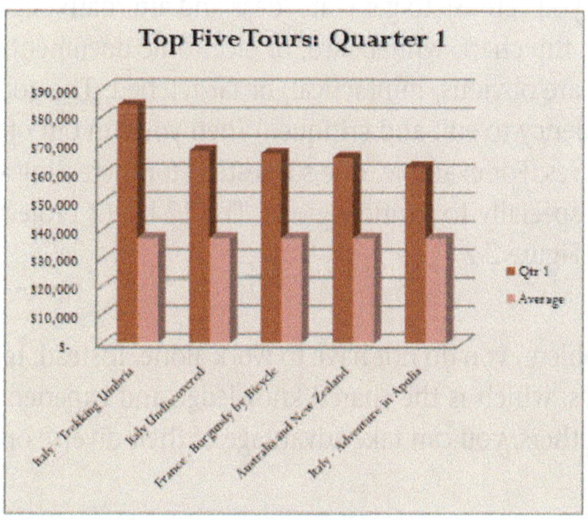

Chart comparing top five tours in Quarter 1

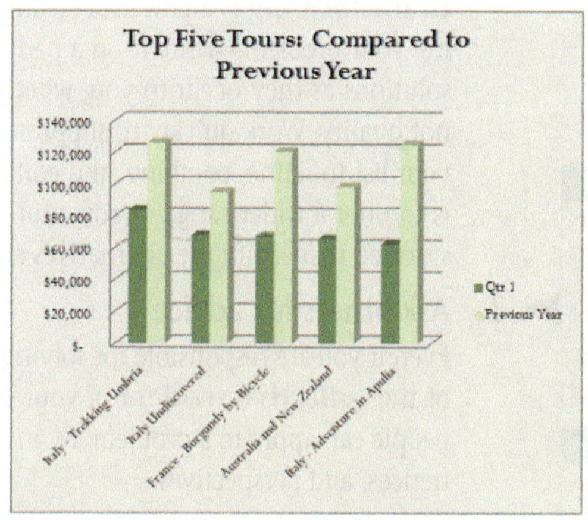

Chart comparing top five tours to previous year

TABLE 2-1: Types of data to collect

type of data	resource	applies to
Financial	Organization records, trade associations, and business databases	Financial problems, such as increasing revenue, decreasing expenses, and setting prices
Task or process	Employee reports and logs	Inefficient processes, such as late orders, missed deadlines, and low production
Product or service	Customer surveys and comments	Decreasing sales, high inventory, and customer dissatisfaction
General advice	Experts, experienced colleagues and managers, outsiders, and secondary sources, such as books and Web sites	Comprehensive problems, such as business mission and focus, and social or interpersonal problems

Objective 10 Part 2

Developing Alternatives

After you research a problem and collect data, start to consider alternatives and solutions. This creative phase of the problem-solving process requires imagination and intuition. Identify as many alternatives and ideas as you can—your eventual solution is only as good as the set of options that you generate. Continue working with other people, especially those who are close to the problem, because they often suggest solutions that might not occur to you. Table 2-2 outlines the do's and don'ts for developing alternatives. case Now that the 12 by 12 project team has gathered data about sales at Quest Specialty Travel and throughout the travel industry, Grace Wong is ready to meet with you and other members of the team to explore alternative solutions.

ESSENTIAL ELEMENTS

QUICK TIP
Innovative ideas often come when you don't expect them, so carry a pad of paper, notebook, or journal with you and record ideas as you think of them.

1. **Think creatively**

   The desire to solve a problem often anchors people to their initial ideas, though this limits the possibilities they consider and detracts from the quality of the final solution. Instead, use your creativity to explore as many ideas as you can. Think of creativity as an exercise in breaking your assumptions. Your goal is to identify new approaches and uncommon ideas.

2. **Brainstorm ideas**

   Brainstorming is a powerful creativity tool you can use to generate ideas and alternatives. Start by defining your problem—write it on a pad of paper, flip chart, whiteboard, or electronic document. List possible solutions as they occur to you, whether they are obvious, impractical, or far-fetched. The goal is quantity, not quality. Work quickly to suppress the tendency to edit and critique. When you run out of ideas, review your list to refine, combine, and edit alternatives. For example, one suggestion for increasing sales at Quest is to offer a wider range of adventure tours, especially to exotic regions. The 12 by 12 project team brainstormed to identify the alternatives shown in Figure 2-2.

QUICK TIP
Remember that you are asking for opinions, not inviting people to assume control of your project.

3. **Ask others for advice**

   Even if you are responsible for solving the problem, you do not have to work alone. Instead, take advantage of the **collective wisdom** of your colleagues, which is the shared knowledge and experience a group of people can apply to a problem. By involving others, you can take advantage of their diverse opinions, experiences, and perspectives.

QUICK TIP
Mapping your ideas visually helps you see relationships, understand and remember your ideas, and avoid the limitations of a traditional outline or list.

4. **Develop a mind map**

   Mind maps are diagrams that represent your ideas and stimulate your creativity. Start a mind map by writing the problem in the center of a physical or digital sheet of paper. As you think of ideas, draw them as branches that project from the problem description (see Figure 2-3). Do this quickly, without pausing to reflect on the ideas, as you do when brainstorming. Add words or concepts that you associate with each idea. Continue to add branches radiating out from the central idea.

YOU TRY IT

Practice developing alternatives by generating a list of alternatives. Open the PS2-Y10.docx document and follow the steps in the worksheet. When you are finished, submit the document to your instructor as requested.

FIGURE 2-2: Brainstorming

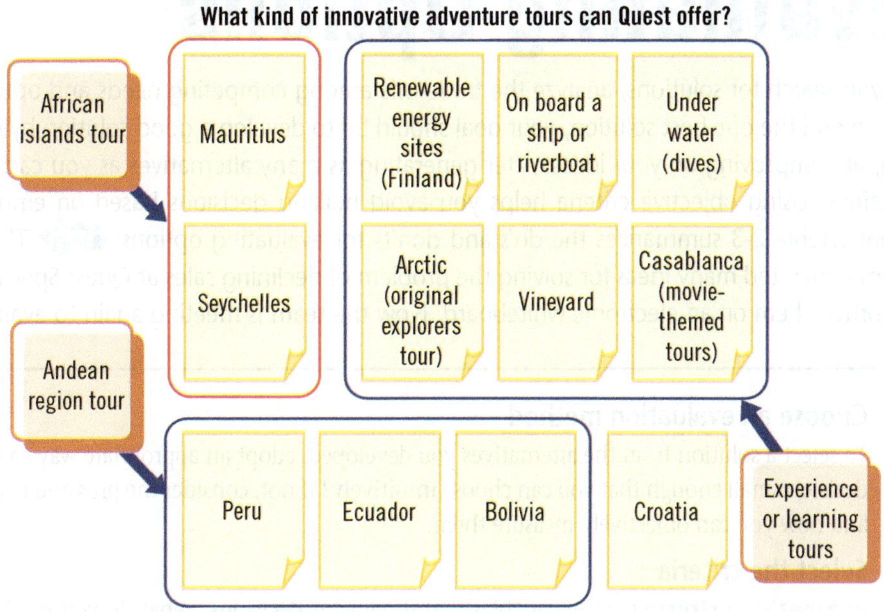

FIGURE 2-3: Mind map

TABLE 2-2: Developing alternatives do's and don'ts

guidelines	do	don't
Think creatively	• Generate as many ideas as possible • Break your assumptions to uncover original ideas • Brainstorm to find new approaches and uncommon ideas • Develop a mind map to see how problems, solutions, and alternatives are connected	• Don't get too attached to your own ideas • Don't settle for the standard approach • Don't rely on your preconceived assumptions • Don't evaluate the ideas you generate yet
Ask others	• Take advantage of the collective wisdom of your colleagues • Consider the opinions and advice of experts and nonexperts	• Don't think you must solve the problem yourself • Don't work on the problem alone
Document ideas	• Keep track of your ideas and those offered by others • Refer to the ideas you documented later	• Don't risk forgetting a great idea by failing to write it down • Don't limit the number or type of ideas you document

Objective 11 Part 2

Evaluating Options

ESSENTIAL ELEMENTS

As you search for solutions, analyze the trade-offs among competing needs and options. Instead of trying to find the one best solution, your goal should be to develop a good solution by evaluating, modifying, and improving on your ideas. After generating as many alternatives as you can, evaluate each one carefully. Using objective criteria helps you avoid making decisions based on emotion or snap judgments. Table 2-3 summarizes the do's and don'ts for evaluating options. case The 12 by 12 project team generated many ideas for solving the problem of declining sales at Quest Specialty Travel, and you recorded them on an electronic whiteboard. Now the team is meeting again to evaluate the options.

1. Choose an evaluation method

To select a solution from the alternatives you developed, adopt an appropriate way to evaluate them. Is the decision small enough that you can choose intuitively? If not, consider the pros and cons of each alternative and how you can objectively measure them.

QUICK TIP Decisions based on a single criterion are often unsatisfactory.

2. Select the criteria

Evaluation criteria are the variables that drive your decisions. What do you need to know about each alternative to make an informed choice? Popular criteria include cost, time, feasibility, usefulness, and appropriateness for the organization. Use more than one of these when evaluating alternatives.

3. Weigh your criteria

If your problem is complex, consider all of its dimensions as you evaluate alternatives. However, not all criteria are equally important. To take the differences into account, assign weights to each option. For example, you might be evaluating locations for a customer appreciation event for Quest Specialty Travel. Two criteria are overall cost and the availability of an event planner at the hotel. Because cost is more significant, you could assign 80 percent of the decision to cost and 20 percent to the event planner. The weights you assign to each criterion determine how much influence each has on the final outcome.

QUICK TIP Have a reality check. Don't assume that the rating is the absolute answer.

4. Rate the alternatives

You can rate the alternatives by ranking each one based on your criteria and the weight you assigned (see Figure 2-4). Another method is to compare each alternative to the others and determine which is superior. You can use an analytical hierarchy matrix to rate alternatives based on these comparisons (see Figure 2-5). When making important decisions, use more than one rating technique. The outcomes might not be identical, but they should be very similar. If not, reevaluate your work.

QUICK TIP Ask trusted colleagues for their opinions; they might see something you overlooked.

5. Make a decision

Choose the best alternative and use it to develop a solution to the problem. Do not be concerned if the selected alternative is not *perfect*. Complex problems rarely have ideal solutions. Make sure you feel comfortable with the alternative you choose.

YOU TRY IT

Practice evaluating options by selecting an option and then explaining why you selected it. Open the PS2-Y11.docx document and follow the steps in the worksheet. When you are finished, submit the document to your instructor as requested.

FIGURE 2-4: Ranking and weighting alternatives

Evaluating Alternatives									
Each alternative = 25%	Easy to do		Popular with customers		Compared to competition		Amount of revenue		
	Points	Score	Points	Score	Points	Score	Points	Score	Total Score
Raise tour prices	5	125	1	25	4	100	5	125	375
Drop unprofitable tours	3	75	5	125	5	125	4	100	425
Offer popular tours more often	3	75	5	125	5	125	5	125	450
Cut tour features	1	25	1	25	2	50	5	125	225

Assign points on a scale, such as 1–5

Multiply points by percentage for each alternative (5 × 25 = 125)

Highest total is the best alternative

Total the scores

FIGURE 2-5: Analytical hierarchy matrix

Options for Increasing Sales	A	B	C	D	Row Sum	Rank
A. Raise tour prices		0	0	1	1	3rd
B. Drop unprofitable tours	1		0	1	2	2nd
C. Offer popular tours more often	1	1		1	3	1st
D. Cut tour features	0	0	0		0	4th

Add the sum of the ratings in the row

Is option A (raise tour prices) preferable to option B (drop unprofitable tours)? If yes, rate this 1. If no, rate it 0.

Is option A preferable to option C (offer popular tours more often)? If yes, rate this 1. If no, rate it 0.

Is option A preferable to option D (cut tour features)? If yes, rate this 1. If no, rate it 0.

Rank the row sums

TABLE 2-3: Evaluating options do's and don'ts

guidelines	do	don't
Examine criteria	• Identify the criteria for your decision, such as cost, time, and usefulness • Choose more than one criteria • Assign weights to each criterion	• **Don't** settle on only one criterion • **Don't** assign the same weight to the criteria
Rate alternatives	• Rank alternatives based on the criteria and assigned weights • Compare each alternative to the others • Reevaluate if you have different outcomes using different techniques	• **Don't** use a single evaluation method for complex problems
Make a decision	• Choose the best alternative and use it to develop a solution to the problem • Select a good alternative instead of waiting for the ideal solution	• **Don't** be concerned if the selected alternative is not perfect • **Don't** make a decision you are not comfortable with

Objective 12 Part 2

Implementing the Solution

Moving from planning to implementation is a significant milestone when you are solving a problem. This is when you begin to make decisions, take actions, and put your plans into practice. Keep everyone informed of your intentions as you move ahead by communicating clearly and frequently. Take action and remember that in most cases, it is better to act decisively with a good solution than it is to plan endlessly looking for the perfect one. Table 2-4 offers do's and don'ts for putting solutions into practice. case Based on the results of the 12 by 12 team's work, Grace Wong has decided to offer popular tours more often in an effort to increase sales for Quest Specialty Travel.

ESSENTIAL ELEMENTS

1. **Get approval from the problem owner**

   Before you implement a solution, consult with the problem owners and make sure they support your idea. Discuss the process you followed, explain the options you considered, and make your case for the solution you chose. If a problem owner is uncomfortable with the solution you recommend, work together to identify an acceptable option.

2. **Develop a plan**

   Outline the steps to apply your chosen alternative. List the resources you need, including people, money, facilities, and influence. Estimate how much time the solution will take, and develop a schedule. Define the expected outcome, and consider what the situation should look like when the problem is solved. Work with other people in your team, if necessary, to identify all parts of the plan. See Figure 2-6.

3. **Notify stakeholders**

   How you communicate your decisions significantly affects how others accept your proposed solution. Internal staff and managers need to understand how each decision relates to their jobs and missions. As you begin to implement your solution, let people know what you are doing so they can take action. Your communication should include the elements shown in Figure 2-7.

4. **Anticipate opposition**

   Decisions that cause change can upset or threaten others in the organization. To avoid this, build support for your solution before you put it into practice. Preview your plan to reassure people who resist change. Clearly explain the nature of the problem, and show why your solution is the most responsible way to deal with it.

5. **Take action**

   Until the solution takes effect, your decision is little more than a good intention. After making decisions and securing approvals, start to take specific actions. Projects suffer from inertia, so it usually requires extra effort to keep your plan moving. However, once you start, it becomes easier to manage.

QUICK TIP

Make sure that your plan leads you to this desired end state.

YOU TRY IT

Practice implementing solutions by identifying why a solution was not successful. Open the PS2-Y12.docx document and follow the steps in the worksheet. When you are finished, submit the document to your instructor as requested.

FIGURE 2-6: Develop a plan

Константин Чагин/Photos.com

FIGURE 2-7: Communicate with stakeholders

Topics to discuss with stakeholders:

What the decision is
How the solution will be put into place
How it will be monitored and evaluated
How changes will be decided on and made

TABLE 2-4: Implementing the solution do's and don'ts

guidelines	do	don't
Communicate with others	• Involve the problem owner in the decision • Describe the steps you followed to make a decision • Communicate clearly and frequently • Notify staff and managers	• Don't go forward with the solution if the problem owner is uncomfortable • Don't withhold information in the hopes of having everyone agree
Develop a plan	• Outline the steps to take to put the solution into place • Identify the resources you need • Draft a realistic schedule • Reconsider your goals	• Don't underestimate the amount of time you need to complete each step of the plan • Don't move forward if your plan doesn't meet your goals
Anticipate opposition	• Build support for your solution • Continue to communicate about your plans and progress	• Don't ignore the opposition • Don't block out opposing points of view, but don't abandon the solution either
Take action	• Start following your plan soon after making a decision	• Don't let inaction end your efforts to solve the problem

Unintended consequences: when solving one problem spurs new ones

Anyone with an e-mail account has been frustrated by spam—junk e-mail sent out in bulk to clog your inbox with advertisements for often phony or fraudulent products. Recently, the flood of spam slowed to a trickle when a group of servers in San Jose, California, were disconnected from the Internet. These servers were considered the source of 40 percent of the world's spam. Shortly after that, the antivirus developer McAfee reported that botnets had taken control of about 12 million new IP addresses, or Internet accounts. A *botnet* refers to a collection of software robots, or bots, that run independently on computers without revealing themselves to the owner. They take advantage of computing resources and often gather e-mail addresses for spamming. What triggered the dramatic increase in bots? McAfee researchers concluded they were a response to the server shutdown in San Jose. The new bots were patrolling for new e-mail addresses, which will eventually lead to new floods of spam. "The question is not whether spam will return to previous levels," the McAfee report said, "but rather when it will return."

This is an example of the law of unintended consequences, a truism maintaining that any purposeful activity produces some unintended consequences. The classic example is of a road bypass built to relieve traffic congestion but results in two busy streets instead of one. As you consider solutions, keep in mind that at least one of them is likely to produce an unintended side effect.

Source: Freakonomics, "The Unintended Consequences of Attacking Spam," *The New York Times*, May 6, 2009.

Objective 13 Part 2

Monitoring and Managing the Solution

ESSENTIAL ELEMENTS

Complicated problems are seldom solved by making a simple decision. Most solutions involve related choices, tasks, and the participation of others. Monitor and manage these activities to ensure a successful outcome. Managers, coworkers, and other stakeholders expect you to deal professionally and competently with interruptions, delays, and unexpected events. Planning for and identifying trouble quickly helps you minimize the disruption and problems it causes. Table 2-5 summarizes the do's and don'ts of managing solutions. case Under Grace Wong's management, the 12 by 12 project team has started to rework schedules and develop promotional materials to offer Quest's most popular tours more often. Grace asks you to help monitor this solution.

1. **Identify key variables**

   Solutions to problems are abstract ideas, not tangible objects you can pick up, hold, and inspect, which makes them difficult to monitor. Instead, identify the key variables or observable indicators that show whether your solution is succeeding or failing. These are often symptoms of the problem itself, such as tour enrollment, and are factors that should improve. Decide which variables are appropriate for your solution and monitor them. For example, you might track weekly tour enrollment in Quest's most popular tours.

> **QUICK TIP**
> Typically, the necessary amount of management and control decreases over time.

2. **Select an appropriate level of monitoring**

   The level of monitoring, follow-up, and control varies for each problem. See Figure 2-8. Complicated solutions require close contact, while simpler problems need less attention. Budget time for monitoring by asking yourself if the solution requires a full-time commitment, daily activity, or only occasional monitoring.

3. **Involve others with the process**

   Engage others to help with your solution. Ask stakeholders and others to monitor changes and watch for problems. Let people know what you changed and the outcomes you expect so they can observe the right indicators. Also advise them about what action to take if something seems out of place. Follow up with these observers to keep them aware and interested. See Figure 2-9.

> **QUICK TIP**
> Stay connected with the issues because much can change in a short time.

4. **Be persistent**

   Spend some time every day monitoring, managing, and working on the problem. In most cases, it is better to spend an hour or two every day managing your project than devoting a full day once a week. Consistency and persistence will contribute to a successful conclusion.

5. **Make corrections promptly**

   Unforeseen complications or issues can cause your solution to go off track. If you detect a problem, it is usually best to make adjustments promptly. Problems tend to grow bigger with time and harder to tame. If you need to change your plans, be sure to communicate them clearly to everyone involved. Then monitor indicators very closely to ensure that the correction is working.

YOU TRY IT

Practice monitoring and managing the solution by describing how you would monitor a problem and solution. Open the PS2-Y13.docx document and follow the steps in the worksheet. When you are finished, submit the document to your instructor as requested.

FIGURE 2-8: Levels of monitoring

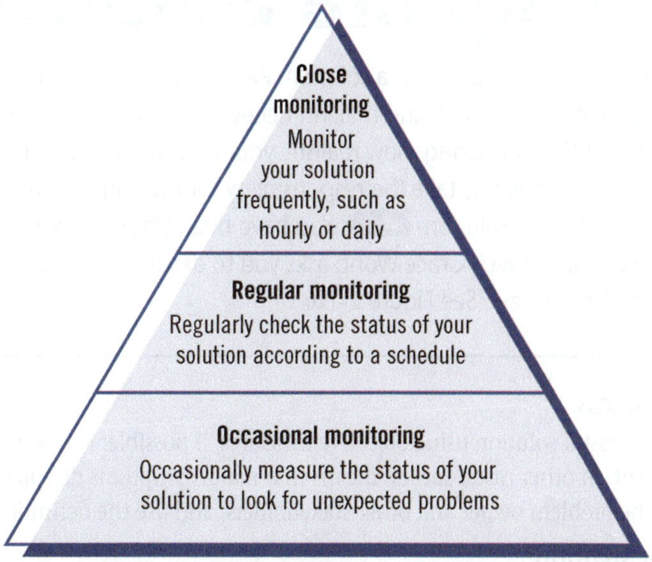

FIGURE 2-9: Involve others with your solution

Marcus Clackson/Photos.com

TABLE 2-5: Managing solution do's and don'ts

guidelines	do	don't
Identify variables	• Identify signs that your plan is working • Track objective measures of the solution's success • Watch for symptoms of the original problem	• **Don't** assume your plan is solving the problem; make sure it is by measuring the results
Select a level of monitoring	• Monitor complicated solutions closely • Monitor simple problems occasionally • Spend at least some time every day monitoring, managing, and working on the problem • Continue to put your solution into place as you planned	• **Don't** forget to budget for monitoring time in your work schedule • **Don't** monitor the solution only one day a week
Involve others	• Ask stakeholders and others to help you monitor changes • Let people know what you changed and the outcomes you expect	• **Don't** let yourself be the only one monitoring the solution • **Don't** forget to let others know what to do if they detect a problem
Correct problems	• Make adjustments as soon as possible • Communicate the changes to everyone involved	• **Don't** overlook signs that the solution is not working or the problem is returning

Objective 14 Part 2

Verifying the Solution

ESSENTIAL ELEMENTS

Expect surprises when you implement a solution. Part of being an effective professional is staying involved with a project until it is completed and making necessary corrections along the way. Ask yourself and others how well the solution is working, how realistic your objectives are, and what is not working as expected. When you identify a deficiency, take the responsibility for making a correction. Table 2-6 outlines the do's and don'ts of verifying the solution. case You have been tracking tour enrollments for the most popular tours at Quest Specialty Travel. Grace Wong asks you to develop a presentation that describes the progress of the project and its success. See Figure 2-10.

1. **Define success**

   Define a successful solution using objective measures, if possible. For example, Quest wants to increase sales by 12 percent. In other cases, success means that major symptoms disappear. Discuss your definition of success with the problem owner and other stakeholders, and use the definition when you verify your work.

2. **Test your solution**

   Though a solution seems to be working superficially, it might break down under stress. Test your solution to make sure it is successful. Determine a **worst-case scenario** and try to simulate it. However, avoid introducing hazards or additional problems. Does increasing sales by 12 percent really solve Quest's income problems? Or do the extra expenses offset the gains? Play what-if to make sure your solution is robust.

3. **Avoid the problem in the future**

   Consider how well your solution holds up over time. What short- and long-term effects do your decisions have on the organization? What else can you do to improve the longevity of your solutions? Who can monitor and maintain the solution in the future? Document the problem so that the organization does not make the same mistakes again.

4. **Learn from the process**

   When you solve a problem, you and the organization should learn from the experience. Identify what you did correctly and what you might have done differently. You can apply many of the lessons you learn in other situations. Your company should also benefit from your efforts. Take the time to document your results and make them available to others to reference in the future.

5. **Take credit for your success**

   Your abilities to solve problems and make decisions are among your most valuable professional skills. When you successfully complete a project, let others know what you and your team accomplished. The problem owner, stakeholders, or your direct supervisor might not be aware of all that you have done. Communicate your success with them professionally through a written report, oral presentation, or combination of the two.

QUICK TIP
Identify how you would conduct the same project if you had to redo it.

QUICK TIP
Take credit for your success and share it with others who helped you.

YOU TRY IT

Practice verifying the solution by testing a solution with a worst-case scenario. Open the PS2-Y14.docx document and follow the steps in the worksheet. When you are finished, submit the document to your instructor as requested.

FIGURE 2-10: Communicating progress

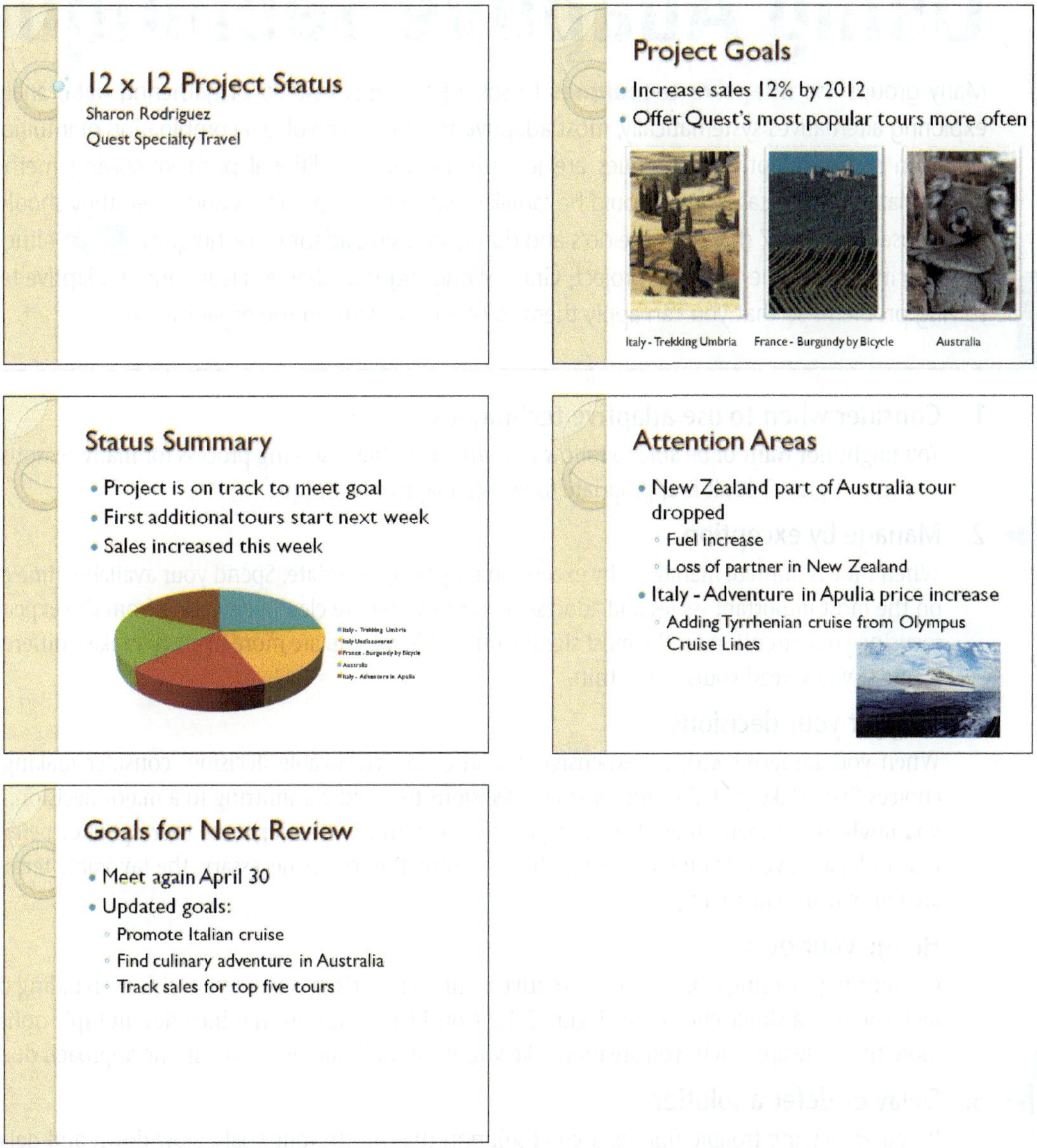

Used with permission from Microsoft Corporation

TABLE 2-6: Verifying solutions do's and don'ts

guidelines	do	don't
Define success	• Compare the current state to the goal state • Measure the changes that determine your success • Define success with the stakeholders and problem owner	• **Don't** forget to define success for the problems you solve • **Don't** consider the problem solved because major symptoms disappear
Test solution	• Test the solution by considering the worst-case scenario • Stress the system and see if you still have the desired results	• **Don't** look at superficial parts of the solution only • **Don't** create a dangerous or problematic test
Avoid problems	• Consider how long your decisions will affect the organization • Train someone else to monitor the solution as necessary	• **Don't** overlook long-term effects • **Don't** hold yourself back by making yourself the only person who knows how to manage the problem and solution
Learn from success	• Make sure you and the organization learn from the success • Document your results	• **Don't** fail to take credit for your contributions to the success

Objective 15 Part 2

Using Adaptive Techniques

Many groups use **adaptive techniques** to solve problems. Instead of gathering data, analyzing it, and exploring alternatives systematically, most adaptive techniques involve a combination of intuition, logic, and common sense. Adaptive techniques are less precise than traditional problem-solving methods, but are appropriate in many cases. You should be familiar with these approaches and when they should and should not be used. Table 2-7 describes the do's and don'ts for using adaptive techniques. case Although Quest is meeting its goals in the 12 by 12 project, Grace Wong suggests that you learn about adaptive techniques for solving problems so that you can apply them to other problems in the organization.

ESSENTIAL ELEMENTS

1. **Consider when to use adaptive techniques**
   You might not want or be able to follow a complete problem-solving process for many reasons. In the cases shown in Figure 2-11, it is appropriate to use an adaptive technique.

QUICK TIP
The most obvious problems are not always the most important problems.

2. **Manage by exception**
   When time is limited, managing by exception may be appropriate. Spend your available time concentrating on the most important issues and address symptoms that are clearly deviating from the expected norm. By focusing your attention on the most significant problems, you are more likely to make a difference than you would if you spread yourself too thin.

3. **Stagger your decisions**
   When you are faced with an expensive option or an irrevocable decision, consider making incremental choices first. Make partial or intermediate decisions to avoid committing to a major decision. For example, you might recommend that Quest renegotiate new terms with a Japanese tour operator before dropping a tour in Japan. Even if you later decide that dropping the tour is necessary, the favorable terms you negotiated provided some savings.

4. **Hedge your bets**
   Committing to a single option or alternative is inherently risky. Spread your risk by avoiding decisions that lock you into a single choice. See Figure 2-12. Consider a solution that includes multiple options. By using more than one approach, you are more likely to have some success—even if one approach doesn't work.

QUICK TIP
Monitor the problem, however, so it doesn't escalate, and set a time limit so you don't delay indefinitely.

5. **Delay or defer a solution**
   If you are having trouble finding a good solution that meets your goals, slow down and delay selecting a single course of action. Use the time to develop other options and gather more information. Occasionally, the problem will resolve itself. More often, the symptoms continue to grow, or events change the nature of the problem. For example, Quest might wait to promote popular tours until customers feel the economy is improving in general.

YOU TRY IT

Practice using adaptive techniques by finding solutions for common problems. Open the PS2-Y15.docx document and follow the steps in the worksheet. When you are finished, submit the document to your instructor as requested.

FIGURE 2-11: Appropriate times to use adaptive techniques

Consider using adaptive techniques when:

- You have a limited amount of time to work
- An exhaustive analysis is not needed
- The risks are minimal and downside costs are low
- The solution is easily reversible

FIGURE 2-12: Avoid decisions that lock you into a single choice

Pawel Gaul/Photos.com

TABLE 2-7: Adaptive techniques do's and don'ts

guidelines	do	don't
Manage by exception	• Spend your available time concentrating on the most important issues • Use your limited time addressing factors deviating from the expected norm	• **Don't** focus on small or insignificant problems, even if they are easier to solve • **Don't** commit to a plan you cannot fulfil
Stagger decisions	• Make incremental changes when faced with expensive or disagreeable alternatives	• **Don't** make a complete commitment to a major decision if you are not prepared to do so
Spread risk	• Look for a solution that includes multiple options	• **Don't** make decisions that lock you into a single choice
Delay decision	• Slow down and delay committing yourself to a course of action • Find time to develop other options and gather more information	• **Don't** ignore the problem while you are deferring the decision

Solving problems in a blink

In his recent book, *Blink, the Power of Thinking Without Thinking*, Malcolm Gladwell explores intuition, hunches, and other abilities to make decisions in the blink of an eye. Gladwell claims that spontaneous decisions—one type of adaptive technique—can be better than those explored with scientific analysis and precision. He attributes this ability to an unconscious technique he calls "thin-slicing": the ability to sense what is important from a very narrow period of experience. *Blink* provides many examples of this phenomenon. A famous Greek statue known as the *kouros* was said to be excavated in Greece. However, when it was exhibited at the J. Paul Getty Museum in California, many museum visitors remarked that something was not right—the statue didn't look like it had ever been in the ground. The visitors' "blink moment" was later discovered to be correct: the statue was a fake. Gladwell argues that professionals often collect too much information, and that experts can make better decisions in snap judgments than they do after months of evaluating data. Experienced physicians often use thin-slicing to diagnose diseases with uncommon symptoms. Effective salespeople use the technique as they meet customers and discuss their needs. In both cases, the intuitive decisions might be correct only because years of training, practice, and experience have been condensed to useful information that can be retrieved without conscious effort.

Source: Malcolm Gladwell, Blink, The Power of Thinking Without Thinking, Little, Brown, 2005.

Objective 16 Part 2

Developing Ethical Solutions

Ethics are standards of behavior that direct how people should act. Ethics involves making moral decisions and choosing between right and wrong. When applied to problem solving, ethical behavior leads to appropriate decisions, not necessarily the optimal ones. As you work to solve problems, consider the situation from an ethical, as well as practical, perspective. Table 2-8 summarizes the do's and don'ts of developing ethical solutions. case One consequence of concentrating tours in a few areas is that adventure travel can create ecological stresses. You and Grace discuss the ethical implications of your decision and look for ways to relieve the pressures on the environment for Quest's top five tours. See Figure 2-13.

ESSENTIAL ELEMENTS

1. **Identify ethical issues**

   Most decisions have an ethical dimension, so you should identify and consider the ethics of each decision you make. Could your decision harm someone else? Should you consider more than simply finding the most efficient solution? What are the long-term implications of your decisions? Consider other people and groups that have a stake in the outcome, and keep their perspectives and interests in mind.

2. **Compare costs and benefits**

   Your solutions can create both benefits and costs for yourself and others. So-called tough decisions include elements of both. Making decisions involves weighing the pros and cons and choosing the best trade-offs. Identify the options that produce the most good and do the least harm. Many professional organizations develop codes of ethics, which are often available online.

QUICK TIP The ideal solution is usually one that benefits everyone involved.

3. **Consider other people**

   Your decisions frequently affect others in an organization. People will remember how you treat them long after the problem that you are working on has been forgotten. Be sensitive to how your actions affect others—both those within and outside of your immediate workgroup. Make decisions that cause the fewest drawbacks for others.

QUICK TIP Ask whether your solution simply moves the problem to another area.

4. **Serve broad interests**

   Look beyond your own objectives and consider the organization as a whole. Consider each alternative and the people who would be affected by it. Solutions that serve the interests of a broader group are preferable to those that only benefit certain individuals. See Figure 2-14.

5. **Be true to yourself**

   When you solve problems, you are contributing to your reputation—either positively or negatively. Not only will you be judged on the success of your solution, but also on the steps you took to accomplish the task. As you make decisions, ask yourself if the option you are considering is consistent with the sort of person you want to be. Always assume that other people will be aware of what you are doing. Never compromise your values for some short-term benefit.

YOU TRY IT

Practice developing ethical solutions by making an ethical decision based on a scenario. Open the PS2-Y16.docx document and follow the steps in the worksheet. When you are finished, submit the document to your instructor as requested.

FIGURE 2-13: Questions to ask before making a decision

Questions to ask				
Is this decision fair?	Will I feel better or worse about myself after I make this decision?	Does this decision break any organizational rules?	Does this decision break any laws or ethical standards?	How would I feel if this decision were broadcast on the news?

FIGURE 2-14: Consider the organization as a whole when you make decisions

Jacob Wackerhausen/Photos.com

TABLE 2-8: Ethical solutions do's and don'ts

guidelines	do	don't
Identify ethical issues	• Consider whether your decision benefits everyone involved • Look for ethical alternatives to the most efficient or practical solution if necessary	• Don't make decisions that cause harm to others • Don't forget that others have a stake in the outcome of your decision
Consider costs and benefits	• Weigh the pros and cons of each decision, including ethical factors • Determine whether the end result justifies the means • Find options that produce the most good and do the least harm	• Don't select an option that has far more costs than benefits
Consider other people	• Be sensitive to how your actions affect others inside and outside the organization	• Don't treat others poorly as you make decisions and solve problems; they are unlikely to forget
Serve broad interests	• Consider the objectives of the organization as well as your own • Look for solutions that serve the interests of a broad group	• Don't make a decision solely on how it benefits you
Be true to yourself	• Remember that you are judged on the success of your solution and on the steps you took to accomplish the task	• Don't compromise your values for a short-term benefit

Technology @ Work: Mashups

A **mashup** is a Web application that combines features or information from more than one source. Figure 2-15 shows the Joblighted Web site, a mashup between Google Maps and online job boards to show where employers are advertising job openings. You can click a pin on the map to display job information, or you can click a source to show on the map only job openings from that source. Businesses are using mashups to develop views of information that aid in decision making. Business mashups typically combine data from internal and public sources, and publish the results within the company for employees to use. They must also meet business software requirements for security, reliability, and usability. case Grace Wong has heard about Web mashups, and wonders if Quest could develop an in-house version that uses mapping Web sites and local data about weather, events, and travel information. She asks you to learn the basics of mashups and their benefits to business.

ESSENTIAL ELEMENTS

1. **Use the best of the Web**

   Mashups are often created from parts of Web applications and services and result in innovative resources. Because they present information in new ways, they can help you to make decisions, especially quick decisions that depend on factors such as weather, traffic, and other volatile systems. For example, if your company does business overseas, it could create a mashup between translation services such as AltaVista's Babel Fish or Google Translate, which translate selected data and Web pages, and local news so you can find the latest news in your native language.

QUICK TIP

Like automobile dashboards, business dashboards display current information about an organization's performance.

2. **Find mashups by type**

   The two main types of mashups are consumer and business, and the two types overlap. Consumer mashups include mapping, photo and video, search, shopping, and news. News mashups use sources such as the *New York Times* or the BBC and syndication technologies such as Really Simple Syndication (RSS) to provide personalized news summaries on your desktop.

   Business mashups generally help employees process information or decision makers view information in new ways. For example, online retailers can combine customer orders with credit card approval and protection systems from banks to offer secure online payment for orders. Managers can view mashups called **dashboards**, windows that graphically summarize information about how a business is operating.

3. **Create a mashup**

   Online tools such as Masher (*www.masher.com*), and Kofax Technologies (*www.kofax.com*) let you create mashups online. To create a mashup using Masher, follow the steps on the Masher home page. See Figure 2-16. Select a source of media, including image and videos, mash (or combine) them using Masher's tools, and then post the results on a social network site.

YOU TRY IT

Learn more about mashups. Open the PS2-TechWork.docx document and follow the steps in the worksheet. When you are finished, submit the document to your instructor as requested.

FIGURE 2-15: Joblighted, a mashup of Google Maps and online job services

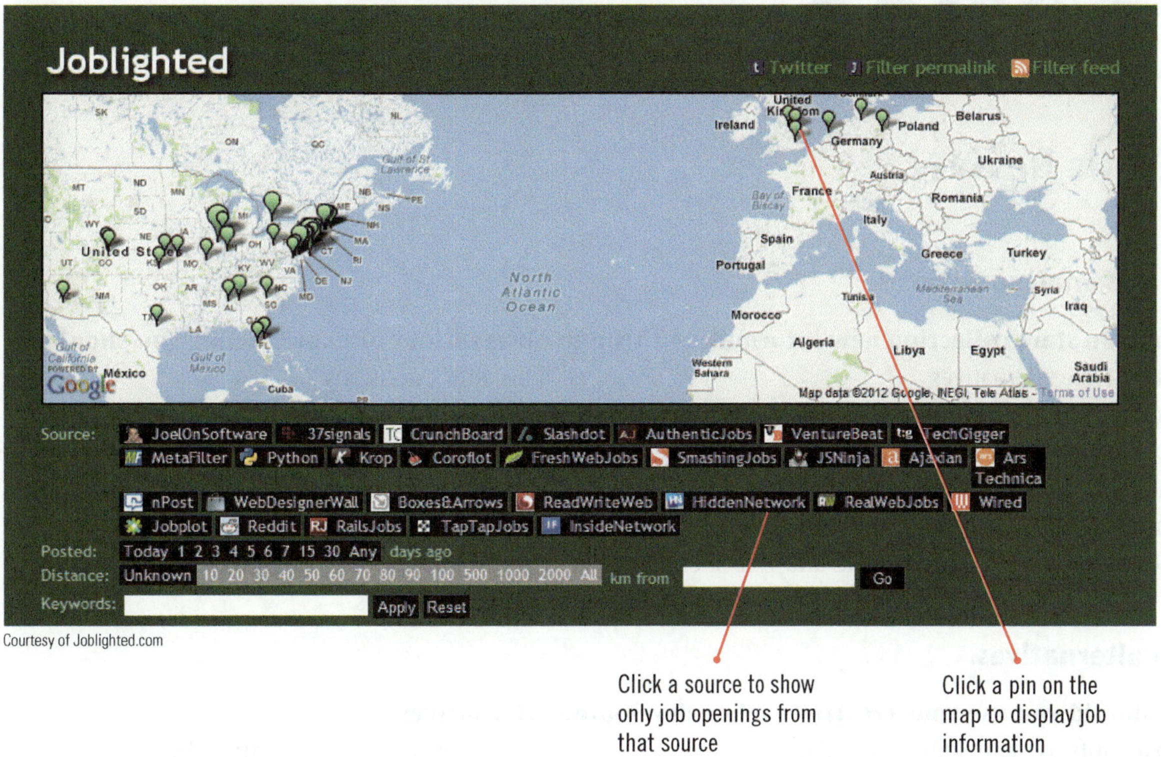

Courtesy of Joblighted.com

FIGURE 2-16: Masher, an online tool for creating mashups

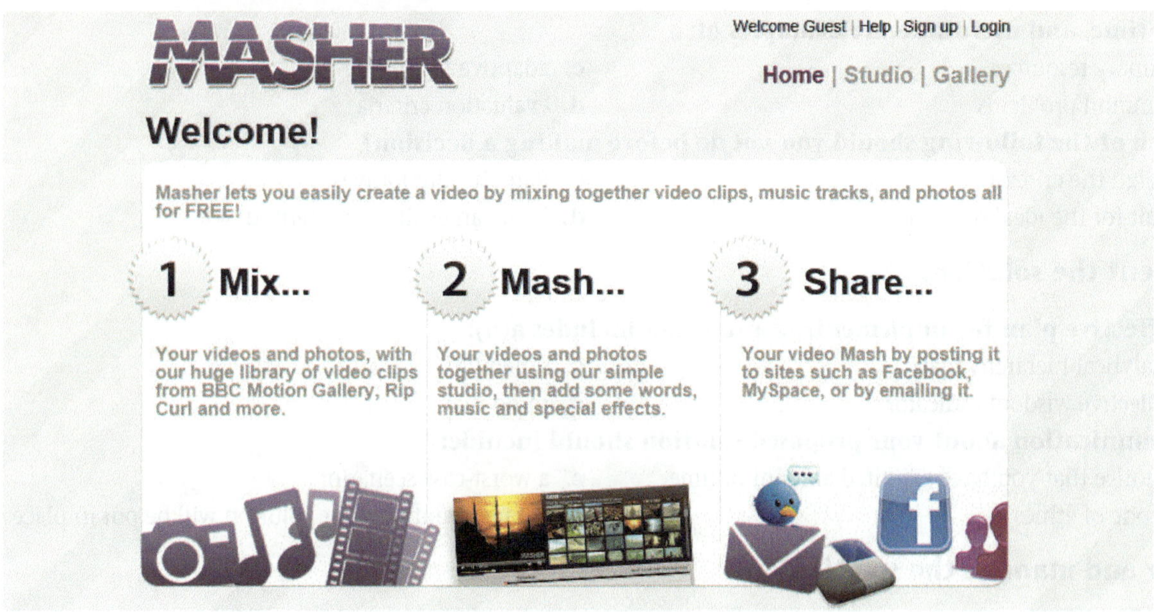

Courtesy of Masher.com

Practice

Soft Skills Review

Gather and analyze data.

1. **Before you start collecting new information through observations or experiments, you should:**
   - **a.** analyze the alternatives
   - **b.** look for sources of existing information
   - **c.** make quick decisions
   - **d.** subscribe to new sources of information
2. **What kind of data should you collect to solve a problem of customer dissatisfaction with a product or service?**
   - **a.** Employee reports and logs
   - **b.** Secondary sources, such as books and Web sites
   - **c.** Customer surveys and comments
   - **d.** Organization records, trade associations, and business databases

Develop alternatives.

1. **Why should you use your creativity when developing alternatives?**
   - **a.** To identify as many ideas as possible
   - **b.** To enjoy the experience
   - **c.** To stay anchored to your initial ideas
   - **d.** To delay a decision
2. **Which of the following is a useful creativity tool for generating ideas?**
   - **a.** Mind map
   - **b.** Mindstorm
   - **c.** Brain wave
   - **d.** Mashup

Evaluate options.

1. **Cost, time, and usefulness are examples of:**
   - **a.** primary resources
   - **b.** common problems
   - **c.** adaptive techniques
   - **d.** evaluation criteria
2. **Which of the following should you *not* do before making a decision?**
   - **a.** Weigh the criteria
   - **b.** Wait for the ideal solution
   - **c.** Rate the alternatives
   - **d.** Select an evaluation method

Implement the solution.

1. **An effective plan for implementing a solution includes a(n):**
   - **a.** analytical hierarchy matrix
   - **b.** collective wisdom indicator
   - **c.** schedule
   - **d.** mind map
2. **Communication about your proposed solution should include:**
   - **a.** a notice that you have a limited amount of time
   - **b.** a code of ethics
   - **c.** a worst-case scenario
   - **d.** details about how the solution will be put in place

Monitor and manage the solution.

1. **Which of the following is *not* a variable you might track when monitoring a solution?**
   - **a.** Expert advice
   - **b.** Daily sales data
   - **c.** Production logs
   - **d.** Customer surveys

2. What should you do if your solution is not causing expected improvements?

a. Wait for the problem to solve itself

b. Adjust the solution promptly

c. Abandon the solution

d. Stop monitoring efforts

Verify the solution.

1. When testing a solution, you should:

a. create the most stressful test possible, even if it is dangerous

b. stick to the superficial part of the solution

c. consider the worst-case scenario

d. make the results confidential

2. Why might you give a presentation after verifying a solution?

a. To communicate your progress

b. To entertain your colleagues

c. To provide an opportunity for brainstorming

d. To defer a decision

Use adaptive techniques.

1. In which of the following scenarios is an adaptive technique *not* appropriate?

a. You have a limited amount of time to work

b. The solution is easily reversible

c. The risks are minimal and costs are low

d. You need an exhaustive analysis

2. Negotiating new terms with a tour operator instead of dropping the tour is an example of:

a. using your intuition

b. managing by exception

c. risk analysis

d. staggering a decision

Develop ethical solutions.

1. Ethical problem solving leads to solutions that:

a. produce the most good while doing the least harm

b. serve narrow interests

c. are perfect

d. have more costs than benefits

2. Which of the following is *not* an example of an ethical dilemma?

a. Cut expenses, though many employees will lose their jobs

b. Reduce quality, even if it makes a product less safe

c. Sell new products abroad, though they are banned in this country

d. Increase sales of services, though the services are new

Technology @ work: Mashups

1. What is a mashup?

a. A matrix for making decisions

b. A way to use groups to solve problems

c. An informal way to make decisions based on intuition or common sense

d. A Web application that combines features or information from more than one source

2. A business might create a mashup to:

a. develop views of information that aid in decision making

b. learn how to manage by exception

c. test solutions using worst-case scenarios

d. schedule Web conferences

Critical Thinking Questions

1. **To increase sales at an electronics store, your manager is advertising a popular music player at an unusually low price. When customers arrive at the store requesting the music player, the manager wants you and other sales people to steer customers to a more expensive alternative. Should you go along?**
2. **Built-in obsolescence means designing products that will degrade over time or otherwise need to be replaced. Many products depend on built-in obsolescence to ensure sales, such as light bulbs, batteries, and electronic devices. Do you think selling products with built-in obsolescence is an ethical way to do business?**
3. **Some people are habitually indecisive. They let others make decisions and then follow along whether they agree or not. Why do you think they behave this way?**
4. **Do groups make better decisions than individuals? What are the pros and cons of working in a group to make decisions? Which do you prefer and why?**
5. **Culture can influence how organizations and people make decisions. For example, a recent study of Japanese and American business students compared how the students used software to purchase a car. The results contradict popular stereotypes and suggest that the Japanese students used a more intuitive process to make decisions, while the Americans relied on statistics and analysis. Suppose someone you know is about to work for a company in another culture. What advice would you give them about making decisions?**

Independent Challenge 1

Lawrence Media in Nashville, Tennessee, specializes in promotional products for businesses, such as corporate apparel, executive gifts, and product giveaways. As an assistant to Ken Lawrence, the founder of the company, you often attend meetings to discuss sales and marketing strategies. Lawrence Media has a new line of digital organizers that companies can buy and provide to customers and sales people as promotions. Ken needs to decide on the best way to sell the organizers. Figure 2-17 shows the decision matrix he has created and asks you to help him complete it.

- **a.** Open the **PS2-IC1.docx** document and follow the steps in the worksheet.
- **b.** Proofread the document carefully to fix any grammar or formatting errors.
- **c.** Submit the document to your instructor as requested.

FIGURE 2-17

Options for Selling Digital Organizer	A	B	C	D	Row Sum	Rank
A. On company Web site						
B. In quarterly catalog						
C. Face-to-face sales calls						
D. In special flyer						

Independent Challenge 2

You work with Carla Marcus, the owner of Sage Realty Services in Winnetka, Illinois. Employee morale is low, and Carla wants to take her staff on a company retreat to boost morale and brainstorm ways to stimulate sales. She wants to have the retreat in a place that offers meeting facilities, access to entertainment, and access to business resources such as computers, copiers, and meeting facilitators. She has narrowed her choices to four locations, and created a table to rank and weigh each choice. Figure 2-18 shows the table. Carla asks you to help her evaluate the alternatives.

a. Open the **PS2-IC2.docx** document and follow the steps in the worksheet.
b. Proofread the document carefully to fix any grammar or formatting errors.
c. Submit the document to your instructor as requested.

FIGURE 2-18

Company Retreat									
Each alternative = 25%	Transportation cost		Meeting facilities		Entertainment		Business resources		
	Points	Score	Points	Score	Points	Score	Points	Score	Total Score
Orlando									
New York									
Smoky Mountains									
Las Vegas									

Real Life Independent Challenge

You can apply the decision-making techniques you learned in this part to the decisions you need to make in other parts of your life, such as what job to accept, whether to buy or rent a house or apartment, and whether to continue your formal education. Select a decision you need to make, and then identify possible solutions.

a. Select a decision you need to make. Choose one that demands careful consideration and analysis.
b. Use one of the tools presented in this lesson to generate possible alternatives. For example, brainstorm a list of alternatives or create a mind map.
c. Use a tool such as a decision table to rate the alternatives.
d. Use a different tool to rate the alternatives, and then compare the results.
e. Now that you've applied logic to your decision, do you intuitively agree with the results?

Team Challenge

You are working for Colorado Green Builders, a company in Boulder, Colorado, specializing in sustainable building. The goal of your company is to design and build structures that use energy, resources, and materials efficiently, protect the health of occupants, improve the productivity of employees, and reduce waste, pollution, and environmental degradation. Your manager, Amanda Karlson, asks you and your team to consider whether Colorado Green Builders should accept a new project. The project involves building an information center in the Colorado Rocky Mountains. The building will be "off the grid," meaning that the building will be self-sufficient and will not rely on public utilities for power or water. Amanda suggests you follow the steps below to make your recommendations:

a. Individually, learn what is involved in green building and creating off-the-grid structures. Outline a plan of up to six steps for building the information center.
b. Meet as a group to discuss what would happen if the project fails miserably. Compile a list of the reasons for the failure.
c. Sort the list into categories, such as technology obstacles, community opposition, and lack of knowledge.
d. Revise your plan to correct its flaws and to avoid the potential problems.
e. Submit the plan to your instructor as requested.

Be the Critic

You are working for Kaboodle Software, a company that designs useful desktop gadgets for computer users. Your boss, Peter McNally, is planning a major overhaul of the company Web site. Peter is trying to decide whether to hire an outside Web design firm to create the Web site or do it in house using company programmers. To help make the decision, Peter listed the pros and cons of his two alternatives, as shown in Figure 2-19. In the end, Peter made a gut decision and now plans to revise the Web site in house. Analyze Peter's decision, noting its weaknesses, and send a list of the weaknesses to your instructor.

FIGURE 2-19

Hire an Outside Web Design Agency?	
Pros	**Cons**
Quality of work	High cost
Expertise	Don't know our products
Work more quickly	Not as flexible
Have graphical resources	Loss of control

Part

3 Thinking Critically

Files You Will Need:

PS3-Y18.docx
PS3-Y19.docx
PS3-Y20.docx
PS3-Y21.docx
PS3-Y22.docx
PS3-Y23.docx
PS3-Y24.docx
PS3-TechWork.docx
PS3-IC1.docx
PS3-IC2.docx

Suppose you were building a bridge across a river. You would determine how people would cross the bridge—by foot, car, or train, for example—find the best spots for the foundations on either side of the river, and take measurements. You might consider a few styles of bridges, and then select the one that meets your needs. You would draw designs on paper and build at least one model to make sure the bridge could bear the load of traffic as it crossed. Finally, after creating schedules and enlisting help from experts, you would dig the first hole for the bridge foundation. All of these activities involve analyzing, evaluating, and making objective decisions to make sure the result is sound and successful. The same is true for critical thinking. In this part, you explore what it means to think critically and how to become a critical thinker. case At Quest Specialty Travel, you have been working with Grace Wong, the vice president of finance, to solve the problem of declining sales. Your project team is now tracking the progress of the solution: increasing the enrollment of Quest's most popular tours. These tours include trips to Italy, France, and Australia. So far, the enrollment for the France and Australia tours have improved steadily. In fact, the Burgundy by Bike tour is now one of the top five all-time best sellers. However, sales for the active tours in Italy remain flat, despite the region's popularity. Grace asks you to help her determine the reasons for the flat sales.

OBJECTIVES

17 Understand critical thinking
18 Identify arguments
19 Assess the credibility of an argument
20 Explore weaknesses in an argument
21 Overcome obstacles to critical thinking
22 Avoid deductive reasoning fallacies
23 Avoid inductive reasoning fallacies
24 Become a critical thinker

Objective 17
Part 3

Understanding Critical Thinking

One characteristic that differentiates humans from other animal species is the ability to think, reason, and make informed judgments about observations and facts. Thought and thinking are natural, sometimes automatic mental processes that include reasoning, remembering, imagining, and reflecting, for example. **Critical thinking** generally requires more analysis, evaluation, discipline, and rigor. The goal of critical thinking is often to improve choices and reduce the risk of adopting or acting on a flawed assumption. case Grace Wong says that investigating the reasons for the flat sales of Italian tours requires critical thinking. She advises you to learn more about critical thinking to help her solve the sales problem.

DETAILS

Ask yourself the following questions as you prepare to improve your critical thinking:

- **What is critical thinking?**
  Critical thinking is the thoughtful, deliberate process of deciding whether you should accept, reject, or reserve judgment about a particular idea. It is also a measure of your confidence in the idea itself. Use critical thinking whenever you make a decision, solve a problem, take an action, or decide what to believe. Although the word *critical* can mean to find fault or to criticize, critical thinking is not a negative activity. Rather, it is a process where you ask questions, challenge assumptions, examine claims, and identify alternatives or answers. See Figure 3-1.

- **What is a claim?**
  A **claim** is a statement that someone says or writes about a topic. The claim can be true or false. Many statements are not claims. For example, when you greet someone or ask a question, the statements are generally not either true or false. In contrast, you can measure the amount of truth in a claim. For example, if a colleague claims the Quest tours to Italy are the most popular, you can refer to tour sales to determine if that claim is true. When you are presented with a claim, you decide whether to accept, reject, or investigate it.

- **What is an issue?**
  When you are solving problems or engaged in other activities that demand critical thinking, you are examining and thinking about an issue. In general terms, an **issue** is any controversial subject that you discuss, dispute, or review. An issue is different from a simple topic of conversation because it raises questions or concerns. For example, the Italian tours at Quest are an issue—their sales should be increasing, but they are not, which raises concerns about the tours.

- **What is an argument?**
  In common usage, *argument* means a heated discussion between people. In the context of critical thinking, an **argument** is a set of one or more claims that support a particular conclusion. The claims are sometimes called *premises*. When you try to persuade someone to adopt your point of view, you typically make an argument and offer evidence that helps prove your claim as true. You should also evaluate other peoples' claims carefully and decide whether you accept their arguments.

- **What is the difference between facts and opinions?**
  Thinking critically demands that you distinguish between fact and opinion. Typically, a **fact** is a claim that is considered to be true. An **opinion** is a claim that someone believes is true. Opinions may or may not be factual, even though people often assert their opinions as facts. Figure 3-2 compares facts and opinions. If you can collect data about and analyze a claim, it is said to be a **factual matter**. This term suggests that you are not certain the claim is a fact, but could prove or disprove if necessary.

QUICK TIP
Some speakers signal their opinions by saying, "I think," or "The way I see it." If they don't, evaluate their claims and question whether they are facts or opinions.

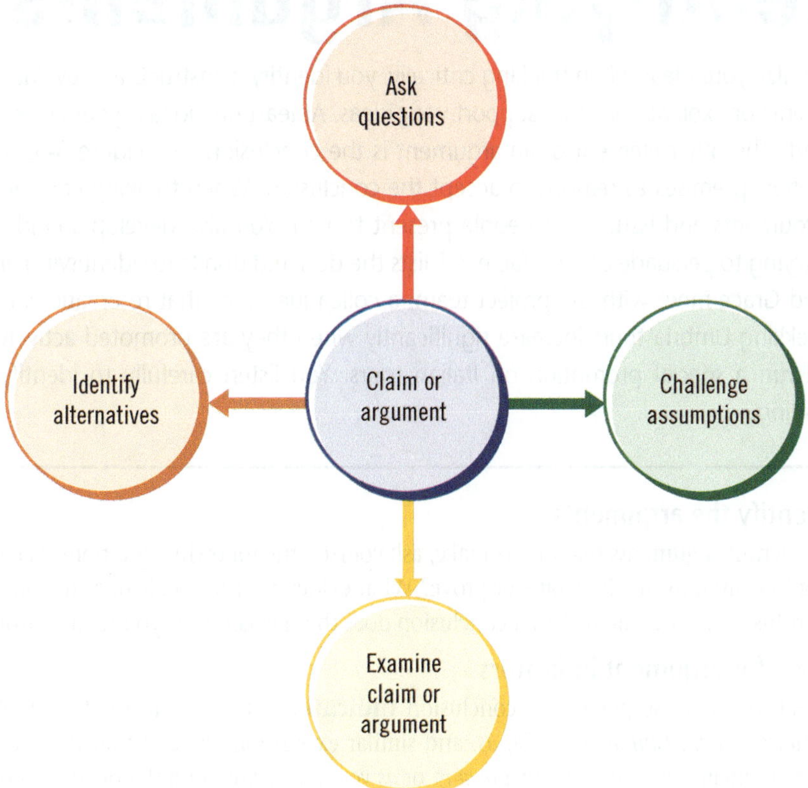

FIGURE 3-1: Steps in critical thinking

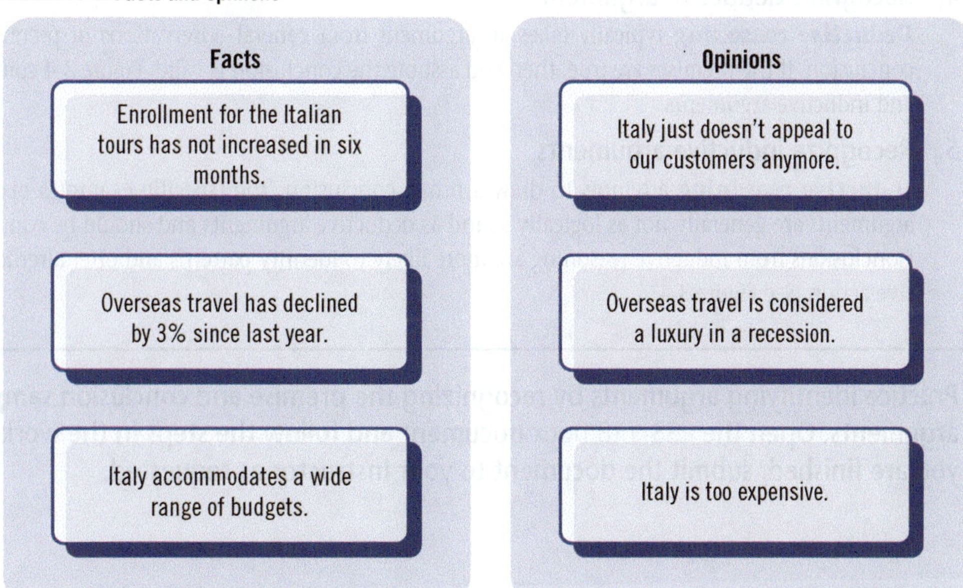

FIGURE 3-2: Facts and opinions

Objective 18
Part 3

Identifying Arguments

To organize your ideas when thinking critically, you identify, construct, and evaluate arguments, which are statements or explanations that support your ideas. At least one idea is your **premise**—what you claim or contend. The other element of an argument is the conclusion. See Figure 3-3. A well-constructed argument offers premises as reasons to accept the conclusion. When thinking critically, you identify and analyze arguments and issues that people present to you. You also develop sound and rational arguments when trying to persuade others. Table 3-1 lists the do's and don'ts for identifying arguments. case When you and Grace meet with the project team, a colleague notes that reservations for the Trekking Tuscany and Trekking Umbria tours increase significantly when they are promoted actively. He argues that Quest should run a special promotion on Italian tours. You listen carefully to identify his arguments before responding.

ESSENTIAL ELEMENTS

QUICK TIP
People sometimes omit an obvious conclusion, assuming you can recognize it on your own.

1. Identify the arguments

To identify arguments that others make, ask yourself the following questions: What is the other person trying to communicate, illustrate, or prove? What evidence or rationale does the other person present to support his or her argument? What conclusion does the speaker want you to draw from his or her argument?

2. Look for argument indicators

Speakers often use premise or conclusion **indicators** as signals to catch your attention. Words such as *because, since, assuming that, for, as,* and similar expressions suggest that the speaker is stating a premise. Phrases including *as a result, that means,* or *as you can see* are examples of conclusion indicators.

QUICK TIP
Making assertions without giving reasons is characteristic of dogmatic or biased thinking, which you can avoid by supporting your arguments with evidence.

3. Differentiate between an argument and an assertion

When analyzing issues, be sure to differentiate between arguments and assertions. An **assertion** is a simple statement that does not include any supporting evidence. For example, "Customers like culinary tours," is an assertion. If the follow-up statement provides evidence or a rationale for the statement, it becomes an argument.

4. Recognize deductive arguments

Deductive reasoning typically takes an argument from general observations or premises to a specific conclusion. If the premises are true, then you assume the conclusion is valid. Figure 3-4 compares deductive and inductive arguments.

5. Recognize inductive arguments

Inductive reasoning attempts to draw a broad conclusion from specific examples or premises. These arguments are generally not as logically sound as deductive arguments and should be considered carefully. Conclusions from inductive reasoning are more likely to identify patterns and offer alternatives than decisive action. See Figure 3-4.

YOU TRY IT

Practice identifying arguments by recognizing the premise and conclusion sample arguments. Open the PS3-Y18.docx document and follow the steps in the worksheet. When you are finished, submit the document to your instructor as requested.

FIGURE 3-3: Identifying arguments

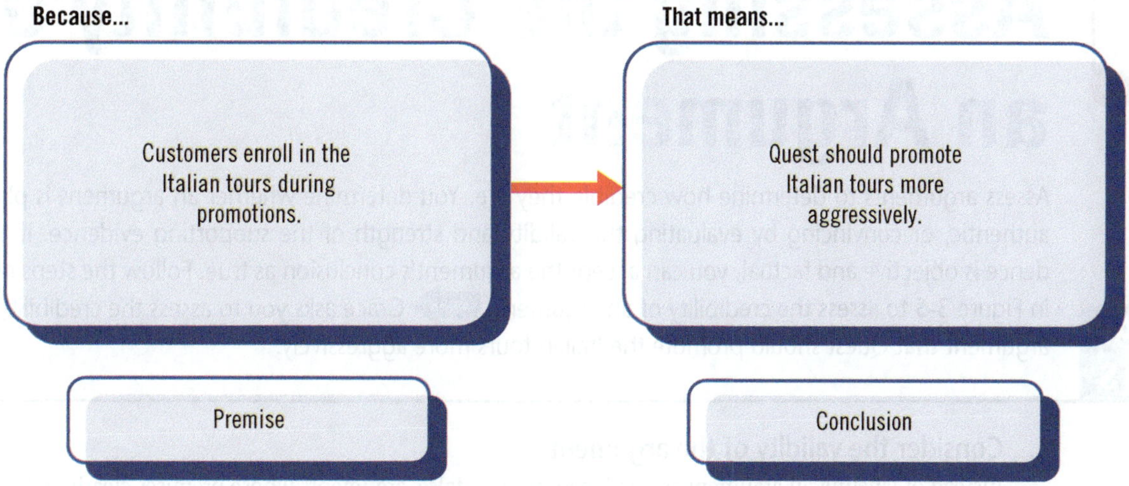

FIGURE 3-4: Comparing deductive and inductive arguments

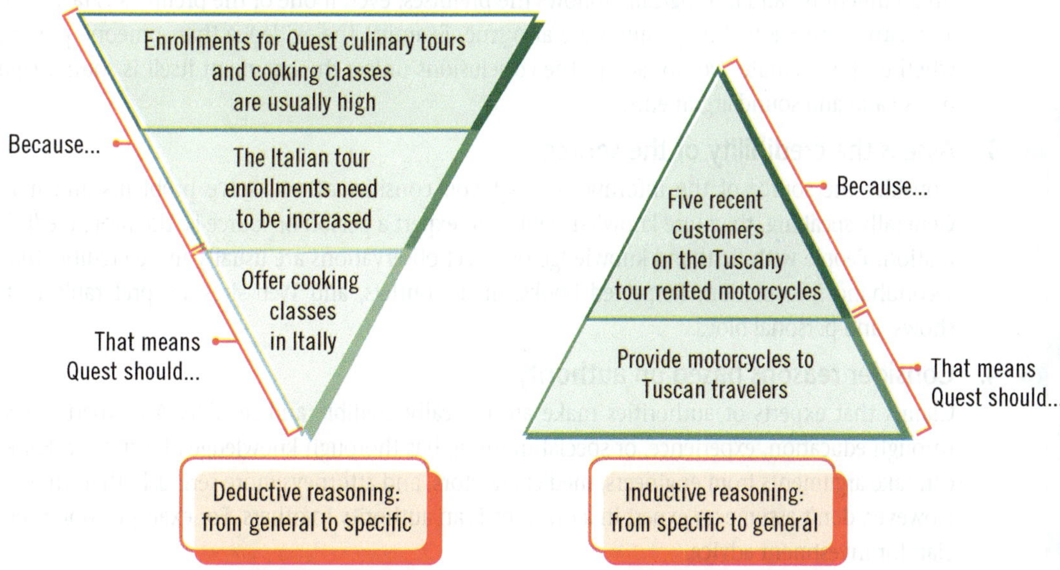

TABLE 3-1: Identifying arguments do's and don'ts

guidelines	do	don't
Identify argument elements	• Consider what someone is trying to communicate, illustrate, or prove • Look for the evidence or rationale the other person presents to support an argument • Evaluate the conclusions • Listen for premise and conclusion indicators • Distinguish between assertions and arguments	• Don't make an argument without verifying your claims • Don't accept another's conclusion without evaluating it • Don't confuse an assertion, which doesn't include supporting evidence, with an argument, which does
Use deductive reasoning	• Draw a conclusion from general observations if the premises are true	• Don't offer a conclusion based on faulty information
Use inductive reasoning	• Use the conclusions of inductive reasoning to identify alternatives and patterns	• Don't rely on inductive arguments, which are not as strong as deductive arguments

Objective
19
Part 3

Assessing the Credibility of an Argument

ESSENTIAL ELEMENTS

Assess arguments to determine how credible they are. You determine whether an argument is plausible, authentic, or convincing by evaluating the validity and strength of the supporting evidence. If the evidence is objective and factual, you can accept the argument's conclusion as true. Follow the steps outlined in Figure 3-5 to assess the credibility of an argument. case Grace asks you to assess the credibility of the argument that Quest should promote the Italian tours more aggressively.

1. **Consider the validity of the argument**
   Instead of labeling an argument as good, bad, true, or false, arguments whose premises clearly support their conclusions are said to be valid. A **valid argument** has a conclusion that logically follows from the premises. If an argument is valid and the premises are true, the conclusion must be true.
2. **Make sure the argument is sound**
   An argument is valid if it logically follows the premises, even if one of the premises is false. It is considered a **sound argument** if its premises are also true. Examine the evidence that someone presents and judge whether it is accurate. Do not accept the conclusions unless the argument itself is sound. Figure 3-6 compares valid and sound arguments.
3. **Assess the credibility of the source**
   Consider the source of the information that you consider as you solve problems and make decisions. Generally speaking, the more knowledgeable and expert a person or source is, the more credible their information. People with firsthand knowledge or direct observations are usually more credible than those with secondhand information. Respected books, media outlets, and Web sites are preferable to tabloids, talk shows, and personal blogs.
4. **Consider reasons based on authority**
   Claims that experts or authorities make are typically credible and reliable. An expert is someone who, through education, experience, or special training, has thorough knowledge of a subject. For example, you can take arguments from engineers, medical doctors, and attorneys more seriously than those of laypeople. However, don't assume an expert in a one area is an authority in others. For example, don't rely on a physician for investment advice.
5. **Compare the argument to your background knowledge**
   Compare claims to your own **background knowledge**, which is the collection of beliefs, facts, experiences, and observations you have amassed during your life. Common sense is also part of your background. You are more likely to dismiss claims that conflict with your background knowledge, though you should keep an open mind. Accept compatible claims as plausible and worthy of additional consideration.

QUICK TIP
A source can be a document, a person, a speech, an observation, or anything used to obtain knowledge.

QUICK TIP
Experts are not always right, so evaluate their arguments as you do arguments from others.

QUICK TIP
The term *information literacy* describes the ability to recognize, analyze, and judge the quality of information.

YOU TRY IT

Practice assessing the credibility of an argument by identifying a sound argument. Open the PS3-Y19.docx document and follow the steps in the worksheet. When you are finished, submit the document to your instructor as requested.

FIGURE 3-5: Assessing the credibility of an argument

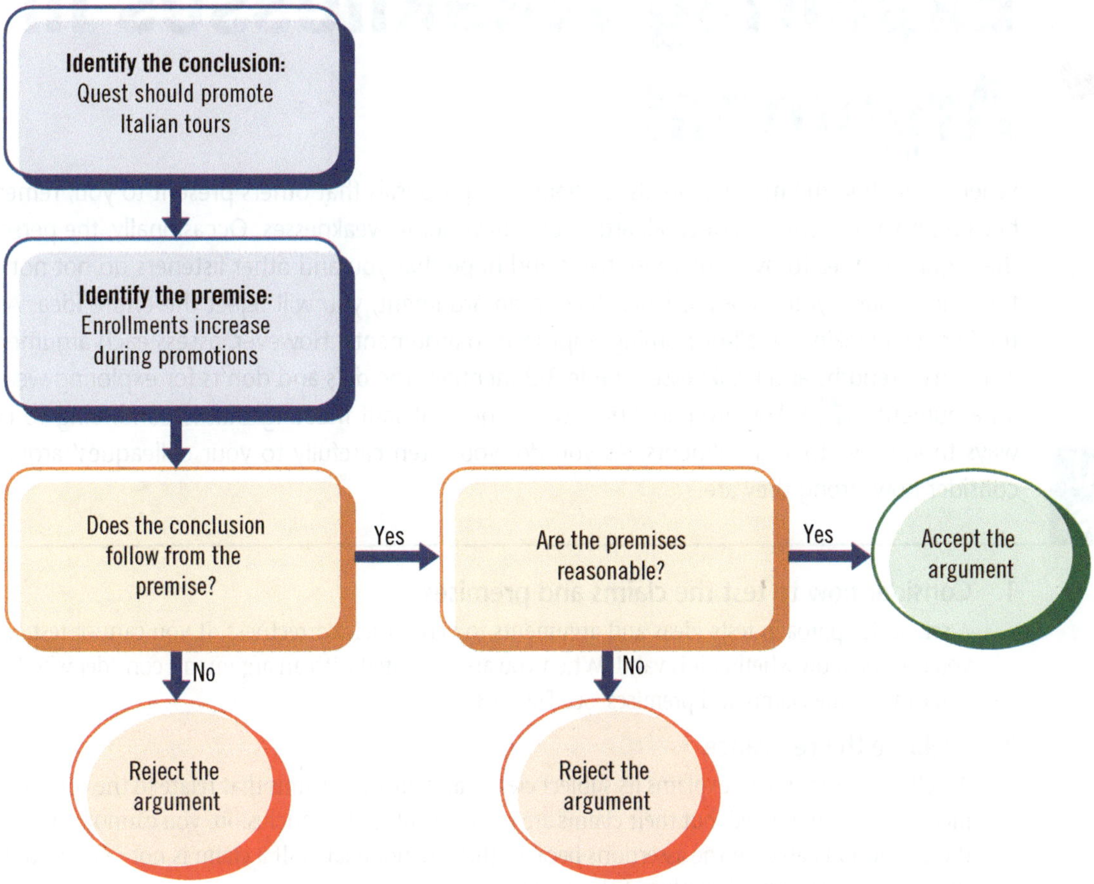

FIGURE 3-6: Valid and sound arguments

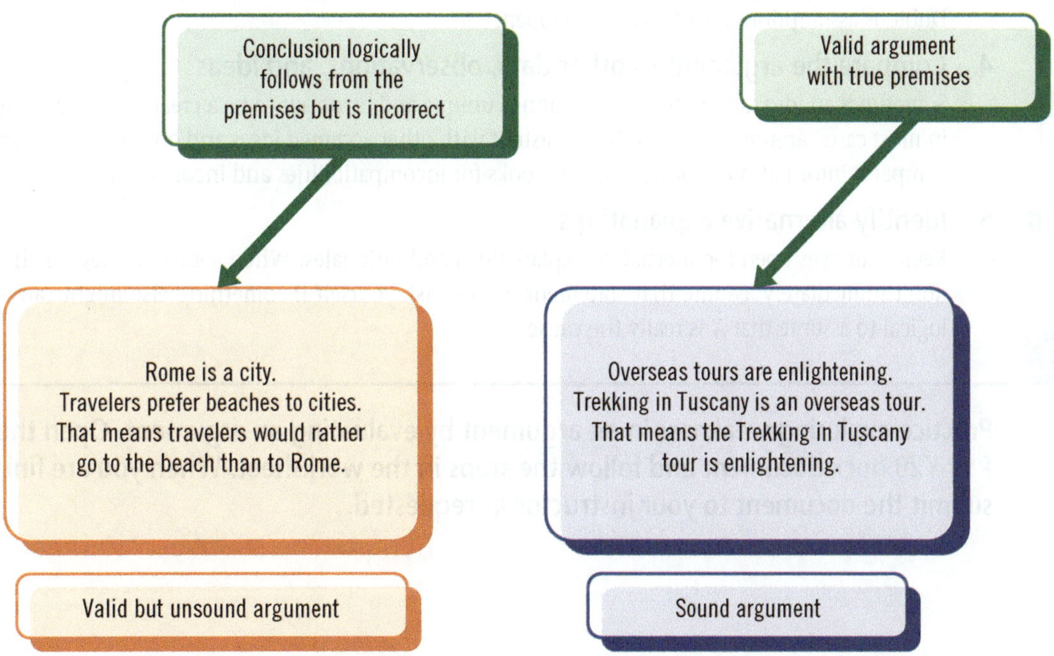

Objective 20
Part 3

Exploring Weaknesses in an Argument

When evaluating the merits of ideas, evidence, or proposals that others present to you, remember that because no argument is perfect, all arguments have some weaknesses. Occasionally, the person making the argument tries to overlook these flaws and hope that you and other listeners do not notice. Often, the fear is that if you see a particular flaw in an argument, you will reject the entire idea. As a critical thinker, avoid taking an all-or-nothing approach to arguments. However, assess each argument according to its strengths and weaknesses. Table 3-2 identifies the do's and don'ts for exploring weaknesses in an argument. case You are participating in a general staff meeting that is continuing to brainstorm ways to improve tour enrollments. As you do, you listen carefully to your colleagues' arguments and consider how strong they are.

ESSENTIAL ELEMENTS

1. **Consider how to test the claims and premises**
   A scientific approach tests ideas and arguments to verify their correctness. If you cannot test an assertion, you cannot know whether it is valid. When you are presented with an argument, consider whether and how you can test the claims and premises. See Figure 3-7.
2. **Evaluate the relevance**
   A well-crafted argument explains its subject clearly and presents claims that relate to the conclusion. If arguments are well presented, but their claims are not relevant to the conclusion, you cannot reasonably predict the conclusion based on the assertions because they are not related. If a claim is not relevant to the conclusion, you can discount the value of the argument.
3. **Look for dubious assumptions**
   One argument is normally considered to be stronger than another if it requires fewer assumptions. An **assumption** is a proposition or claim that you take for granted as though it were known to be valid. Dubious assumptions are unlikely to happen.
4. **Compare the argument to other data, observations, and ideas**
   Sometimes an idea, alternative, or solution is unique and turns out to be a creative breakthrough. However, in most cases, arguments should be consistent with other accepted ideas and observations. A critical thinker compares information to other data and looks for incompatibilities and inconsistencies.
5. **Identify alternative explanations**
   Keep your eyes open for alternative explanations and rationales. When someone suggests that *X* causes *Y*, don't immediately assume that statement is true. Ask yourself if something else might cause *Y*, or if it is logical to assume that *X* is really the cause.

QUICK TIP
If events happen at the same time, they might be coincidences or correspondences, but one does not necessarily cause the other.

YOU TRY IT

Practice exploring weakness in an argument by evaluating an argument. Open the PS3-Y20.docx document and follow the steps in the worksheet. When you are finished, submit the document to your instructor as requested.

FIGURE 3-7: Evaluating argument weaknesses

TABLE 3-2: Exploring argument weaknesses do's and don'ts

guidelines	do	don't
Test claims	• Take a scientific approach by verifying ideas and arguments	• **Don't** accept an assertion if you cannot test it
Evaluate relevance	• Check to make sure the claims relate to the conclusion	• **Don't** buy into an argument if it is well presented but the claims are not related to the conclusion
Look for assumptions	• Give more weight to arguments with fewer assumptions	• **Don't** accept dubious assumptions
Consider consistency	• Look for arguments consistent with accepted ideas and practices	• **Don't** ignore ideas, alternatives, or solutions that might be unique and turn out to be a creative breakthrough

Objective 21
Part 3

Overcoming Obstacles to Critical Thinking

You develop critical thinking as a skill over time through practice and repeated application. Learn to recognize typical obstacles to critical thinking so you can anticipate and work through them. Table 3-3 lists the do's and don'ts for overcoming obstacles to critical thinking. case Grace Wong is not convinced that Quest needs to promote the Italian tours more aggressively. When she checked the advertising expenses, she found the Italian tours are already being promoted heavily. She asks you to help you find the root of the problem, which will require additional critical thinking. You prepare to overcome typical obstacles so you can help Grace find a solution.

ESSENTIAL ELEMENTS

QUICK TIP
Being flexible, adaptable, and open minded when working with others helps you avoid egocentric thinking.

1. Avoid egocentric thinking

Being egocentric means seeing the world from your own point of view, assuming you are the norm or center. This thinking limits your ability to appreciate other points of view or see past your limitations.

2. Be aware of your social conditioning

Social conditioning encourages you to accept the beliefs, traditions, and values of your social group. Social conditioning helps you feel part of the greater whole, but it can also prevent you from considering unpopular alternatives. Challenge yourself to move beyond your social conditioning and consider other ways of thinking and interpreting.

3. Identify outliers

Past experiences with other people, places, and situations that are extremely good or bad are **outliers**. They can bias your expectations in the future. For example, if your first experience flying in a commercial jet involved stormy weather, turbulence, and rough landings, you might not want to fly again. However, that flight was an outlier, so you should not expect future flights to be similar.

QUICK TIP
If you notice yourself accepting a common idea without much consideration, you have likely normalized it in your mind.

4. Avoid normalization

People who assume that their ideas are normal because they have been exposed to them repeatedly are normalizing the ideas. Critical thinking looks past the tendency to normalize and requires you to question your own thoughts and beliefs. Critical thinking, like creative thinking, demands that you see problems with a fresh perspective. In fact, keeping critical thinking separate from creative thinking can be an obstacle to solving problems. See Figure 3-8.

5. Respect your emotions

Respect your emotions, but consider their logic and appropriateness for the decisions that you are trying to make. Avoid emotional thinking, which makes it difficult to distinguish between emotions and thoughts.

YOU TRY IT

Practice overcoming obstacles to critical thinking by reacting to a scenario. Open the PS3-Y21.docx document and follow the steps in the worksheet. When you are finished, submit the document to your instructor as requested.

FIGURE 3-8: Creative and critical thinking

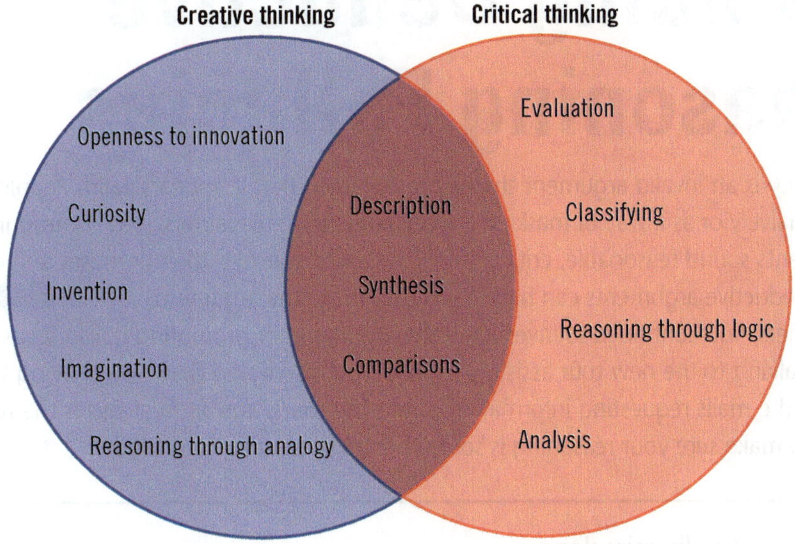

TABLE 3-3: Overcoming obstacles do's and don'ts

guidelines	do	don't
Avoid egocentric thinking	• Be aware of your own point of view	• **Don't** assume your point of view is the norm or exclusively right
Recognize social conditioning	• Challenge yourself to move beyond your social conditioning and consider alternative ways of thinking and interpreting	• **Don't** let social conditioning prevent you from considering unpopular alternatives
Understand outliers	• Understand that past extreme experiences can bias future behavior	• **Don't** let past experience necessarily determine your reactions to similar experiences in the future
Avoid normalization	• Look past the tendency to normalize ideas • Question and challenge thoughts and beliefs when appropriate	• **Don't** keep critical thinking separate from creative thinking
Respect emotions	• Respect your emotional reactions to arguments	• **Don't** give emotion more weight than logic and reason

Critical thinking and feeling

Rational thoughts and emotional feelings are usually considered as separate mental processes, perhaps even occurring in opposite sides of the brain. In early brain studies, scientists said that the rational mind is like a computer, and computers do not have feelings. Recently, however, researchers discovered that we cannot understand how we think without understanding how we feel. "When you look at the actual anatomy of the brain, you quickly see that everything is connected," says Elizabeth Phelps, a scientist at New York University. Antonio Damasio, a neuroscientist at USC, studied people with brain injuries that prevented them from perceiving their emotions. He found that they could not make effective decisions. According to Jonah Lehrer in *The Boston Globe*, "Some made terrible investments and ended up bankrupt; most just spent hours deliberating over irrelevant details, such as where to eat lunch." Researchers now use sophisticated imaging techniques to monitor brain activities. They find that decisions involve emotional reactions as well as logical thought. In fact, Jonathan Haidt, a social psychologist at the University of Virginia, wrote, "It is only because our emotional brains work so well that our reasoning can work at all."

Source: Lehrer, Jonah, "Hearts and Minds," *The Boston Globe*, April 29, 2007.

Objective 22
Part 3

Avoiding Deductive Reasoning Fallacies

A **fallacy** is an invalid argument that is presented so that it appears valid. People frequently use fallacies either naively or as a way of masking a weak conclusion. Because skilled communicators can make flawed arguments sound reasonable, critical thinkers should consider their premises and conclusions with special care. Deductive arguments can have flaws that make the arguments invalid. case After talking to Grace and others, you continued to investigate the argument for promoting Italian tours more heavily. However, when talking to the new tour assistant in Italy, you discovered that she is having trouble returning phone calls and e-mails requesting information about the tours. You suspect this is the root of the problem, but want to make sure your reasoning is sound before presenting it to Grace.

ESSENTIAL ELEMENTS

1. **Avoid the slippery slope**
   A slippery-slope argument says that if one event happens, another serious or drastic event will inevitably follow. If someone presents a slippery slope to you, politely ask how they arrived at their conclusions. See Figure 3-9.

2. **Be aware of false dilemmas**
   A false dilemma presents a limited number of options (frequently, two choices), though more options are available. The options are offered in black and white terms—one is good and the other is bad. For example, "Either we pay the higher hotel rates to our provider or we discontinue all of our tours in France," is a false dilemma. The goal of a false dilemma argument is usually to have you accept a particular conclusion.

   QUICK TIP
   To respond to a false dilemma argument, suggest that other options should be considered before making a decision.

3. **Straighten out circular reasoning**
   An argument that uses circular reasoning has a claim or premise that is little more than a restatement of the conclusion. It is logically flawed because the argument does not include independent claims or assertions. The argument is used to prove itself. Note that people often use this fallacy when expressing their opinions. See Figure 3-10.

   QUICK TIP
   This is sometimes called "begging the question."

4. **Clear up equivocation**
   Using ambiguous or vague words in an argument is known as **equivocation**, and may or may not be intentional. At one of the stops on a Quest tour in Latin America, a sign reads, "Fine for public sunbathing." A tourist assumed that it was fine to openly lie out in the sun. The word *fine* has more than one meaning, which led to the confusion. If you are unsure of someone else's meaning, be sure to ask before acting on their argument.

YOU TRY IT

Practice avoiding deductive reasoning fallacies by evaluating arguments. Open the PS3-Y22.docx document and follow the steps in the worksheet. When you are finished, submit the document to your instructor as requested.

FIGURE 3-9: Slippery slope fallacy

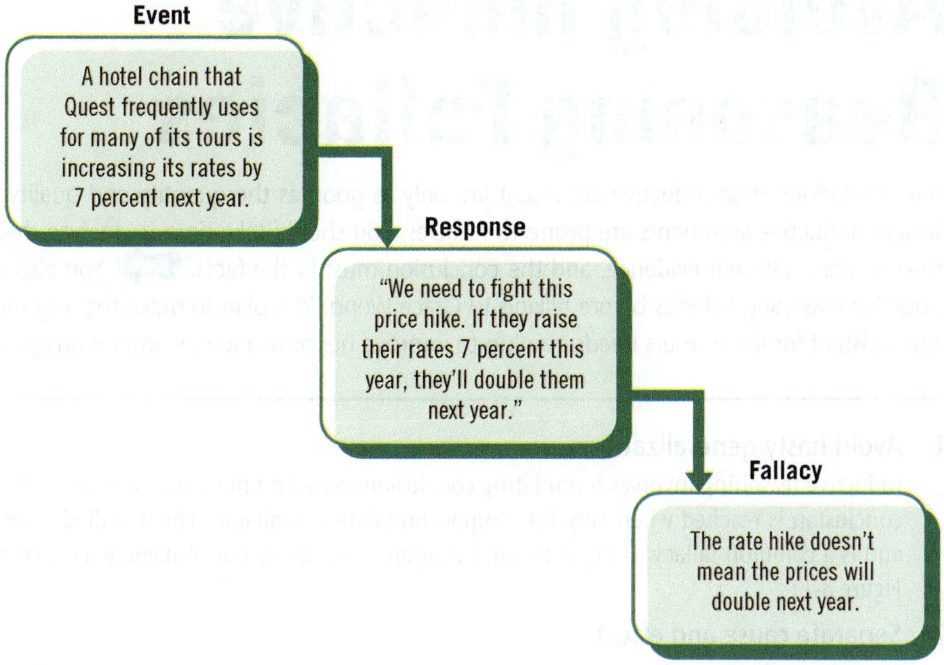

FIGURE 3-10: Circular reasoning

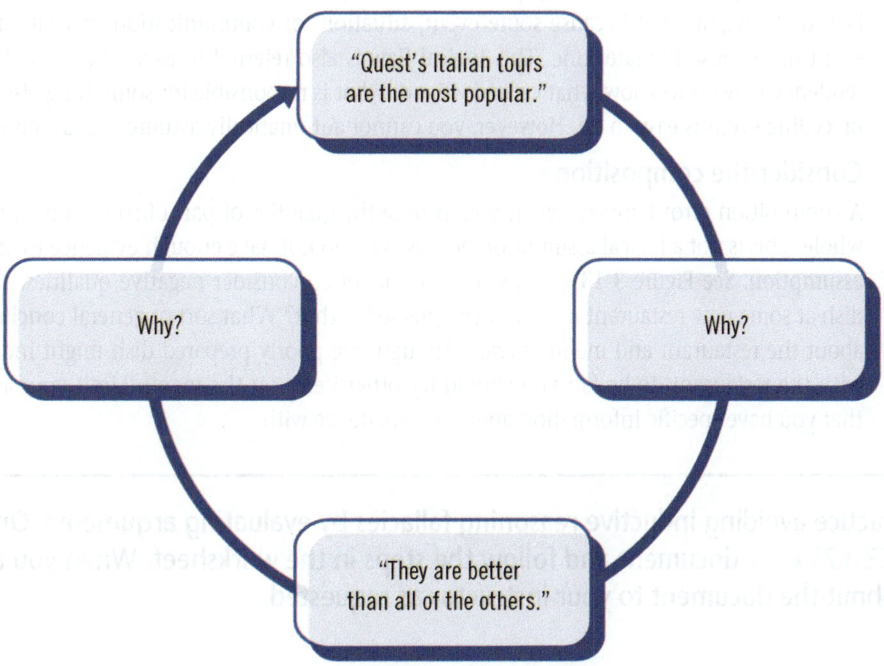

Objective 23

Part 3

Avoiding Inductive Reasoning Fallacies

The conclusions of an inductive argument are only as good as the quantity and quality of the premises. Because inductive arguments are prone to fallacies, you should take time to analyze them. The premises must contain sufficient evidence, and the conclusion must fit the facts. case You also want to consider inductive reasoning fallacies before talking to Grace Wong. You plan to make the argument that the new tour assistant for Italian tours needs training to improve her time and customer management skills.

ESSENTIAL ELEMENTS

1. **Avoid hasty generalizations**

   Inductive reasoning involves formulating conclusions based on limited observations. Sometimes, a broad conclusion is reached when very little supporting data is available. This is called a hasty generalization and is a common fallacy. Hasty generalizations are often made out of negligence, biases, or laziness. See Figure 3-11.

QUICK TIP

Collect enough data so that the conclusions are reasonable and practical.

2. **Separate cause and effect**

   Arguments often examine multiple events, occurrences, or situations to determine if they are related. A common error is to assume that when two or more events happen at the same time, one causes the other. See Figure 3-12. The fallacy occurs because the conclusion is reached without sufficient evidence to determine the real cause and effect. When an argument suggests that A causes B, ask yourself if there is anything else that can be the cause. Is the evidence sufficient to accept the conclusion?

3. **Look for false causes**

   The Latin expression *post hoc, ergo propter hoc* literally means "after this, therefore because of this." It is a fallacy that suggests that because some event, situation, or communication precedes another that the first event must cause the later one. This logical flaw is also referred to as a *false cause*. People have a natural tendency to want to know what caused what or what is responsible for something else, and assigning it to a preceding event is easy to do. However, you cannot automatically assume that a causal link exists.

4. **Consider the composition**

   A composition error happens when you assume the qualities of part of something are also qualities of the whole. This is not a logical assumption because you do not have enough evidence to make the more general assumption. See Figure 3-13. Composition errors often consider negative qualities. Have you ever tried a dish at some new restaurant and not been pleased with it? What sort of general conclusion might you draw about the restaurant and menu overall? Though one poorly prepared dish might indicate larger problems with the restaurant, to be fair you should try other items on the menu. Limit your assumptions to things that you have specific information about or experience with.

YOU TRY IT

Practice avoiding inductive reasoning fallacies by evaluating arguments. Open the PS3-Y23.docx document and follow the steps in the worksheet. When you are finished, submit the document to your instructor as requested.

FIGURE 3-11: Hasty generalization

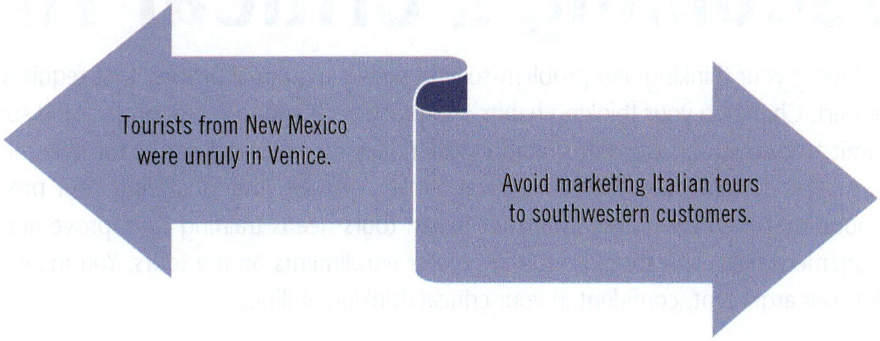

FIGURE 3-12: Separating cause and effect

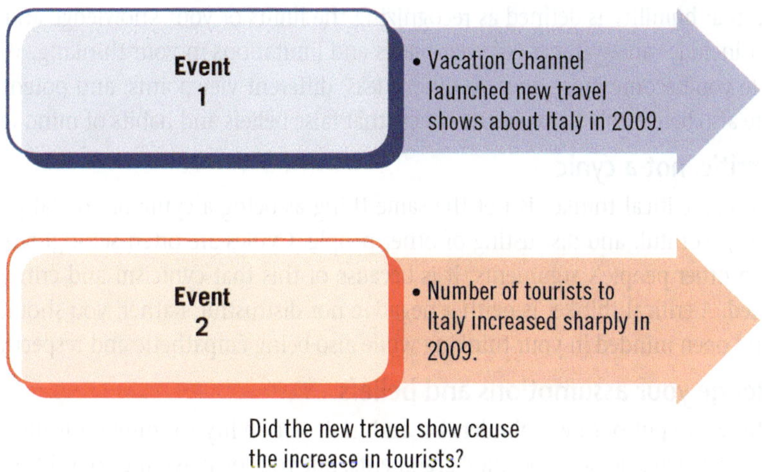

FIGURE 3-13: Composition error

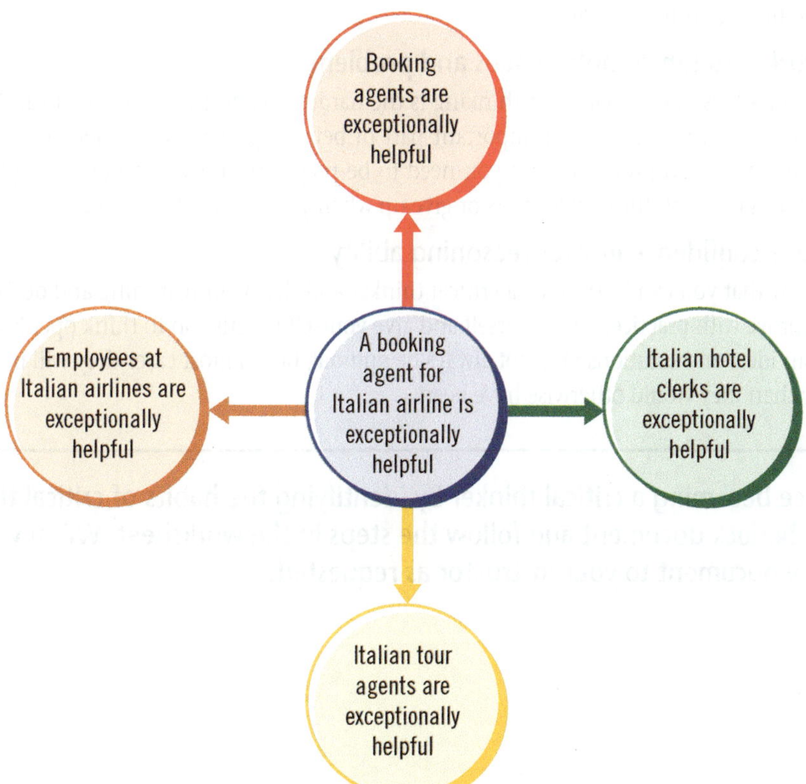

Objective 24 Part 3

Becoming a Critical Thinker

Developing your thinking and problem-solving skills is a gradual process that requires conscious effort on your part. Changing your thinking habits and practices is a long-range project and something you should commit to throughout your life. Table 3-4 identifies the do's and don'ts for becoming a critical thinker. Figure 3-14 illustrates the habits of critical thinkers. case After analyzing your premises and data, you conclude that the new tour assistant for Italian tours needs training to improve her time and customer management skills. This should result in greater enrollments on the tours. You meet with Grace Wong to make your argument, confident in your critical thinking abilities.

ESSENTIAL ELEMENTS

1. **Develop intellectual humility**

   Intellectual humility is defined as recognizing the limits of your knowledge and understanding of a situation. It includes an awareness of your biases and limitations in your thinking. When you are intellectually humble you become more open to other ideas, different viewpoints, and potential solutions to problems. You are also better able to avoid the effects that false beliefs and habits of mind tend to have.

2. **Be a critic, not a cynic**

   Becoming a critical thinker is not the same thing as being a cynic or critical person. A cynic is generally negative, scornful, and distrusting of other people. Cynics are often self-righteous and quick to point out flaws in other people's arguments. It is because of this that cynicism and critical thinking are sometimes confused. A critical thinker is neither negative nor distrustful. Rather, you should be inquisitive, questioning, and open minded in your thinking while also being empathetic and respectful of other people.

3. **Challenge your assumptions and beliefs**

   Sometimes we put our own blinders on and limit our ability to think critically. You can overcome this by not only challenging other peoples' arguments, but your own assumptions, ideas, and beliefs as well. Don't always believe and accept everything you see for the first time. Ask yourself what you want to see or hear and how that influences any incoming information. Hold yourself to the same intellectual standards that you have for other people.

4. **Work through complex issues and problems**

   Thomas Edison once said that thinking is the hardest job on the planet. Critical thinking is certainly hard work; however, it is also an important part of being a professional. There are no simplistic solutions to complex human problems, and you need to be prepared to work through complex issues. Don't become comfortable with the easy answers or give up when you become frustrated.

5. **Have confidence in your reasoning ability**

   Know that you can learn to be a critical thinker and that your reasoning and decision-making abilities can improve with practice. Trust yourself and give yourself permission to think openly and honestly. Know that your ideas and solutions may not always be optimal, but in most cases they will be "good enough" and better than they would otherwise have been.

YOU TRY IT

Practice becoming a critical thinker by identifying the habits of critical thinkers. Open the PS3-Y24.docx document and follow the steps in the worksheet. When you are finished, submit the document to your instructor as requested.

FIGURE 3-14: Critical thinking habits

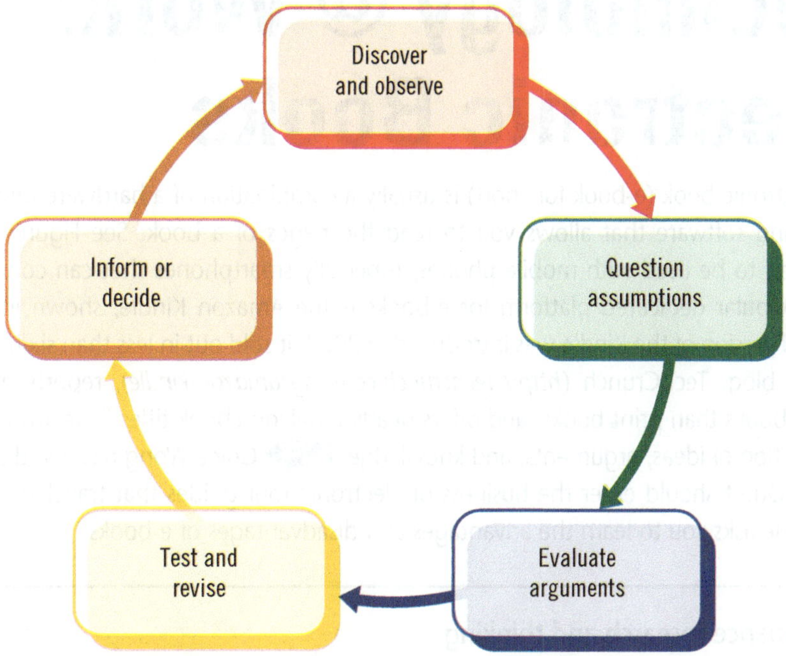

TABLE 3-4: Becoming a critical thinker do's and don'ts

guidelines	do	don't
Develop intellectual humility	• Recognize the limits of your own knowledge and understanding • Be aware of your biases and limitations	• Don't grow overconfident about your habits or conclusions
Be critical	• Be inquisitive, questioning, and open minded in your thinking while also being empathetic and respectful of other people • Challenge your own assumptions, ideas, and beliefs	• Don't be cynical when you should be critical • Don't be negative or distrustful
Have confidence in your critical thinking	• Practice critical thinking • Accept solutions that are good enough instead of perfect	• Don't be intolerant of uncertainty

Guesstimating is critical thinking

According to *Guesstimation: Solving the World's Problems on the Back of a Cocktail Napkin* by Lawrence Weinstein and John A. Adam, one way to become a critical thinker is to guesstimate—giving approximate answers to mathematical questions such as the amount of space required to gather all the people in the world in one place (answer: the equivalent of a large city). As Tony Mann, professor of mathematical science at the University of Greenwich, says, "This is a useful life skill - we all have to make judgments based on approximations and 'guesstimates' . . . Similar thought processes might help one to . . . evaluate the real risk underlying a medical scare story in the press. Employers sometimes use such questions to assess candidates for appointments, believing that they provide evidence of problem-solving skills." The book provides puzzles and strategies for solving them. For example, one question is, "If you put all the miles that Americans drive every year end to end, how far into space could you travel?" To answer the question, you systematically break the problem into small parts to come up with a reasonable ballpark guess. Americans drive about 12,000 miles per year. There is, perhaps, one car for every two people, or about 150 million cars in the U.S. Multiply that by 12,000 miles to calculate the result of two trillion miles, which gets you very far into space. Pluto is only three billion miles from Earth, so you could go well beyond that.

Why guesstimate when you could just search for the answer on Google? "I hate to tell you this, but not everything on the Web can be believed," explains Lawrence Weinstein, one of the authors. Learning to guesstimate also helps you judge problems. "It gets people out of a crisis mode of thinking," he said.

Sources: Angier, Natalie, "The Biggest of Puzzles Brought Down to Size," *The New York Times*, March 30, 2009, and Mann, Tony, "Guesstimation," *The Times Higher Education*, June 5, 2008.

Technology @ Work: Electronic Books

An electronic book (e-book for short) is usually a combination of a hardware device you can hold in your hand and software that allows you to read the pages of a book. See Figure 3-15. Some e-books are designed to be used with mobile phones, especially smartphones that can connect to the Internet. The most popular dedicated platform for e-books is the Amazon Kindle, shown in Figure 3-16. When the original version of the Kindle was introduced in 2007, it sold out in less than six hours. The influential technology blog, TechCrunch (*http://techcrunch.com/tag/amazon-kindle*), reports that "Amazon sells more Kindle books than print books, and offers nearly a million ebook titles." Electronic books can increase the distribution of ideas, arguments, and knowledge. case Grace Wong has heard about e-books, and wonders if Quest should enter the business of electronic tour guides that travelers could take with them on trips. She asks you to learn the advantages and disadvantages of e-books.

ESSENTIAL ELEMENTS

1. **Enhance research and thinking**
   Unlike conventional, printed books, you can search e-books electronically using hyperlinks, similar to the way you use the Web. That could make it easier to do research and find the connections among ideas, evidence, and arguments, which enhances thinking.

2. **Provide a more engaging medium**
   E-books can include multimedia such as sound, video, and more vivid graphics than are usually produced in printed books. Readers can annotate and highlight e-texts without permanently marking the book. They can also adjust font size, lighting, and other settings to create a more comfortable and engaging reading experience.

3. **Require electronic device and software**
   Even if you read e-books on a laptop computer or mobile phone, you need special software to do so, whereas traditional books do not need special equipment or software. Traditional books are also easier to carry and transport than e-book devices, which require a source of power. Furthermore, e-books are more fragile than printed books and are susceptible to physical damage.

4. **Change the reading experience**
   Traditional books enhance the tactile and visual experience. Scanning and quickly paging through a book can be a more effective way to learn new information than searching electronically. Unlike glancing at the front or back cover of a book, it is difficult to gain a sense of an e-book by viewing its first page or promotional material.

YOU TRY IT

Learn more about electronic books. Open the PS3-TechWork.docx document and follow the steps in the worksheet. When you are finished, submit the document to your instructor as requested.

FIGURE 3-15: Handheld e-book for children

Courtesy Design Continuum

FIGURE 3-16: Amazon Kindle

Practice

Soft Skills Review

Understand critical thinking.

1. **A(n) ______________ is a written or spoken statement that someone makes about a particular topic that is either true or false.**
   a. opinion
   b. hasty generalization
   c. claim
   d. fallacy
2. **What is an argument?**
   a. Claims that support a particular conclusion
   b. An act based on a flawed assumption
   c. Any subject of controversy
   d. The limit of your own knowledge

Identify arguments.

1. **Which of the following is *not* a premise indicator?**
   a. In my opinion
   b. Because
   c. Assuming that
   d. As a result
2. **What type of reasoning takes an argument from general observations or premises to a specific conclusion?**
   a. Inductive
   b. Deductive
   c. Conductive
   d. Cause-and-effect

Assess the credibility of an argument.

1. **An argument that logically follows its true premises is a:**
   a. credible argument
   b. valid argument
   c. good argument
   d. sound argument
2. **If an argument is valid and the premises are true, the conclusion must be:**
   a. sound
   b. weak
   c. true
   d. false

Explore weaknesses in an argument.

1. **What should you do when someone makes an assertion?**
   a. Test the assertion
   b. Accept the assertion
   c. Assume it is correct
   d. Look for a premise indicator
2. **What is a proposition or claim that is taken for granted as though it were known to be valid?**
   a. An assertion
   b. A sound argument
   c. An assumption
   d. A conclusion

Overcome obstacles to critical thinking.

1. **Which of the following is *not* an obstacle to critical thinking?**
   a. Normalization
   b. Creative thinking
   c. Social conditioning
   d. Being egocentric
2. **What is an outlier?**
   a. An extreme experience in the past
   b. Someone far outside the norm
   c. An emotional reaction to a logical problem
   d. A goal in critical thinking

Avoid deductive reasoning fallacies.

1. **What do you call an invalid argument that is presented to appear valid?**
   - **a.** Outlier
   - **b.** Hasty generalization
   - **c.** Unsound
   - **d.** Fallacy
2. **What type of argument asserts that if one event happens, another event will inevitably occur as a result?**
   - **a.** Slippery slope
   - **b.** Outward path
   - **c.** Composition error
   - **d.** Rubik's cube

Avoid inductive reasoning fallacies.

1. **An inductive argument is one that makes general conclusions based on:**
   - **a.** general behavior
   - **b.** social conditioning
   - **c.** fallacies
   - **d.** specific instances or observations
2. **What type of reasoning error assumes that if part of something has a particular quality, the whole shares that quality?**
   - **a.** Composition
   - **b.** *Post hoc, ergo propter hoc*
   - **c.** Equivocation
   - **d.** Metaphor

Become a critical thinker.

1. **Which one of the following is *not* a habit of critical thinkers?**
   - **a.** Intellectual humility
   - **b.** Methodical reasoning
   - **c.** Cynicism
   - **d.** Questioning assumptions
2. **What quality do you have when you understand the limits of your own knowledge?**
   - **a.** Intellectual humility
   - **b.** Scientific reasoning
   - **c.** Valid arguments
   - **d.** Social conditioning

Technology @ work: Electronic books

1. **Which of the following is an advantage e-books offer over conventional books?**
   - **a.** Can transport without a power source
   - **b.** Can search electronically using hyperlinks
   - **c.** Can absorb greater physical damage
   - **d.** Can judge an e-book by its cover
2. **Which of the following is an advantage traditional books offer over e-books?**
   - **a.** Include multimedia
   - **b.** Can annotate without making permanent marks
   - **c.** Can adjust font size
   - **d.** Do not need special equipment or software

Critical Thinking Questions

1. **"Critical thinking is the opposite of creative thinking." Do you agree? Provide examples of why you agree or disagree.**
2. **Google's motto is "Don't be evil." Is that the same as "Be good?"**
3. **Suppose your colleague, Marco, says that he will be in Chicago or St. Louis on Friday. On Friday morning, your boss says, "Where is Marco? He's supposed to be in Chicago, but he's not there." You reply, "If he's not in Chicago, then he's in St. Louis." Is your argument valid?**
4. **Suppose that in your hometown, the number of college graduates who work for banks declined by 20 percent in the last two years. During the same period, the number of college graduates who work for graphic design studios increased by 25 percent, even though the studios offer smaller starting salaries than banks. How do you account for this behavior?**
5. **How are critical thinking and decision making related? Consider styles of decision making such as using intuition or more systematic approaches. Also consider the habits of critical thinkers. How do those habits contribute to more successful decisions?**

Independent Challenge 1

Lawrence Media in Nashville, Tennessee, specializes in promotional products for businesses, such as corporate apparel, executive gifts, and product giveaways. As an assistant to Ken Lawrence, the founder of the company, you often attend meetings to discuss sales and marketing strategies. A recent problem is that the corporate apparel line has not been selling well in the last six months. Ken asks you to attend a team meeting to discuss the problem and suggest solutions. Figure 3-17 shows some of the suggestions made during the meeting.

- **a.** Open the **PS3-IC1.docx** document and follow the steps in the worksheet.
- **b.** Proofread the document carefully to fix any grammar or formatting errors.
- **c.** Submit the document to your instructor as requested.

FIGURE 3-17

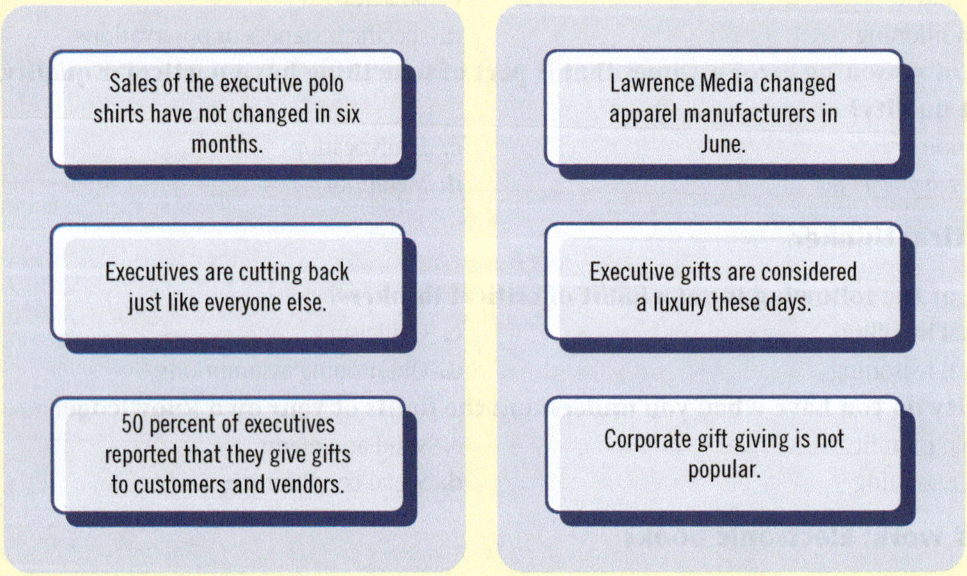

Independent Challenge 2

You work with Carla Marcus, the owner of Sage Realty Services in Winnetka, Illinois. Carla is taking her staff on a company retreat to brainstorm ways to stimulate sales. She asks for suggestions on selling more houses and office space. Figure 3-18 shows a suggestion. Carla asks you to help her evaluate the suggestion.

- **a.** Open the **PS3-IC1.docx** document and follow the steps in the worksheet.
- **b.** Proofread the document carefully to fix any grammar or formatting errors.
- **c.** Submit the document to your instructor as requested.

FIGURE 3-18

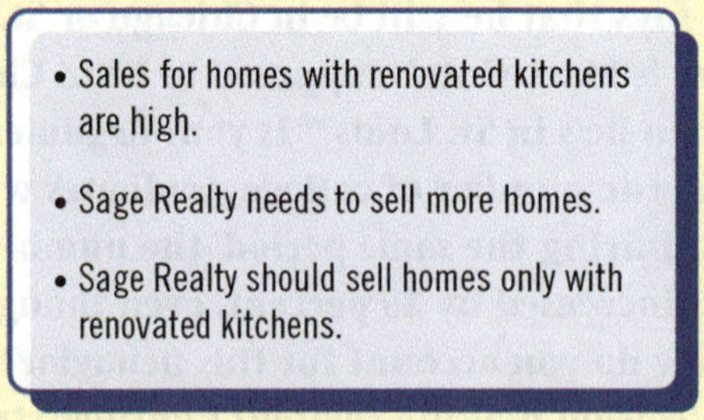

Real Life Independent Challenge

You can apply the critical-thinking techniques you learned in this part to develop your leadership skills. Develop your self-awareness by completing the following exercise.

- **a.** Create a timeline of your life history. What are the major events in your life?
- **b.** Identify your role models. Are these people in your current or past life? What did you learn from them?
- **c.** Describe your strengths and weaknesses.
- **d.** Describe the way you typically solve problems.
- **e.** Identify at least three of your core values. How do they shape the decisions you make?
- **f.** Describe your approach to persuading others or allowing yourself to be persuaded. What types of arguments work best with you?

Team Challenge

You are working for Colorado Green Builders, a company in Boulder, Colorado, specializing in sustainable building. The goal of your company is to design and build structures that use energy, resources, and materials efficiently, protecting the health of occupants and improving the productivity of employees while reducing waste, pollution, and environmental degradation. Your top competitor is a company named Whole Environments, and you are both submitting bids on three lucrative contracts. Your manager, Amanda Karlson, asks your team to find a way to win the contract. Which of the following motivating actions should your team choose and why? Select your responses individually and then discuss them in your team.

- **a.** Offer your team data from the green building trade association showing how Colorado Green Builders uses more environmentally friendly methods and products than Whole Environments.
- **b.** Offer a whitewater rafting adventure tour for any team member who wins a contract.
- **c.** Announce that Colorado Green Builders is downsizing. The team member who does not contribute to a winning bid will be fired.
- **d.** Hold a team meeting to brainstorm how to win the contracts. What has anyone learned from customers recently? Do they like the buildings and structures from Colorado Green Builders? What can be improved and how?

Be the Critic

You are working for a natural history museum and one of the members of the board wants to include a whale exhibit in the museum, which usually exhibits only dinosaurs and fossils. He provided the argument mapped out in Figure 3-19. Analyze the argument, noting its weaknesses, and send a list of the weaknesses to your instructor.

FIGURE 3-19

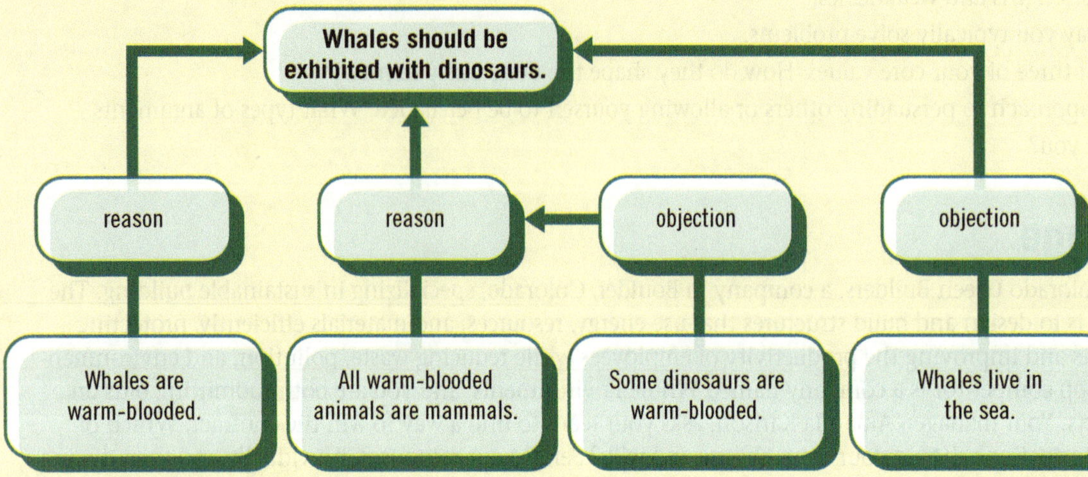

Part 4

Group Decision Making and Problem Solving

Files You Will Need:

PS4-Y26.docx
PS4-Y27.docx
PS4-Y28.docx
PS4-Y29.docx
PS4-Y30.docx
PS4-Y31.docx
PS4-Y32.docx
PS4-TechWork.docx
PS4-IC1.docx
PS4-IC2.docx

When confronted with a complex problem or one that affects many people, organizations usually form a group to study the problem and make decisions that lead to a solution. In contrast to an authoritarian style once common in corporations, group decision making and participatory management have grown in popularity over the past few decades. Today, many companies regularly use team-based approaches for organizational tasks. Although you solve problems in similar ways whether you are working alone or as a member of a group, your task can be complicated or enhanced by group dynamics. This unit introduces you to the basics of group dynamics and the ways teams can work together effectively to solve problems. **case** You have been working with Grace Wong, the vice president of finance at Quest Specialty Travel, to solve business problems for the company. Grace suspects that Quest's future financial health depends on expanding its services to corporate travelers. She talks to Quest employees who were members of other problem-solving groups and asks them to join a new team exploring business travel services. Grace asks you to be a member of the new team.

OBJECTIVES

25 Understand group dynamics
26 Evolve from a group to a team
27 Use divergent thinking
28 Use convergent thinking
29 Reach closure
30 Avoid common group traps
31 Work with large groups
32 Build sustainable agreements

Objective 25
Part 4

Understanding Group Dynamics

When working on complex tasks, you cannot do them all yourself. Organizations use groups and teams to make decisions, solve problems, and accomplish goals. A **group** is made up of two or more people who interact with each other, share expectations and obligations, and develop a common identity as a group. Real groups, as opposed to random collections of individuals, also have social or professional bonds and common interests, values, or backgrounds. The way that people work and interact with each other is known as **group dynamics**. Other terms used to describe groups include "teams," "clubs," "cliques," "squads," and "committees." case Before the new Quest group meets for the first time, Grace Wong suggests that you learn about the benefits of successful groups.

DETAILS

Organizations are embracing group projects and teamwork for the following reasons:

- **Diversity**

  A group of people can bring a rich diversity of culture, age groups, gender, and other variables to a common table. This diversity gives a group a more varied perspective and appreciation for different ideas and enhances the types of solutions it can come up with. Figure 4-1 illustrates the types of expertise group members can offer when discussing a topic or solving a problem.

- **Rich experience base**

  Each member of a group brings unique experiences with them. This includes differences in formal and informal education, work experience, responsibilities, and exposure to ideas from outside of the organization. Bringing together a group of people with a rich set of experiences can be very powerful.

- **Enhanced organizational memory**

  Organizations have a unique history and culture that a group must function in. People who have worked for a company for some time develop an **organizational memory** as they learn about the various processes, personalities, and subtleties of how the organization operates. When a group is formed, it can take advantage of its rich organizational memory. Someone on the team is likely to know who to talk with, what resources are available, or how to get something done. See Figure 4-2.

> **QUICK TIP**
> Organizational memory can include an organization's physical archives, electronic databases, and members' knowledge.

- **Error detection**

  When you bring people together to work on a common task, you introduce multiple levels of error checking. Mistakes and omissions that may have otherwise gone unnoticed are more likely to be caught by other team members.

- **More creative solutions**

  Each individual in a group will approach a problem differently than everyone else. This leads to a larger number of unique and creative solutions. Functional teams can be an excellent source of ideas.

- **Greater acceptance of decisions and outcomes**

  When someone is involved in a decision-making process, they are more likely to accept and support its outcome. Committees are often formed when broad acceptance of an outcome is necessary. Even those who are not part of the group will be more accepting if someone from their department or work unit is involved in the decision process.

FIGURE 4-1: Using a group's expertise to explore a topic

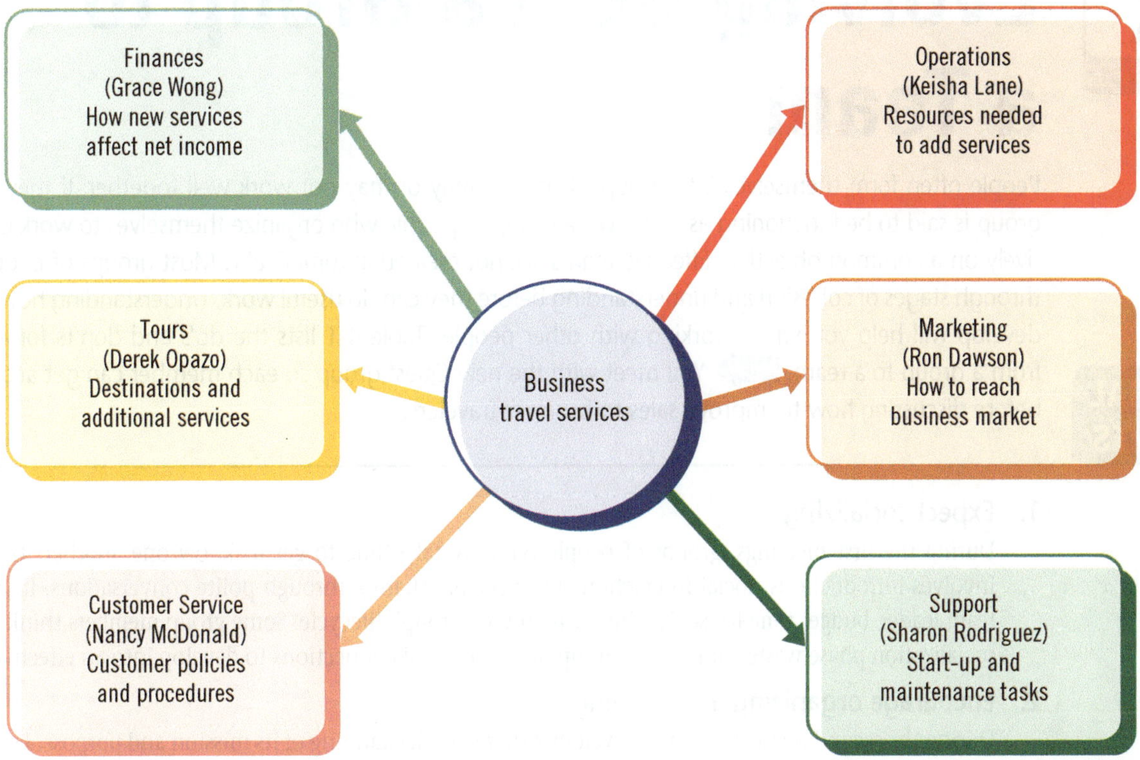

FIGURE 4-2: Organizational memory

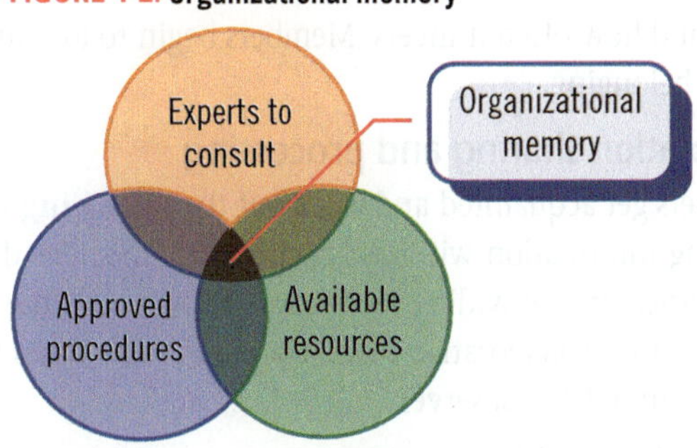

Star power or team effectiveness?

Using a popular management approach, many managers assign tasks to staff members according to their skills, personalities, and experience. This style of leadership, called a differentiated style, is used by coaches who treat their superstars differently from other players. For example, they might assign a locker to a star player separate from other players or allow the star more time with the trainer. In contrast, team-focused leadership treats a staff or other group as a whole. A recent study compared the two styles and reached a surprising conclusion. "Most managers believe that you *should* treat everybody differently," says Angelo Kinicki, a researcher at the University of Miami. "But our results reveal that, while that approach may seem to make sense...in a team setting, it can actually lead to negative effects." Kinicki uses the Phoenix Suns basketball team as an analogy. "Think about the Suns for moment," Kinicki says. "They have 12 players on the roster, and you have one true superstar in Amare [Stoudemire]. But if you do all these special things for him, if you treat him different than everybody else, the other teammates are before long going to say, 'Hey, this isn't right. This isn't fair.'" The unexpected results of Kinicki's research show that teams in organizations work the same way. Treat all members of team the same way, and they work more effectively in the group. Treat them differently, and resentments and other problems emerge.

Source: Staff, "Successful Small Team Leadership: Manage the Group, Not the Individuals," Knowledge@W.P. Carey, May 27, 2009.

Objective
26
Part 4

Evolving from a Group to a Team

People often form themselves into groups, but they may or may not work well together. If they do, the group is said to be functioning as a **team**—a group of people who organize themselves to work cooperatively on a common objective. Effective teams are not created automatically. Most groups of people pass through stages of cohesion and understanding before they can do useful work. Understanding how groups develop will help you when working with other people. Table 4-1 lists the do's and don'ts for evolving from a group to a team. case You meet with the new Quest group so each member can get acquainted before discussing how to improve sales to business travelers.

ESSENTIAL ELEMENTS

1. Expect socializing

During the first meetings, groups of people typically take time to get to know one another. This phase involves introductions, social interaction, and personal sharing through polite conversations. If you are a team leader, budget time for socializing early in your group's lifecycle. Some group members think that the socialization phase wastes time, but a group needs personal connections to develop into an effective team.

2. Encourage organizing and forming

During the second phase, the group develops a shared understanding of its mission and purpose. People also begin to assume group roles, including asserting their dominance and competing for influence over the group's direction. This power struggle often occurs even if the group has a formal leader or chair. In time, the group comes to an understanding about how it operates and makes decisions, what the expectations for participation are, and how often it meets. Members begin to identify with the group during this phase and develop a sense of belonging.

QUICK TIP
Avoid making important decisions before the group works out a pecking order. Priorities can change as informal leaders emerge.

3. Facilitate information sharing and processing

After group members get acquainted and work out their **pecking order**, as shown in Figure 4-3, they feel comfortable sharing information with each other. This includes disclosing sensitive material, responding openly to one another, and providing feedback. At this point, the group can begin to schedule meetings, work sessions, and other collaborative time. The group also starts to work on its assigned tasks and looks more like a team to an outside observer.

4. Collaborate to solve problems

Assuming a group successfully completes earlier phases, it eventually develops teamwork and **synergy**, which is achieved when two or more people work together to produce something greater than the sum of their individual efforts. During the collaboration phase, group members can complete tasks efficiently, work together on complex problems, and make shared decisions. They respect each other, develop a desire to cooperate, and take pride in the group's accomplishments instead of only their own. Not all groups evolve to the collaboration phase, but those that do are usually very productive and effective.

YOU TRY IT

Practice evolving from a group to a team by analyzing descriptions of group meetings. Open the PS4-Y26.docx document and follow the steps in the worksheet. When you are finished, submit the document to your instructor as requested.

FIGURE 4-3: Pecking order and assumed roles

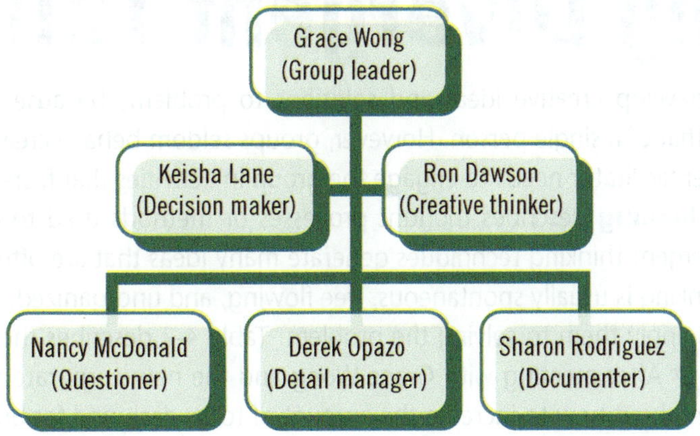

TABLE 4-1: Evolving to a team do's and don'ts

guidelines	do	don't
Phase 1: Socialize	• Allow time for a new group to get acquainted • Develop the personal connections that make teams successful	• Don't skip this phase because you think it wastes time
Phase 2: Organize	• Agree on a shared mission and purpose • Reach an understanding about how to run and participate in group meetings • Set a schedule • Identify with the group	• Don't let a power struggle over the group's leadership get in the way of the group's mission • Don't rush this preliminary phase • Don't make important decisions during this phase
Phase 3: Share	• Share information with other group members • Respond openly to others in the group • Provide feedback • Schedule work sessions and other collaborative meetings	• Don't disregard the pecking order the group has established
Phase 4: Solve problems	• Collaborate on tasks • Work on solving complex problems • Make shared decisions • Encourage respect and cooperation	• Don't be discouraged if your group does not reach this level of teamwork

Consensus decisions and groupthink

If your group is discussing a change that directly affects most people in the organization or a solution that requires cooperation and unity, consensus decision making can be invaluable. In the early days of the Internet, for example, before the World Wide Web was developed, a group of computer scientists worked out the rules for exchanging information on the Internet. As Stephen Crocker, an Internet pioneer explains, "Instead of authority-based decision making, we relied on a process we called 'rough consensus and running code.' Everyone was welcome to propose ideas, and if enough people liked it and used it, the design became a standard." Consensus was appropriate because the computer scientists had to cooperate in a unified effort to make the technology useful, and their decisions affected everyone who used the Internet. On the other hand, groupthink can lead to a false consensus, which is when everyone accepts a decision, but some members have reservations or objections that they keep to themselves. This often occurs when some members of a group have more authority or experience than others. In a commencement speech to West Point graduates, Defense Secretary Robert Gates urged the nation's future Army officers to question authority, challenge conventional wisdom, and work to avoid the dangerous groupthink that often takes root in military circles, according to *The Wall Street Journal*. In such cases, it is difficult to speak out against the consensus opinion, though doing so might bring about the changes the group or organization needs.

Sources: Crocker, Stephen D., "How the Internet Got Its Rules," *The New York Times*, April 6, 2009; Dreazen, Yochi J. and Cole, August, "Gates Tells West Point Graduates to Question Authority," *The Wall Street Journal*, May 23, 2009.

Objective 27
Part 4

Using Divergent Thinking

Groups can develop creative ideas and solutions to problems because their collective knowledge is greater than that of a single person. However, groups seldom behave creatively on their own. The team leader or other facilitator needs to engage the group in activities that foster creativity and collaboration. **Divergent thinking** describes thought processes or methods used to generate ideas. As the name suggests, divergent thinking techniques generate many ideas that are often not related to one another. Divergent thinking is usually spontaneous, free flowing, and unorganized. Later, the group can organize the ideas and apply them to solving the problem. Table 4-2 describes the do's and don'ts of divergent thinking. case After meeting with Grace Wong and the new corporate travel team, you are ready to generate ideas about how to increase the amount of tours designed for business travelers.

ESSENTIAL ELEMENTS

1. **Brainstorming**

   One of the most popular and well-known techniques for divergent thinking is brainstorming, which was introduced in Unit B. Groups use brainstorming to generate ideas and solutions to problems. The group considers a question, task, or project, and then generates as many ideas as possible, usually in a short period of time. Every idea is recorded, and no idea is disregarded, criticized, or analyzed. As ideas are suggested, they often stimulate others. The group continues to contribute ideas until everyone has exhausted their creativity.

2. **Group mind mapping**

   Mind mapping, also introduced in Unit B, uses simple graphics to generate, visualize, and organize creative ideas. A group member lists a main idea or problem at the center of a page, white board, or flip chart. Each participant is invited to share reactions and ideas. These are drawn as radial lines or spokes. When someone's idea builds, or piggybacks, on another, it is drawn as a branch in a tree structure. The visual nature of a mind map helps some people to think about a problem more creatively and may yield different results than traditional brainstorming. The map itself is a useful record of the group's contributions. See Figure 4-4.

3. **Free writing**

   Free writing is a form of brainstorming where group members focus on a subject and then write about it nonstop for a short period of time. Participants write any idea that occurs to them without pausing to consider the value of the idea or to proofread or edit their writing. This exercise is designed to encourage creativity and explore alternatives. When done as a group, free writing can be followed by a brainstorming or mind mapping session to collect ideas for the group.

4. **Journaling**

   People often think of creative ideas spontaneously and can easily forget them if they do not act on them or record them. Distribute journals to members of a group and ask each to write down thoughts and ideas. A journal can be an inexpensive spiral notebook or specialty blank book. Team members can keep the journal at their desks to note ideas when they occur to them. They can share the ideas with the group at a later meeting or submit them directly to a team leader. The quantity of ideas generated through journal writing is not as great as some other techniques, but the quality and range of the ideas are often superior.

QUICK TIP

Allow people to submit their entries anonymously if the question is controversial or politically charged.

YOU TRY IT

Practice using divergent thinking by generating solutions to a problem. Open the PS4-Y27.docx document and follow the steps in the worksheet. When you are finished, submit the document to your instructor as requested.

FIGURE 4-4: Group mind map

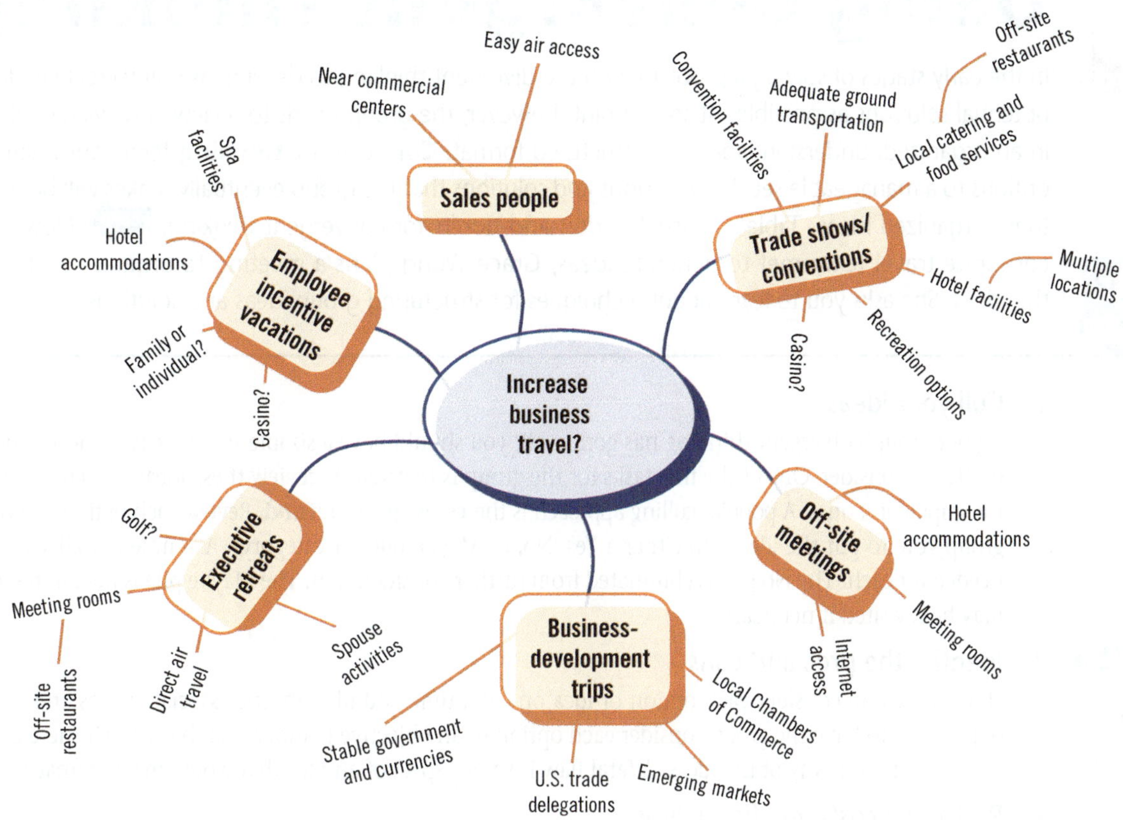

TABLE 4-2: Divergent thinking do's and don'ts

guidelines	do	don't
Brainstorming	• Generate ideas and solutions as a group • Record ideas	• Don't disregard, analyze, or reject an idea during brainstorming
Mind map	• Visualize and organize creative ideas as a group • Draw ideas as a tree or spoke-wheel diagram • Retain the mind map as a record of the group's ideas and decisions	• Don't get bogged down in the mechanics of drawing a mind map • Don't evaluate ideas until you are finished
Free writing	• Use to stimulate individual creativity • Write thoughts about a subject nonstop for a short time • Follow up with a group brainstorming or mind mapping session	• Don't pause to edit, proofread, or review as you are writing
Journal writing	• Use to record spontaneous thoughts and ideas • Share journal contents with the group	• Don't expect to generate as many ideas with a journal as with brainstorming or mind maps

Mind mapping software

You can use digital tools to boost your divergent thinking. Bubbl.us (*www.bubbl.us*) is a free Web application that lets you conduct brainstorming sessions online. You write your thoughts in graphical bubbles and connect those to other bubbles without the distraction of drawing and formatting. Bubbl.us helps you brainstorm quickly instead of getting bogged down in the mechanics of creating and linking bubbles. MindMeister (*www.mindmeister.com*) is a simple, free tool that lets you quickly create mind maps just by pressing the directional arrow keys on your keyboard. XMind (*www.xmind.net*) is also free, but lets you create fishbone, organizational, tree, and logic charts in addition to mind maps.

Objective 28
Part 4

Using Convergent Thinking

In the early stages of solving a problem, you use divergent thinking to develop as many creative ideas and potential solutions as possible. At some point, however, the group needs to review and evaluate the ideas in an organized, understandable, and structured format. **Convergent thinking** techniques narrow the options to a manageable set. The decisions and solutions that the group eventually makes will be based on these organized ideas. Table 4-3 lists the do's and don'ts for convergent thinking. case Now that the corporate travel team met to generate ideas, Grace Wong plans a meeting to organize and evaluate the ideas. She asks you to learn about techniques for structuring group ideas and solutions.

ESSENTIAL ELEMENTS

1. Cull your ideas

If your group's divergent thinking has gone well, you should have a sizable set of ideas, options, and possibilities to consider. One of the first tasks for the group is to carefully review these ideas and cull, or remove, the impractical ones. A popular culling approach is the **three-pile method**. Review each option and have the group vote to put the idea into either a Yes, No, or Maybe pile (or category). A simple plurality of votes is needed for each. The No pile is eliminated from further consideration. The Maybe pile is held in reserve and may be revisited if necessary.

QUICK TIP
Identify pros and cons in an informal discussion, or more formally with someone recording the feedback for all to see.

2. Identify the pros and cons

Have the group consider each option or idea one at a time and identify the associated pros and cons. The objective is to have the group consider each option in an objective manner. Ask the group if there is a **fatal flaw** inherent in any of the ideas. A fatal flaw is some aspect of an idea that would make it unacceptable.

3. Perform a cost-benefit analysis

Each idea that is proposed will have some benefit to the group or organization. It will also have some associated costs. Good ideas typically have benefits that outweigh their costs. Costs and benefits may take different forms such as monetary return, cost savings, improved efficiency, reduced problems, and others, and comparing one to another may be tricky. A **decision balance sheet** is a formal way of organizing an idea's costs and benefits. See Figure 4-5.

QUICK TIP
An impact analysis alone should not drive the final decision, but can help to better differentiate between alternatives.

4. Create an impact analysis

It is easy to consider ideas, options, and potential solutions by themselves and not consider other related factors. Use an **impact analysis** to broaden your view. Have the group list the consequences of each idea. Who or what would each option affect? Would the consequences be minimal or manageable? Which idea would cause the least amount of loss or harm? See Figure 4-6.

5. Use reverse brainstorming

Brainstorming is usually thought of as a divergent thinking technique. However, when used in reverse it can be a helpful convergent tool. Present each idea or option to the group and ask everyone to identify possible weaknesses or problems. The goal is not to come up with new ideas, but to generate criticisms instead. This exercise forces people to take a hard look at each option and helps minimize problems associated with groupthink. The group can reexamine the ideas to generate possible solutions for each of the weaknesses identified.

YOU TRY IT

Practice using convergent thinking by generating solutions to a problem. Open the PS4-Y28.docx document and follow the steps in the worksheet. When you are finished, submit the document to your instructor as requested.

FIGURE 4-5: Decision balance sheet

Should Quest expand to provide tours and services for the business traveler?

	Gains	Losses
Quest Specialty Travel	Add to customer base	Detract from current customers
	Develop new sources of revenue	Increase expenses
	Build on current tours	Manage conflicts
	Create stability	Manage change
	Increase sales to both sets of customers	Dilute current services
Customers	Can select from a full range of services	Might be confused about company focus
	Can combine business and personal travel	Might not be willing to pay higher prices for business services

FIGURE 4-6: Impact analysis

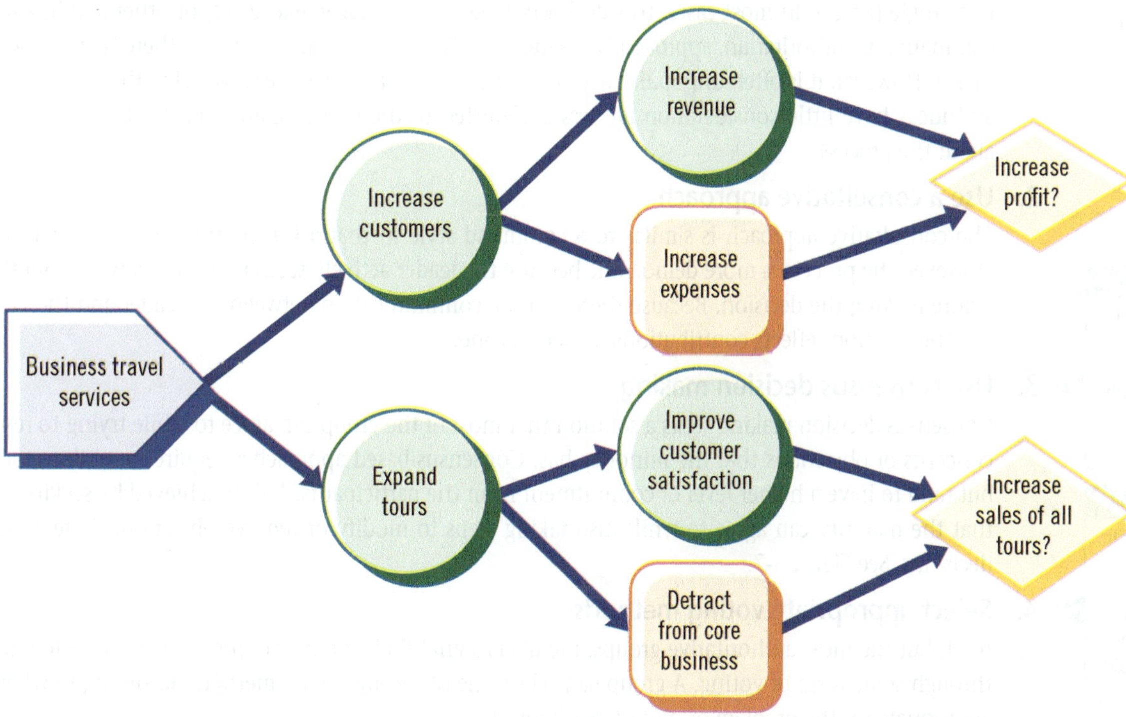

TABLE 4-3: Convergent thinking do's and don'ts

guidelines	do	don't
Cull ideas	• Review ideas and eliminate some • Reduce number of ideas to a manageable amount • Use three-pile method to have group vote on each idea	• **Don't** reject ideas arbitrarily; use criteria the group agrees on
Analyze ideas	• List the pros and cons of each idea • Perform a cost-benefit analysis • Create a decision balance sheet • Create an impact analysis • List the consequences of each idea • Use reverse brainstorming to identify weaknesses and avoid groupthink	• **Don't** overlook the fatal flaw in an idea • **Don't** focus on one type of cost or benefit—consider different forms • **Don't** consider ideas, options, and potential solutions on their own—consider related factors • **Don't** introduce new ideas

Objective 29
Part 4

Reaching Closure

Some groups and teams are designed to be ongoing concerns that continue to work together and move from one issue or project to another. Other groups address a particular concern and are disbanded when that problem is solved. In both cases, it is common for the group to artificially prolong a process and not reach closure as efficiently as it could. A team leader needs to provide direction and help the group to develop closure and make necessary decisions. Table 4-4 lists common approaches for groups to make final decisions. case The corporate travel team has met a few times and generated detailed suggestions for providing tours to the business traveler. For the next meeting, you and the other members plan to decide whether to pursue the new business and if so, what approach to take.

ESSENTIAL ELEMENTS

QUICK TIP
This is sometimes called a "dictator approach" to decision making.

1. Use a command style

In some settings, a group may examine an issue and develop ideas for it, but the final decisions are left up to a single person. In most cases, this decision maker is a manager, executive, or other administrator. The command, or authoritarian, approach is the most efficient way to reach closure as there is only one decision maker. However, it is often unpopular with the other participants. People who feel as though their opinions and ideas have little consideration are less committed to the outcome and may harbor negative feelings about the process.

2. Use a consultative approach

The consultative approach is similar to a command style in that a leader still makes the final decisions. However, the process is more democratic because the leader actively seeks input and advice from the group before making the decision. Because there is more communication between the leader and the group, ideally the solution reflects contributions from everyone.

QUICK TIP
Consensus doesn't mean allowing someone to hold a group hostage with an unreasonable demand.

3. Use consensus decision making

Consensus decision making seeks a solution that most of the group can agree to while trying to resolve any concerns or objections that the minority has. Consensus-based approaches require more time for closure, but tend to have a higher level of commitment from the participants. This is achieved by seeking solutions that the majority can agree to while also taking steps to modify or remove objectionable features of any decisions. See Figure 4-7.

QUICK TIP
Strengthen a plurality vote by using several rounds. Eliminate options with the least support and vote again.

4. Select appropriate voting methods

In all but the most authoritative groups, members signal their intent and preferences for different options through some form of voting. A group can select one of several voting methods according to what is most appropriate for the problem or project. See Table 4-4.

YOU TRY IT

Practice reaching closure by reviewing a decision and choosing how to reach closure. Open the PS4-Y29.docx document and follow the steps in the worksheet. When you are finished, submit the document to your instructor as requested.

FIGURE 4-7: Reaching closure through consensus

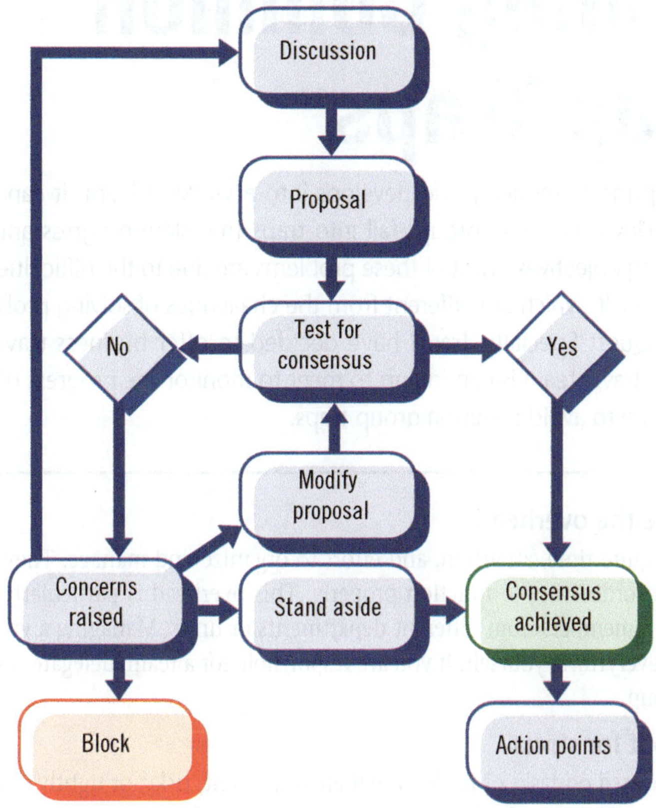

TABLE 4-4: Group decision methods

method	description	purpose
Range voting	• Members assign scores to multiple options rather than voting for a single choice • Scores indicate level of preference • Option with the highest overall average is selected	• Allows people to better express their preferences • Appropriate when group members support several options
Majority rule	• Common decision technique • Selects an alternative based on which one has more than half of the votes	• Efficient technique when choosing between two alternatives • Less efficient with more than two options; another approach might be more practical
Plurality	• The largest block in the group decides the issue • A plurality can be a percentage less than 50 percent	• This technique is useful when a choice is made from multiple alternatives • Because a decision can be made by a relatively small percentage of a group, people may be less accepting of the outcome

Objective 30 Part 4

Avoiding Common Group Traps

When a group meets regularly and develops into a working team, it can solve problems creatively and thoughtfully. However, some groups fall into traps that slow progress and distract members from their problem-solving objectives. Most of these problems are due to the difficulties of participating in or managing the group itself, which are different from the challenges of solving problems on your own. case The managers at Quest Specialty Travel have decided to offer business travel services on a limited basis. The corporate travel team is continuing to meet to monitor the progress of the new project. Grace Wong advises everyone to avoid common group traps.

ESSENTIAL ELEMENTS

QUICK TIP
Focus on what is important, and do not let yourself get caught up in managing overhead.

1. **Organize the overhead**

   Groups require time, attention, and effort to organize and manage. They need communication, scheduling, and coordinating to function properly. This overhead is particularly demanding for large groups or teams with members from different departments or units. Managing a group can be overwhelming if you try to do everything yourself. If you are responsible for a team, delegate responsibilities and tasks to others in the group.

QUICK TIP
Keep an eye on other commitments and deadlines that group members may be facing.

2. **Watch out for stress**

   Groups focused on tasks or projects that are important, risky, or tightly scheduled usually experience stress and anxiety. Stress can lead to making inappropriate decisions, cutting corners, and overlooking relevant options. Reduce stress by using a positive, optimistic tone during meetings. Bringing refreshments to meetings can help people feel more relaxed and motivated. Acknowledge the stressful conditions and discuss them with the rest of the group. Use the pressure as motivation to rise to challenges and perform better than expected.

3. **Avoid the Superman complex**

   If a group develops a collective sense of invulnerability, it has a **Superman complex**. Teams that have been working together for some time and are comfortable with their roles within the group sometimes assume that their decisions are always correct, that their plans are optimal, and that they are not responsible to a larger audience. Occasionally attending meetings of other teams and inviting outside participants to team meetings can help bring perspectives back into focus. With outsiders, conduct a strengths, weaknesses, opportunities, and threat (SWOT) exercise to make sure the group's success is not blinding members to potential problems. See Figure 4-8.

QUICK TIP
If your team is suffering from groupthink, invite an outside expert to play the devil's advocate.

4. **Look out for groupthink**

   Groups can become so cohesive that the members minimize conflict and support consensus without critically considering the merits of ideas and decisions. When individual creativity and independent thinking are lost to group cohesiveness, the condition is known as **groupthink**. In this condition, group members shy away from presenting ideas that may fall outside the group's comfort zone. Figure 4-9 contrasts an ideal group process with one suffering from groupthink.

YOU TRY IT

Practice avoiding common group traps by analyzing a description of a meeting. Open the PS4-Y30.docx document and follow the steps in the worksheet. When you are finished, submit the document to your instructor as requested.

FIGURE 4-8: SWOT analysis

FIGURE 4-9: Groupthink

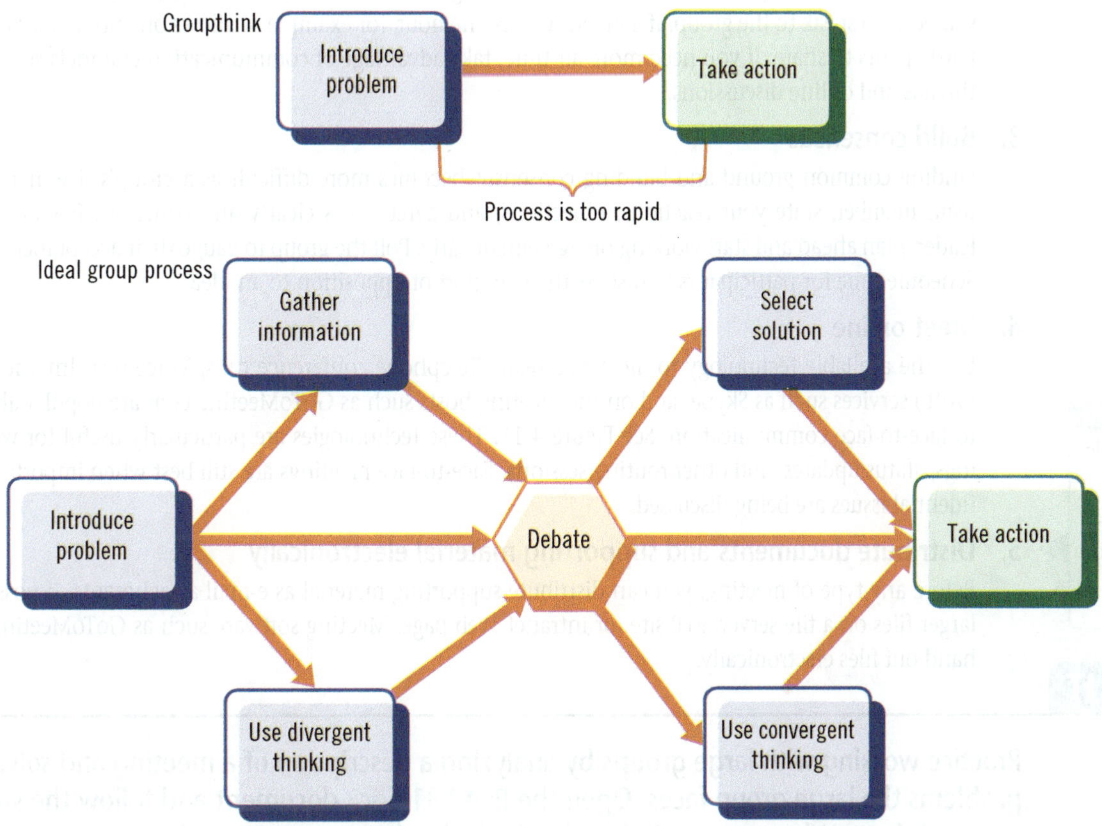

Objective 31
Part 4

Working with Large Groups

A small group in a single location involves little overhead to organize and manage. Large groups and those with members in more than one location, however, require extra time for planning, organizing, and managing. See Figure 4-10. As companies grow, merge, and evolve, they use large and geographically distributed groups more often. Managing and participating in such a group takes additional communication skills. Table 4-5 lists the do's and don'ts for working in large or dispersed groups. case To make sure Quest's new business travel services are successful, Grace Wong wants to work with the New York office of Quest Specialty Travel and important partners in London, Paris, and Tokyo. She asks you to help her organize meetings with the expanded group.

ESSENTIAL ELEMENTS

QUICK TIP
Electronic calendars and schedulers help large groups quickly identify suitable meeting times.

1. **Manage the logistics**

   When organizing and participating in a group of any size, you need to communicate with other team members, schedule and attend meetings, and follow up on task assignments. These activities take more time when the group is large or has members in more than one location. If you are leading such a group, be aware of **logistics**, which refers to how resources such as information and people are provided where they are needed. As a group member, being familiar with software tools such as electronic calendars and schedulers helps you manage your participation.

2. **Expand communication channels**

   In a meeting, you expect to have an opportunity to talk about topics that interest you. However, as a group grows larger, you might find you do not have enough **air time**, which is the amount of time available for someone to speak to the group. If a meeting lasts one hour, for example, it allows one hour of air time for all participants to share. If you need more air time, take advantage of communication channels such as e-mail threads and online discussions.

3. **Build consensus**

   Finding common ground and building consensus becomes more difficult as a group's size increases. As a team member, state your reactions, objections, and agreements clearly and concisely. If you are a team leader, plan ahead and start working on agreement early. Poll the group to gauge their acceptance of an idea. Schedule time for participants to discuss their support or opposition to an idea.

4. **Meet online**

   Use the available technology to meet as a team. Telephone conference calls, Voice over Internet Protocol (VoIP) services such as Skype, and online meeting hosts such as GoToMeeting.com are popular alternatives to face-to-face communication. See Figure 4-11. These technologies are particularly useful for work meetings, status updates, and other routine sessions. Face-to-face meetings are still best when important or confidential issues are being discussed.

QUICK TIP
If files contain confidential contents, find out how to require a user name and password before people can access the material.

5. **Distribute documents and supporting material electronically**

   Before any type of meeting, you can distribute supporting material as e-mail attachments, if possible. Post larger files on a file server, FTP site, or intranet Web page. Meeting software such as GoToMeeting lets you hand out files electronically.

YOU TRY IT

Practice working with large groups by analyzing a description of a meeting and solving problems the large group faces. Open the PS4-Y31.docx document and follow the steps in the worksheet. When you are finished, submit the document to your instructor as requested.

FIGURE 4-10: Large groups require extra time for planning

David Baumber/Photos.com

FIGURE 4-11: Meeting online in a video conference

Andrey Popov/Photos.com

TABLE 4-5: Large group do's and don'ts

guidelines	do	don't
Logistics	• Allow time for group maintenance tasks • Use technology to simplify group management	• **Don't** spend too much time on group maintenance unless you are the team leader
Communications	• Expand the communication channels beyond team meetings • Use e-mail, online discussion forums, and Web conferences • Record meetings as digital video or audio for members who cannot attend • Distribute documents and supporting material electronically	• **Don't** schedule a meeting for every topic that needs to be discussed
Consensus	• Discuss how the team will reach agreement • Work on finding common ground early • Allow plenty of time for a large group to discuss plans and options	• **Don't** delay consensus building • **Don't** rush team members to make a decision

Objective 32
Part 4

Building Sustainable Agreements

The final step a problem-solving group performs is developing an implementation plan, also called an **action plan**, to guide changes, product or service introductions, and complex projects. The action plan summarizes the activities the group and other members of the organization agree to perform to make sure the project succeeds. See Figure 4-12. Recognize that the action plan represents change, and people and organizations tend to resist change. Involve members of the team and others in the organization to build an agreement that can be sustained as the problem is solved. Table 4-6 describes the do's and don'ts for building agreements. case A few days after meeting to discuss Quest's new business travel services with the New York office and partners around the world, you and the rest of the corporate travel team in San Diego meet again to create an action plan.

ESSENTIAL ELEMENTS

QUICK TIP
If the group's solution might be threatening to a decision maker, invite that person to a team meeting to encourage their support.

1. **Overcome fear**

   An action plan represents change, which can threaten someone's job, status, position, budget, or power. Resistance to change increases as a solution becomes more creative and less like habitual activities. See Figure 4-13. Members of your group should discuss their concerns about the plan and understand its benefits before agreeing to it. The group can also work together to identify fears and objections others in the organization might have.

2. **Communicate openly**

   Groups tend to communicate among themselves, forgetting to share their ideas with a larger audience. This is especially true of teams that have worked together in the same location for some time. As your group starts to develop its action plan, take extra steps to share your ideas and progress with stakeholders and decision makers. Use a variety of open meetings, forums, memos, newsletters, and presentations to communicate across the organization.

3. **Manage the pace**

   People are more accepting of change when they have sufficient time to adjust to it. Your group should share ideas and conclusions gradually, allowing time between each new step the group introduces. Welcome discussions about the action plan and its steps, but avoid overwhelming people with major new initiatives all at once.

QUICK TIP
Look at the company calendar and ask people what activities are scheduled for the organization.

4. **Avoid stressful times**

   Be aware of the periods when your organization is typically busy, and avoid starting the steps in the action plan at that time. For example, trying to launch a new project at a public accounting firm in early April when employees are struggling to meet tax deadlines would likely be a disaster. That same initiative introduced in May might have a warm reception.

YOU TRY IT

Practice building sustainable agreements by creating an action plan for a project. Open the PS4-Y32.docx document and follow the steps in the worksheet. When you are finished, submit the document to your instructor as requested.

FIGURE 4-12: Sample action plan

Action	Cost	Time	Schedule	Assigned to
Action Plan: Expand business travel market				
Objectives: To contact 2000 potential business customers and sign 40 of those customers to a tour in one year **Budget:** $1500 start-up budget plus $1000/month				
• Add or expand five tours for business travelers	$1000	24 hours	March 20–April 20	Keisha Lane Ron Dawson Derek Opazo
• Join Association for Business Travelers (Meetings and networking)	$250/yr	4 hrs/month	April, September	Ron Dawson
• Create new brochure	$600	15 hrs	April 20–30	Keisha Lane, Sharon Rodriguez
• Select and hire a telemarketing firm	$300/month	5 hrs/month	May 1–July 1	Ron Dawson
• Advertising (Direct mail and Web)	$550 plus $120/month	9 hrs plus 3 hrs/month	April 16–June 15	Keisha Lane Grace Wong Ron Dawson
• Develop sales presentation	$360	20 hrs	April 20–30	Derek Opazo, Grace Wong
• Train customer service staff	$150	20 hrs	April 16–30	Nancy McDonald Eric Jameson
Start-up expenses	**$2910**	**88 hrs**		
Monthly expenses	**$420**	**12 hrs**		

FIGURE 4-13: Overcoming resistance to change

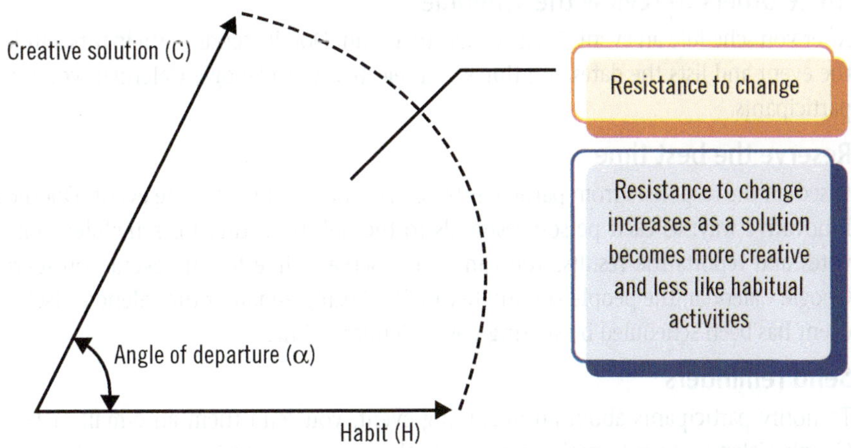

TABLE 4-6: Building agreements do's and don'ts

guidelines	do	don't
Overcome fear	• Recognize that team members and others in the organization might resist change • Discuss the benefits of the change	• **Don't** change tasks, project goals, or parts of the team without discussing them first • **Don't** discourage members of your group from discussing their concerns about the project • **Don't** avoid identifying fears and objections others in the organization might have
Communicate openly	• Share team ideas with a larger audience, such as a department or company • Communicate frequently with decision makers • Hold open meetings and forums, and provide memos, newsletters, and presentations to keep in touch with others outside the team	• **Don't** assume a single communication or tool is sufficient • **Don't** overwhelm the larger audience with too much or too frequent news • **Don't** introduce a new solution during a period that is usually busy for your organization

Technology @ Work: Online Scheduling Tools

Finding time for team meetings or scheduling appointments with another professional can result in dozens of exchanged e-mail messages that are hard to track. Online scheduling tools Doodle and Google Calendar can simplify this time-consuming task. In both online scheduling tools, the meeting organizer uses an online calendar to select times for the meeting. The organizer uses e-mail to notify everyone who needs or wants to attend the meeting. Participants respond by selecting times that are most convenient for them. The organizer can select the time, usually the one that works for most people, or the tool can recommend a time. Figure 4-14 shows Doodle, which conducts polls to schedule events. Figure 4-15 shows Google Calendar, which lets you organize your schedule and share it with others. case Grace Wong wants to offer services such as destination planning and trip coordination to corporate customers. She asks you to learn about online scheduling tools to find out if they would support these services and appeal to Quest's business customers.

ESSENTIAL ELEMENTS

QUICK TIP
If you are setting up many dates and times in Doodle, you can copy and paste the times from one date to the next.

1. **Schedule events**

   If you are organizing a meeting or hosting an event, you can use Doodle or Google Calendar to enter the event on an online calendar. With Doodle, you select more than one day or time convenient for you and other participants. With Google Calendar, you enter the event on a personal calendar.

2. **Invite others to review the schedule**

   After you schedule an event, invite others to attend. Doodle sends participants a link to a poll that describes the event and lists the dates and times you selected. With Google Calendar, you send e-mail invitations to participants.

3. **Reserve the best time**

   Based on the responses from participants, reserve the best time for the event. Doodle takes care of this in an innovative way: as each person responds to the poll by voting for scheduled time, Doodle tabulates the votes and reports the results. You can then reserve a time for the event considering those results. With Google Calendar, the people you invite can RSVP using e-mail or the calendar itself. Let everyone know the event has been scheduled by sharing your calendar online.

QUICK TIP
In Google Calendar, you can set up a calendar for a conference room so you can reserve a meeting space.

4. **Send reminders**

   To notify participants about an upcoming event, you send them an e-mail or text message. You can set Google Calendar to automatically remind others about upcoming events or let them know if event details have changed. If you sign up for a free Google account, you can receive a daily agenda listing your schedule for the day.

YOU TRY IT

Learn more about online scheduling tools. Open the PS4-TechWork.docx document and follow the steps in the worksheet. When you are finished, submit the document to your instructor as requested.

FIGURE 4-14: Scheduling an event in Doodle

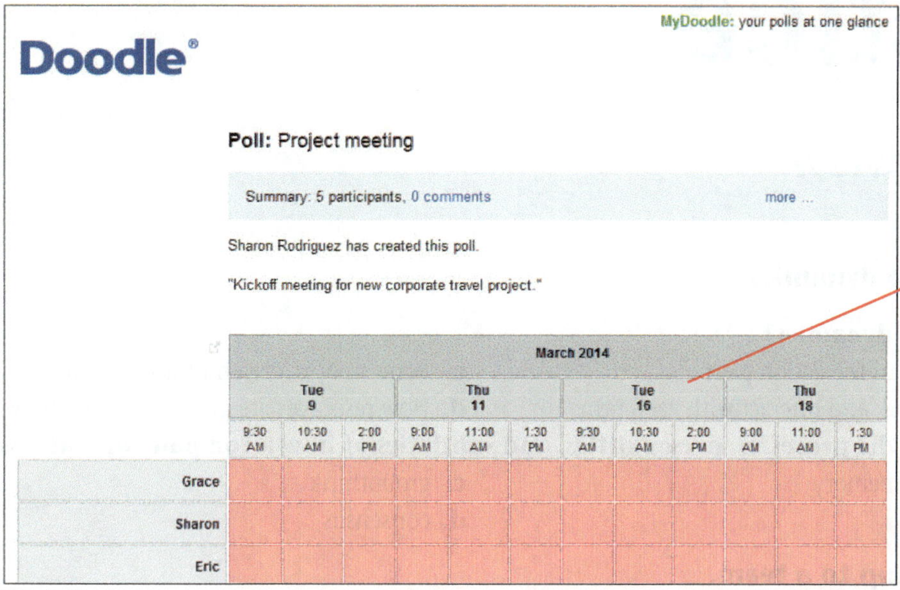

Send these dates and times to participants, and ask them to vote for the best time

© Doodle AG

FIGURE 4-15: Google Calendar

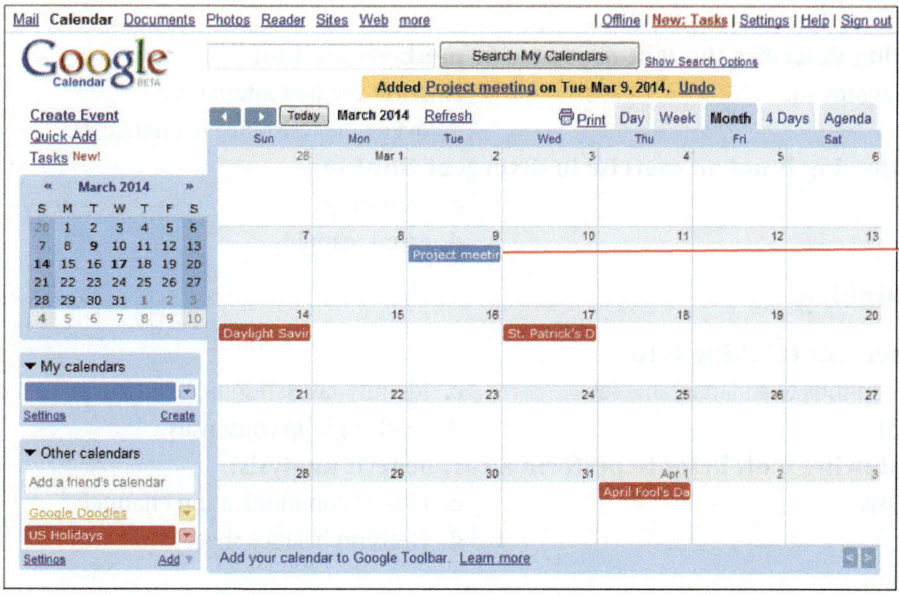

Publish this calendar so meeting participants can schedule the event

Courtesy of Google

Problem-Solving and Decision Making

Practice

Soft Skills Review

Understand group dynamics.

1. **What are group dynamics?**
   a. Changes noted in the action plan
   b. How people work and interact with each other
   c. Ways to organize an idea's costs and benefits
   d. How resources are provided where they are needed
2. **Knowing about the processes, personalities, and subtleties of how a company operates is called:**
   a. organizational memory
   b. logistics
   c. groupthink
   d. consensus

Evolve from a group to a team.

1. **In business, a team is:**
   a. two or more people attending a meeting
   b. a group of people who work together cooperatively on a common objective
   c. a group of people that meet regularly
   d. two or more people who share expectations and obligations
2. **What do successful teams allow time for when the group first starts to meet?**
   a. Online scheduling
   b. Convergent thinking
   c. Creating action plans
   d. Socializing

Use divergent thinking.

1. **Divergent thinking describes thought processes or methods used to:**
   a. design credible arguments
   b. generate ideas
   c. select the best alternative
   d. overcome resistance to change
2. **Which of the following is *not* an exercise in divergent thinking?**
   a. Brainstorming
   b. Free writing
   c. Outlining
   d. Mind mapping

Use convergent thinking.

1. **The goal of convergent thinking is to:**
   a. narrow possible options to a manageable set
   b. avoid groupthink
   c. identify tasks, resources, and expenses
   d. reach a group consensus
2. **Which of the following tools helps to perform a cost-benefit analysis?**
   a. Three-pile analysis
   b. SWOT analysis
   c. Online communication channel
   d. Decision balance sheet

Reach closure.

1. **A team leader who actively seeks advice from the group before making a decision is using:**
   - **a.** a consultative approach
   - **b.** a command style
   - **c.** consensus decision making
   - **d.** an active advice approach
2. **When is majority rule an efficient decision-making technique?**
   - **a.** When using a command style
   - **b.** When group members support several options
   - **c.** When choosing between two alternatives
   - **d.** With small groups

Avoid common group traps.

1. **Which of the following is *not* a common group trap?**
   - **a.** Overhead
   - **b.** Stress
   - **c.** Superman complex
   - **d.** Devil's advocate
2. **When group members avoid presenting ideas that fall outside the group's comfort zone, they are suffering from:**
   - **a.** groupthink
   - **b.** the Superman complex
   - **c.** group analysis
   - **d.** consensus building

Work with large groups.

1. **Which of the following tools is useful when working in a large group or one with members in more than one location?**
   - **a.** Impact analysis
   - **b.** Air time
   - **c.** Online calendar
   - **d.** Electronic book
2. **Before a meeting of a large group, you should:**
   - **a.** ask for extra time to hand out materials
   - **b.** distribute materials electronically
   - **c.** reserve air time
   - **d.** send e-mails to participants explaining that no supporting materials are allowed

Build sustainable agreements.

1. **What is the purpose of an action plan?**
   - **a.** To identify the consequences of each idea
   - **b.** To review ideas and reduce them to a manageable number
   - **c.** To document meeting activities
   - **d.** To summarize the activities the group agrees to perform
2. **Which of the following is *not* a way to build a sustainable agreement?**
   - **a.** Introduce all changes at the same time
   - **b.** Overcome fears
   - **c.** Communicate openly
   - **d.** Manage the pace

Technology @ work: Online scheduling tools

1. **In most online scheduling tools, the meeting organizer uses an online calendar to:**
   - **a.** vote for meeting locations
   - **b.** select times for a meeting
   - **c.** schedule range voting
   - **d.** distribute documents electronically
2. **After participants respond to a meeting invitation, how does Doodle help you select the best time?**
   - **a.** It reserves a conference room
   - **b.** It publishes a group calendar online
   - **c.** It sends electronic RSVPs
   - **d.** It tabulates responses and reports the results

Critical Thinking Questions

1. **This unit provides guidelines for being both a group member and a group leader. Do all groups need leaders? Do teams without leaders offer advantages over teams that have leaders?**
2. **Are divergent thinking techniques as well respected as convergent thinking techniques? Why or why not?**
3. **In what types of situations is individual decision making preferable to group decision making? When is group decision making more effective than individual decision making?**
4. **The consequences of groupthink can be disastrous. Irving Janis, a social psychologist who studied groupthink, identified the Bay of Pigs invasion of Cuba as an example of groupthink because a group of advisers to President Kennedy went along with his decision despite misgivings. The Challenger Space Shuttle is another well-known example of groupthink. A group of NASA officials disregarded an engineer's concerns and decided to launch the shuttle, which resulted in disaster. As a group member, what can you do to avoid groupthink?**
5. **Suppose you are a member of a group asked to find ways to cut costs throughout your organization for the upcoming year. Sales have fallen sharply, and the company is in danger of going out of business. After gathering information, your group concludes that the company will save the most money by freezing pay for a year, despite a tradition of annual salary increases. How can you make sure this is a fair decision? How can you make sure that others in the organization will see it as a fair decision?**

Independent Challenge 1

Lawrence Media in Nashville, Tennessee, specializes in promotional products for businesses, such as corporate apparel, executive gifts, and product giveaways. You work as an assistant to Ken Lawrence, the founder of the company, and are a member of a group examining why the corporate apparel line is not selling well and how to solve that problem. During a recent team meeting, Ken conducted a brainstorming session to generate ideas for improving sales of corporate apparel. Figure 4-16 shows the results of the brainstorming session.

a. Open the **PS4-IC1.docx** document and follow the steps in the worksheet.
b. Proofread the document carefully to fix any grammar or formatting errors.
c. Submit the document to your instructor as requested.

FIGURE 4-16

Spend 30 minutes on Google learning more about current customers	Ask current customers for referrals	Improve quality of the shirts and jackets
Spend 30 minutes on Twitter finding prospective customers	Repeat successful ad from last year	Add something new to the shirts and jackets
Offer golf hats in addition to shirts and jackets	Use all natural fibers in shirts and jackets	Sponsor an athletic event to make shirts and jackets more appealing

Independent Challenge 2

You work with Carla Marcus, the owner of Sage Realty Services in Winnetka, Illinois. As a member of a team working on the problem of slumping real estate sales, you have been offering Carla suggestions on selling more houses and office space. One solution is to improve customer service and increase referrals. Carla asked the team to generate ideas for trying this solution for six months. Figure 4-17 shows the basic ideas the team generated. Carla asks you to organize this information in an action plan.

FIGURE 4-17

Survey customers	Sponsor event for home buyers
Send links or DVDs of virtual tours	Update contact management software
Do in three stages: March 1–15, May 1–15, and September 1–15	Organize follow-up social events with recent customers

a. Open the **PS4-IC2.docx** document and follow the steps in the worksheet.
b. Proofread the document carefully to fix any grammar or formatting errors.
c. Submit the document to your instructor as requested.

Real Life Independent Challenge

You can apply the group decision-making techniques you learned in this unit to develop your group participation and decision-making skills. Most jobs require a variety of skills in these categories. Develop these skills by completing the following exercise.

a. Identify your work and study skills. List the types of activities you have performed in the past six months at work or school. For example, have you worked on a team? Written reports? Attended meetings? Then list the skills required to complete these activities.
b. Identify your experiences outside of work or school. List these experiences and the skills required to perform them.
c. Review the lists you created and identify interpersonal and group skills, such as motivating others, learning to negotiate or network, or organizing a meeting.
d. Which skills do you want to continue to develop and be central parts of your future jobs?

Team Challenge

You are working for Colorado Green Builders, a company in Boulder, Colorado, specializing in sustainable building. You are part of a project team that is supervising the design and construction of a visitor's center in the Rocky Mountain National Park. The goal is to build the visitor's center so that it is self-sufficient. That means it should use no outside resources, if possible, including energy, water, and waste systems. Your manager, Amanda Karlson, suggests that you meet with your team to plan this project.

a. Meet as a team and brainstorm the general categories of resources you need to build the visitor's center so that it is self-sufficient. Consider everything typically found in a public building.
b. Review the resource categories and create a master list.
c. For each category, brainstorm ways to provide the resource without depending on outside systems. For example, if you have a food category, you could create a garden and greenhouse to provide fruits and vegetables without depending on outside suppliers.
d. Review the ideas your team generated, and then use convergent thinking techniques to edit the list. Your goal is to identify all the resources a visitor's center needs using systems that are fairly easy to set up and maintain and are not too expensive.
e. Submit the list to your instructor as requested.

Be the Critic

You are working part-time for a landscaping company planting trees and shrubs in a new neighborhood full of recently built homes. A large shed is located near a creek at the edge of the neighborhood. When you enter the shed, you discover it houses old pesticides, some of which are now outlawed. Concerned that the pesticides could pose a danger to the new neighborhood, you introduced the topic of the pesticides at a staff meeting and asked what you should do. Figure 4-18 shows how people answered your question. Analyze the solutions offered, noting their weaknesses, and send a list of the weaknesses to your instructor.

FIGURE 4-18

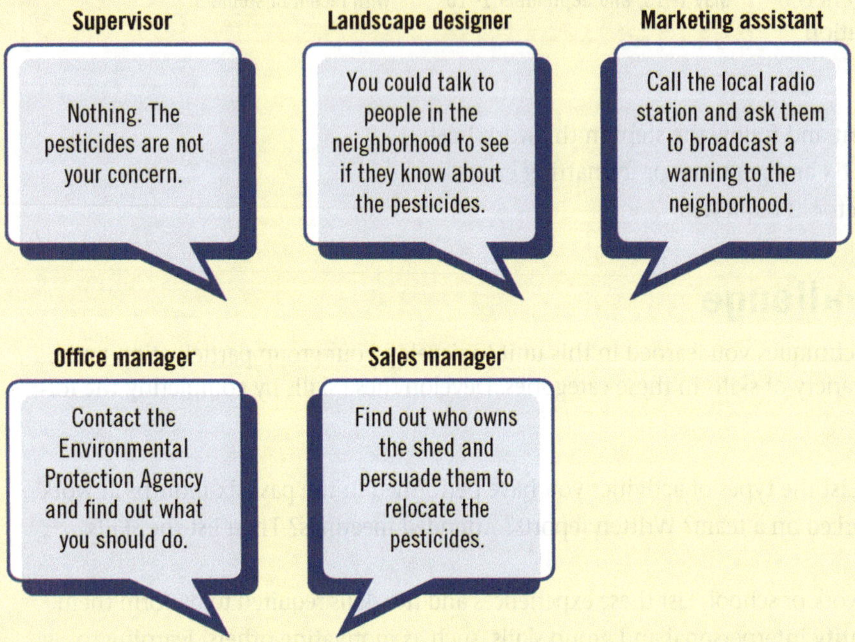

Part 5

Decision Support Tools

Files You Will Need:

PS5-Y34.docx
PS5-Y35.docx
PS5-Y36.docx
PS5-Y37.docx
PS5-Y38.docx
PS5-Y39.docx
PS5-Y40.docx
PS5-TechWork.docx
PS5-IC1.docx
PS5-IC2.docx

One of the earliest uses of computer technology was to support people making complex decisions. The term decision support system (DSS) describes any information system that aids in decision making, such as spreadsheets that compare weekly sales data or software that summarizes data on a so-called dashboard to highlight positive and negative trends. Early DSSs were large, proprietary, and expensive. Today, decision makers use spreadsheets, communication tools, and graphics software to analyze data and options. This part introduces the basic concepts of decision support tools and shows how you can use software to make objective decisions. You need to have some basic spreadsheet knowledge to complete this part. **case** You have been working with Grace Wong, the vice president of finance at Quest Specialty Travel, to help expand the company's services to corporate travelers. The new project is a success so far, though it has introduced some unexpected questions and decisions. Grace asks you to help her organize information and learn to use decision support tools so that she and others can make effective decisions.

OBJECTIVES

33 Understand decision support systems
34 Model decisions quantitatively
35 Describe data objectively
36 Work with formulas and functions
37 Perform what-if analyses
38 Weigh factors
39 Create decision trees
40 Use graphics to display data

Objective 33
Part 5

Understanding Decision Support Systems

A **decision support system (DSS)** is interactive software designed to help you compile useful information from raw data, documents, and business knowledge. You then use this information to identify and solve problems and make decisions. A DSS is ideal for analyzing complex problems that involve sets of data and demand a systematic decision-making approach. case Before you start assisting Grace Wong, she asks you to learn about decision support tools and their benefits.

DETAILS

Decision support tools offer the following benefits for decision makers:

- **Add objectivity to making decisions**
  Decision support software requires you to clearly define the issues, identify relevant information, determine how factors are related, and analyze the results. When you are making a decision, a DSS helps you evaluate all parts of the decision objectively. For example, Quest Specialty Travel can use a graphic such as the one shown in Figure 5-1 to determine which tour to offer first to corporate customers.

- **Improve efficiency for complex decisions**
  Complex decisions typically involve gathering lots of detailed information and then ranking or assigning weights to each factor. A computer can store information and make complex calculations much more efficiently than people can. You use decision support software to maintain, process, and report on the detailed information involved in complex decisions. For example, Quest is considering opening a branch office in Los Angeles or Chicago to serve corporate customers. It can use decision support software to compare expenses such as rent, travel, and employees and weigh factors such as proximity to clients, staff preference, and local attractions.

- **Encourage exploration and discovery**
  Decision support tools help you visualize data, illustrate problems, and graphically represent options and solutions. You can easily adjust variables and model scenarios. For example, Quest employees can use a spreadsheet to compare the income and expenses they have now with those they expect to have with a separate business travel department. Playing "what-if" with data encourages exploration of possibilities and can lead to more creative solutions.

- **Provide support for particular decisions**
  As a member of an organization, you must always be prepared to support the decisions you make. Intuitive decisions can be difficult to defend. When you approach a decision objectively and analyze it, you can demonstrate that you handled the matter professionally. For example, a decision support tool can help to compare the cost and volume of trips to find the best price.

- **Help communicate decisions to other interested people**
  Describing the thought processes that go into making a complex decision or solving an involved problem can be difficult. Decision support tools and their models can help you more effectively communicate your ideas to interested stakeholders. Figure 5-2 shows the steps, processes, and decisions involved in creating a new corporate travel department at Quest Specialty Travel.

QUICK TIP
Recall from Part 1 that when you solve a problem intuitively, you react immediately and instinctively, without following a particular procedure.

FIGURE 5-1: Decision diagram

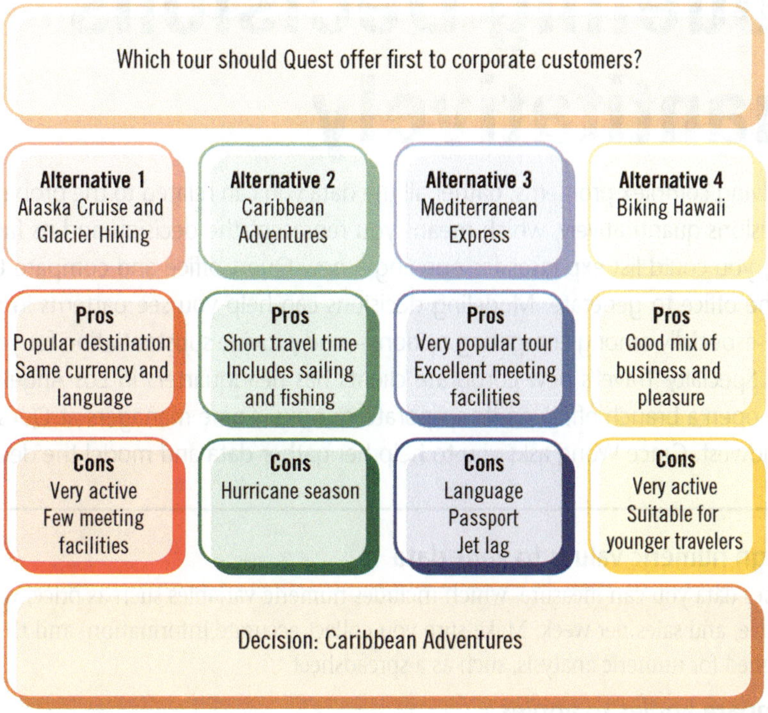

FIGURE 5-2: Comparing cost and volume of trips

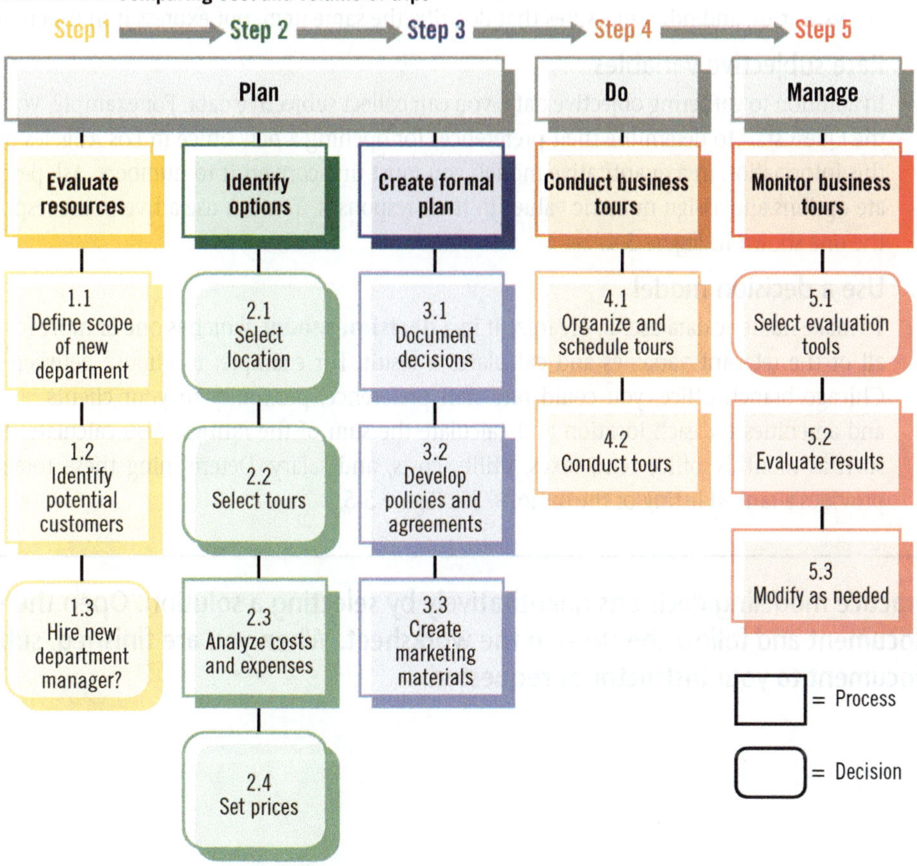

Objective 34
Part 5

Modeling Decisions Quantitatively

When solving complex problems, gather all the data you can related to the problem. Then you can **model** your decisions quantitatively, which means you represent the decision and its factors using numbers. For example, you could list expenses for opening a new Quest office and compare them to the revenue you expect the office to generate. Modeling decisions can help you see patterns in the data, make objective choices—especially among competing options—and provide substantiation for your decisions. case One of Quest Specialty Travel's new corporate clients has headquarters in Los Angeles, California, and wants Quest to open a branch office on its corporate campus. Some managers at Quest want to open an office in the Midwest. Grace Wong asks you to help her gather data and model the decision quantitatively.

ESSENTIAL ELEMENTS

QUICK TIP
Be sure to enter numbers carefully—a typo can ruin an otherwise useful model.

1. **Assign numeric values to your data**
   Gather data you can measure, which includes numeric variables such as price, weight, temperature, square footage, and sales per week. Make sure you collect accurate information, and then enter the data in a tool designed for numeric analysis, such as a spreadsheet.

2. **Compare apples to apples**
   The data you collect is not always available in the same format. For example, to compare salary data, convert an hourly or monthly wage to an annual salary or vice versa. See Figure 5-3. Make similar adjustments for quantities (single units vs. bulk quantities), temperatures (Celsius vs. Fahrenheit), monetary units (dollars vs. euros), and other measures that describe the same item, but express it in different ways.

QUICK TIP
Survey designers recommend five-point scales as the most accurate; fewer points don't offer enough options, and more points create confusion.

3. **Rate subjective variables**
   In addition to gathering objective data, you can collect subjective data. For example, you might want to poll the Quest staff to determine their preferences for opening a new office in Los Angeles or other sites. To use this information in a quantitative model, you must first convert it to numbers. Ask people to rate or evaluate options and assign numeric values to their responses. You can use a five-point response scale similar to the one shown in Figure 5-4.

4. **Use a decision model**
   To make numeric data useful, organize it in a **decision model**, which is one or more formulas that includes all of the relevant variables and calculates a result. For example, to choose between a Los Angeles and Chicago branch office, you could rate staff preference, proximity to your clients, and building features and amenities for each location and calculate the sum of the ratings. Also calculate the sum of variables such as monthly office rent, taxes, utility costs, and salary. Determining these totals for each location provides a ranked listing of the options. See Figure 5-5.

YOU TRY IT

Practice modeling decisions quantitatively by selecting a solution. Open the PS5-Y34.docx document and follow the steps in the worksheet. When you are finished, submit the document to your instructor as requested.

FIGURE 5-3: Comparing data

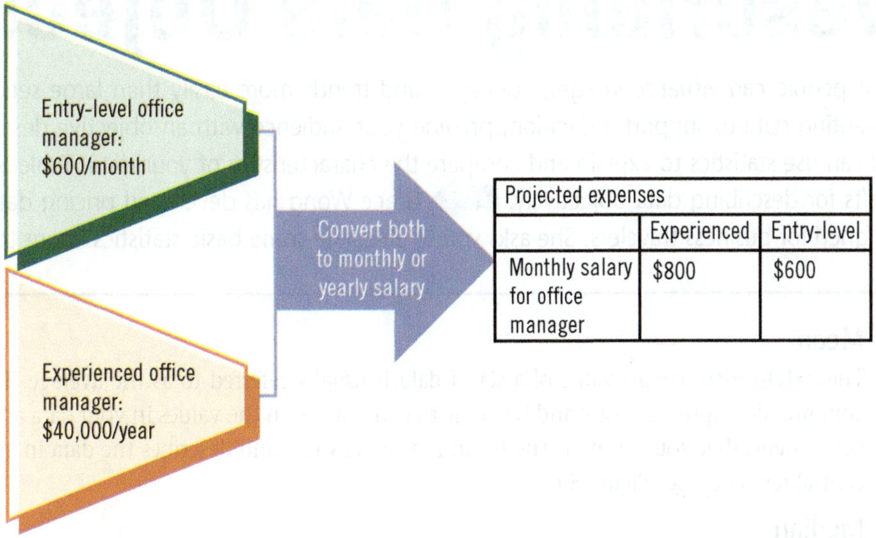

Problem: How much should Quest budget for an office manager in the new Los Angeles office?

FIGURE 5-4: Rating subjective data

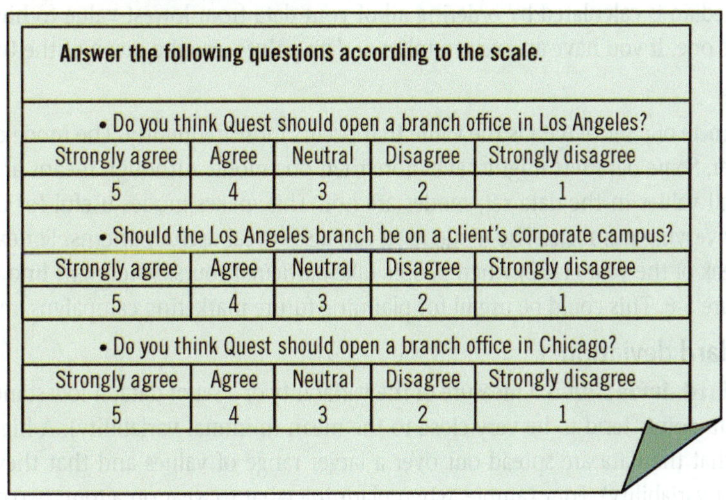

Answer the following questions according to the scale.

• Do you think Quest should open a branch office in Los Angeles?

Strongly agree	Agree	Neutral	Disagree	Strongly disagree
5	4	3	2	1

• Should the Los Angeles branch be on a client's corporate campus?

Strongly agree	Agree	Neutral	Disagree	Strongly disagree
5	4	3	2	1

• Do you think Quest should open a branch office in Chicago?

Strongly agree	Agree	Neutral	Disagree	Strongly disagree
5	4	3	2	1

FIGURE 5-5: Decision model

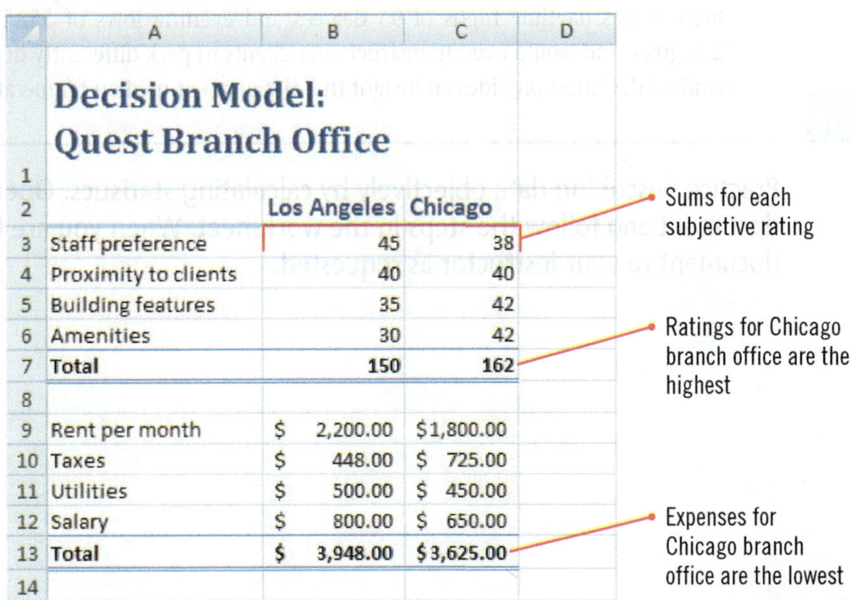

	A	B	C	D
1	**Decision Model: Quest Branch Office**			
2		**Los Angeles**	**Chicago**	
3	Staff preference	45	38	
4	Proximity to clients	40	40	
5	Building features	35	42	
6	Amenities	30	42	
7	**Total**	**150**	**162**	
8				
9	Rent per month	$ 2,200.00	$1,800.00	
10	Taxes	$ 448.00	$ 725.00	
11	Utilities	$ 500.00	$ 450.00	
12	Salary	$ 800.00	$ 650.00	
13	**Total**	**$ 3,948.00**	**$3,625.00**	
14				

Objective 35
Part 5

Describing Data Objectively

Most people can visualize images, concepts, and trends more easily than large sets of numbers. When presenting data to support a decision, provide your audience with an objective description of that data. You can use statistics to explain and compare the characteristics of your data. Table 5-1 lists the do's and don'ts for describing data objectively. case Grace Wong has developed pricing data for the new tours designed for business travelers. She asks you to calculate some basic statistics about the prices.

ESSENTIAL ELEMENTS

QUICK TIP
Technically, you can measure the average in other ways. The mean uses a particular calculation.

1. Mean

The **arithmetic mean** value of a set of data is usually referred to as the average. The mean is the most common descriptive statistic and is simple to compute. Sum the values in your data and divide by the number of items that you counted. The mean is a single value and describes the data in general by showing its central tendency. See Figure 5-6.

2. Median

The **median** value of a set of data is that point that separates the higher values from the lower values. The median is similar to the mean, but is less susceptible to distortion by extremely large or small values. The median is calculated by ordering all of your data from lowest value to highest value and selecting the middle one. If you have an even number of data points, use the mean of the two middle values.

3. Mode

The **mode** of a set of data is the value that occurs most frequently. The mode does not have to be a unique number. Some data sets might have more than one mode. Although means are affected by extremely large or small values in the data set, modes are not. This makes modes useful for describing data that includes widely varying numbers. The mode itself can also reveal useful patterns. For example, if you are measuring the week of the year (1–52) when people take particular tours, you might find that week 14 is the mode, as in Figure 5-6. This could be useful for planning future marketing campaigns and new tour offerings.

QUICK TIP
Data that is normally distributed is sometimes described as having a bell-shaped curve.

4. Standard deviation

Standard deviation is a measure of the variability of a set of data. A low standard deviation indicates that the data points tend to be very close to the mean (minimal variability). A higher standard deviation indicates that the data are spread out over a larger range of values and that they are farther from the mean (greater variability). For example, when planning what to wear on a tour, two destination cities might have the same average temperatures (75 degrees). However, the mean alone might not be enough information. One city has daytime highs of 95 degrees and evening lows of 55. The other varies between 78 and 72 degrees. You would need to instruct your clients to pack differently depending on their destination. The standard deviation provides an insight that the mean or median temperatures do not.

YOU TRY IT

Practice describing data objectively by calculating statistics. Open the PS5-Y35.docx document and follow the steps in the worksheet. When you are finished, submit the document to your instructor as requested.

FIGURE 5-6: Basic statistics

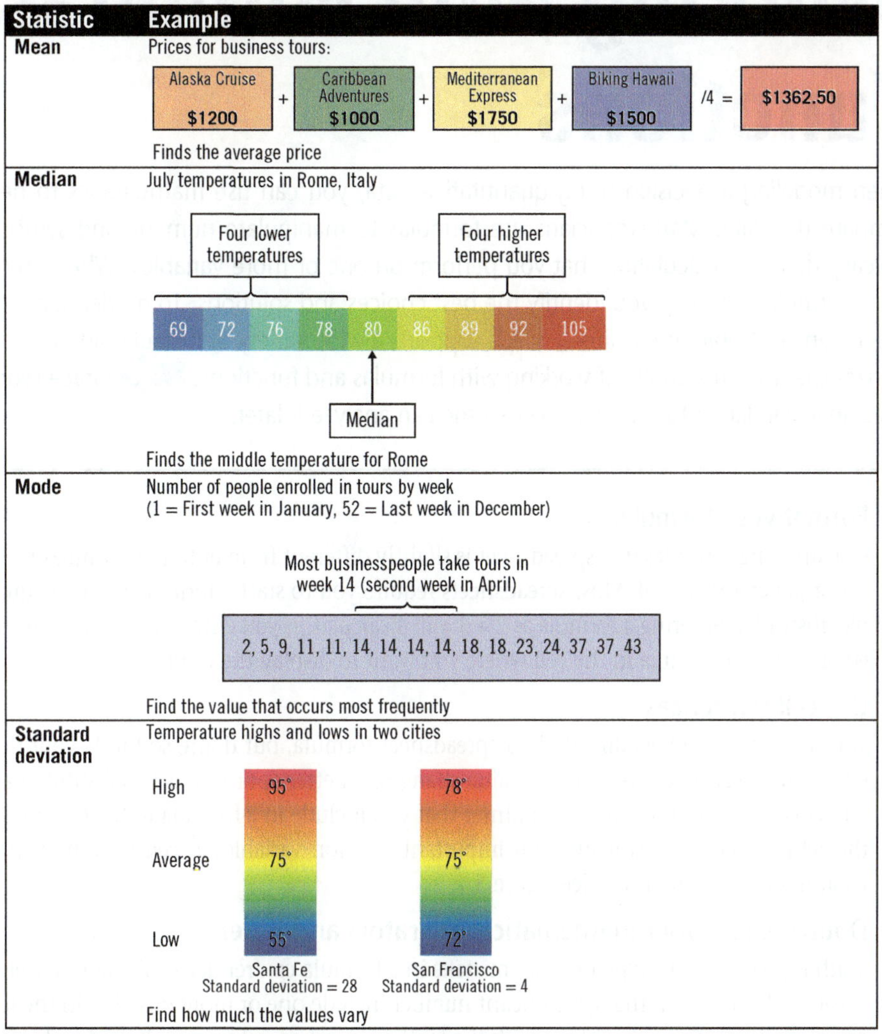

TABLE 5-1: Modeling decisions do's and don'ts

guidelines	do	don't
Mean	• Add the values and divide the sum by the number of values • Calculate the mean to find the tendency in the data	• Don't include extremely high or low values; they are outliers
Median	• Sort values from low to high or high to low, and then find the middle value • Find the median to determine the middle value, which is not affected by extreme values	• Don't confuse the median with the mean
Mode	• Sort values and find the ones that occur most frequently • Use to describe data that includes widely varying numbers	• Don't look for the mode in all sets of data—some don't have a mode
Standard deviation	• Interpret low standard deviations to mean that the values are very close to the mean so they don't vary much • Interpret high standard deviation to mean that the data are spread over a larger range of values and are farther from the mean	• Don't evaluate standard deviations as better or worse—they show which values are more consistent than other values

Objective 36
Part 5

Working with Formulas and Functions

When modeling a decision using quantitative data, you can use mathematics to help you analyze and compare the data. Mathematicians use formulas to manipulate numeric and symbolic data. A formula typically defines a calculation that you perform on one or more variables. When used with decision variables, formulas can help you identify the best choices and solutions. To model quantitative decisions, you can use an electronic spreadsheet, which supports a wide variety of formulas and functions. Table 5-2 summarizes the do's and don'ts of working with formulas and functions. case Grace Wong asks you to enter basic financial data into a spreadsheet so she can analyze it later.

ESSENTIAL ELEMENTS

1. **Format your formulas**
   Constructing formulas in a spreadsheet is slightly different from entering formulas by hand using a calculator or paper and pencil. Most spreadsheets require you to start a formula with an equal sign (=). For example, instead of entering a formula as 2 + 3 = in a calculator, you enter = 2 + 3 in a spreadsheet. You insert the equal sign of a formula in the cell where you want to display the result.

2. **Use cell references**
   You can enter numbers directly in a spreadsheet formula, but doing so limits your flexibility. You have to edit your spreadsheet every time a value changes. A better approach is to substitute hard numbers with cell references. A **cell reference** is a pointer that you include in a formula to tell the spreadsheet where to find the actual data. By organizing your important decision variables as cell references, it is much easier to do what-if and other analyses. See Figure 5-7.

3. **Double-check your mathematical operators and order**
   Math is precise, and a typo or other mistake in a formula can render a calculation useless. Studies of spreadsheet use have shown that a significant number include one or more mistakes in the formulas. Many of the errors are due to simple problems with the mathematical operators and the order of operations. Spreadsheets solve formulas in the order of operations shown in Figure 5-8.

QUICK TIP
Search the Web for lists of spreadsheet functions (e.g., Excel and Google Spreadsheet) and use them as a reference.

4. **Simplify with functions**
   Functions are preprogrammed formulas and simplify common mathematical tasks. Spreadsheet programs include functions to support statistical, engineering, mathematical, financial, and other calculations. In most spreadsheets, you enter an equal sign (=) followed by the function name and its arguments. **Arguments** are the values or cell references that the function uses in its calculations. Argument values are always contained inside parentheses. For example, the following formulas both calculate the same results:

   = D1 + D2 + D3 + D4 + D5 + D6

   = SUM (D1:D6)

   The SUM function automatically adds all of the values in cells D1 through D6 and displays the result.

YOU TRY IT

Practice working with formulas and functions by entering formulas. Open the PS5-Y36.docx document and follow the steps in the worksheet. When you are finished, submit the document to your instructor as requested.

FIGURE 5-7: Entering formulas in a spreadsheet

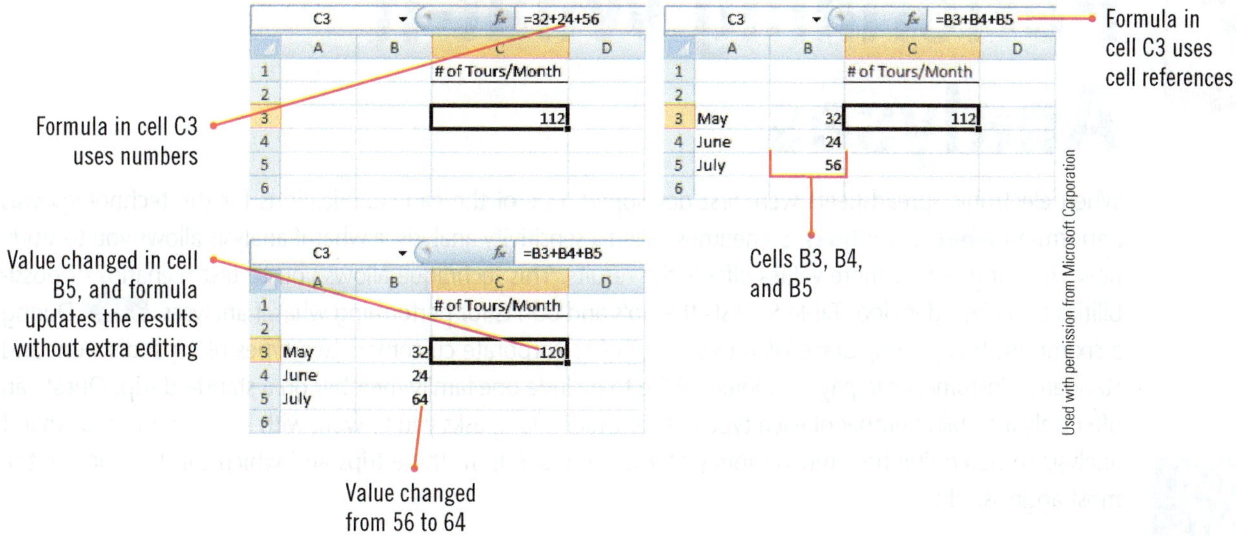

FIGURE 5-8: Order of operations

Order	Operation	Symbol	Example	Description
1.	Exponents	^	(8 ^ 2 + 5 ^ 2) * 10/2 8 ^ 2 = 64 5 ^ 2 = 25	Exponents (^) are solved first
2.		()	(64 + 25) * 10/2 64 + 25 = 89	Expression in parentheses is solved next
3.	Multiplication	*	89 * 10/2 89 * 10 = 890	Multiplication and division are solved left to right
	Division	/	890/2 = 445	
4.	Addition	+		Addition and subtraction are solved left to right
	Subtraction	−		

TABLE 5-2: Working with formulas and functions do's and don'ts

guidelines	do	don't
Format formulas	• Select the cell where you want the formula results to be displayed • Start a formula with an equal sign	• Don't insert the equal sign at the end as you do in manual formulas
Use cell references	• Use cell references in formulas instead of numbers or other values • Prepare for what-if analysis by using cell references	• Don't enter numbers and other values in a formula when you can use cell references instead
Organize operators correctly	• Follow the standard order of operations that your spreadsheet uses	• Don't forget to use parentheses to indicate parts of the formula you want to calculate first
Simplify with functions	• Start with an equal sign followed by the name of the function • Include arguments in parentheses • Use functions to simplify formulas	• Don't add a long string of numbers when you can use the SUM function instead

Objective 37 Part 5

Performing What-If Analyses

When electronic spreadsheets were first developed, one of the early applications for the technology was performing **what-if analyses**. Sometimes called a sensitivity analysis, a what-if analysis allows you to study how changing one or more values affects the results. This technique allows you to test scenarios or possibilities to make a decision. Table 5-3 lists the do's and don'ts for performing what-if analyses. case During a six-month trial period, Grace Wong wants to offer corporate customers two types of trips: discount and standard. Customers can pay an additional fee to include one family member on a standard trip. Quest can offer only a certain number of each type of trip. Grace Wong asks you to work with her to perform a what-if analysis to determine how much money Quest can make from these trips and which trip to promote the most aggressively.

ESSENTIAL ELEMENTS

QUICK TIP
Decision variables are often used in formulas that show results.

1. Identify decision variables

Decision variables are values that could change and affect the results. Statisticians refer to these as independent variables. Identify decision variables by asking whether changing the value would also change the results. If so, treat it as a decision variable. See Figure 5-9.

2. Identify the constants

Constants are elements that are not likely to change much over time. They do not vary in a what-if analysis. If you are calculating the amount of revenue Quest can generate from three types of business trips, the price of each trip is a constant. For example, the price of a discount trip is $1200. That value will not change no matter what else changes in the spreadsheet.

3. Identify output variables

The **output variables** are values in the results that could change if the decision variables change. Output variables are often referred to as dependent variables because their value depends on the independent variables. These are the results that you are calculating and studying with the what-if analysis. As shown in Figure 5-9, Quest can make about $716,000 in six months on business trips. It should also promote discount trips because they generate the most revenue.

QUICK TIP
Consider optimistic, realistic, and pessimistic scenarios.

4. Test several scenarios

Typically, you perform what-if analyses on several scenarios. For each possible scenario, consider a range of values for each decision variable. Enter the values and formulas to see how the values affect your output variables. For example, Figure 5-10 shows two scenarios in a what-if analysis for Quest Specialty Travel.

5. Assess your results using common sense

Double-check your spreadsheet carefully for mistakes or flawed assumptions. Use simple test data to make sure the results are what you expect. If the results seem unreasonable or too good to be true, the spreadsheet probably contains an error. Recalculate the data by hand and ask trusted colleagues to look at your analysis with a critical eye.

YOU TRY IT

Practice performing what-if analyses by using Microsoft Excel's what-if analysis tools. Open the PS5-Y37.docx document and follow the steps in the worksheet. When you are finished, submit the document to your instructor as requested.

FIGURE 5-9: Constants, decision variables, and output variables

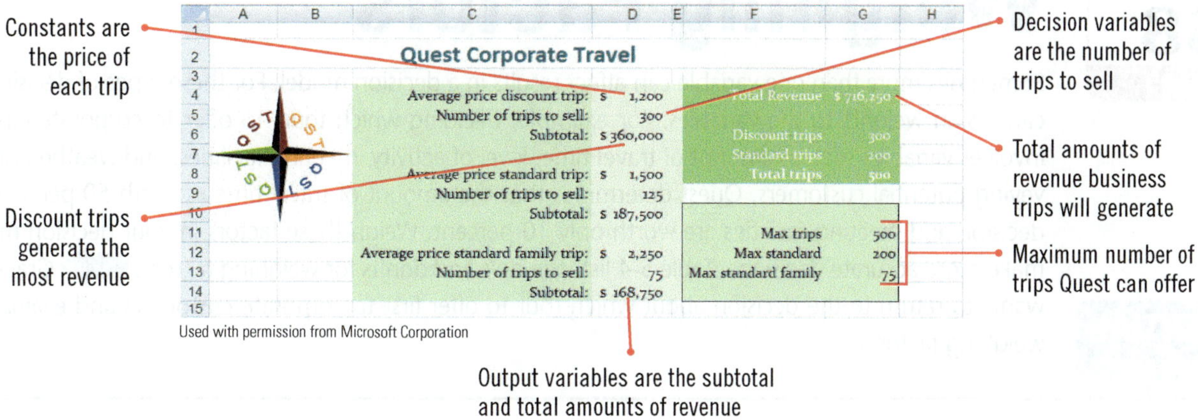

Used with permission from Microsoft Corporation

FIGURE 5-10: What-if analysis with two scenarios

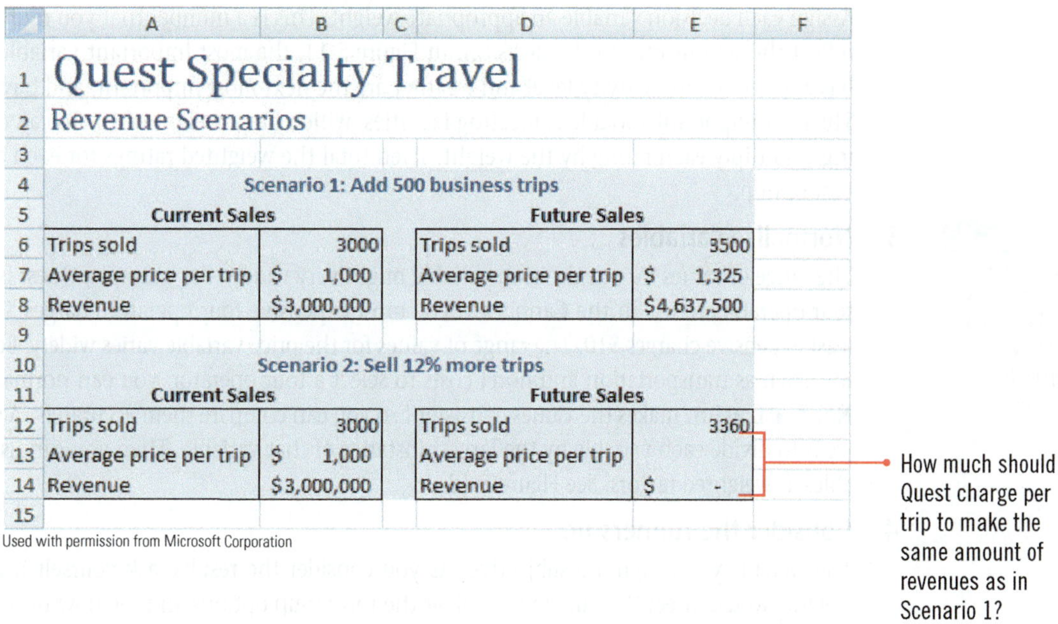

Used with permission from Microsoft Corporation

TABLE 5-3: Performing what-if analyses do's and don'ts

guidelines	do	don't
Decision variables	• Identify values that are likely to change	• Don't assume all values you enter are decision variables
Constants	• Identify values that are not likely to change	• Don't vary the constants in a what-if analysis
Output variables	• Identify results that are likely to change	• Don't enter values for output variables—use formulas
Scenarios	• Create two or more scenarios to test in the what-if analysis	• Don't use only one scenario
Results	• Double-check the decision variables, constants, and formulas • Use test data to check the spreadsheet	• Don't assume that the spreadsheet results are valid—test them carefully • Don't accept results that seem too good to be true

Objective 38
Part 5

Weighing Factors

Sometimes more than one variable can affect results in a decision model. For these types of decisions, you can assign weights to the variables. For example, deciding which tours to offer to corporate customers involves variables such as amount of travel time, level of activity, meeting facilities, and weather. After surveying potential customers, Quest determines that the amount of travel time is worth 50 percent of the decision and meeting facilities are worth only 10 percent. Weigh these factors in your decision model to make more accurate decisions. Table 5-4 lists the do's and don'ts for weighing factors. case Grace Wong wants to return to the decision about which tour to offer first to corporate customers and evaluate it by weighing factors.

ESSENTIAL ELEMENTS

1. Identify the most important decision variables

The most important factors are the decision variables that are most likely to affect your output variables. If your decision includes many independent variables, limit yourself to those that have the most effect on the decision. In Figure 5-11, the four variables are activity level, meeting facilities, travel time, and weather.

2. Determine the appropriate weights

Assign each decision variable an appropriate weight. This is a number that you multiply the variable by to reflect the significance in the decision. In Figure 5-11, the most important variable is travel time, which has a weight of 50. Activity level and weather are the next most important, and have a weight of 20 each. The least important variable is meeting facilities, which has a weight of 10. To calculate the weighted ratings, multiply each rating by the weight. Then total the weighted ratings for each alternative to find the best option.

3. Normalize variables

QUICK TIP
When normalizing, you usually multiply or divide the data by a variable so you can compare the variables fairly.

The range of values for one decision variable might vary widely. For example, Quest is considering five local tour operators to use in the Caribbean. The most expensive tour operator charges $50 per person and the least expensive charges $10. The range of values for the price variable varies widely. Before adding other factors such as transportation and hotel costs to select a tour operator, you can normalize the price variable. **Normalization** makes the values consistent so you can compare them accurately. A simple way to normalize is to divide each variable by the largest instance of that variable. Then you can use the normalized variables as weighted factors. See Figure 5-12.

4. Consider the runners-up

The weights you assign are subjective. As you consider the results, ask yourself if a small change in the weights would affect the outcome. Look at the runner-up options and see how near they are to the leader. Values close to the top value are often important decision variables.

YOU TRY IT

Practice weighing factors by assigning weights and calculating results. Open the PS5-Y38.docx document and follow the steps in the worksheet. When you are finished, submit the document to your instructor as requested.

FIGURE 5-11: Assigning weights

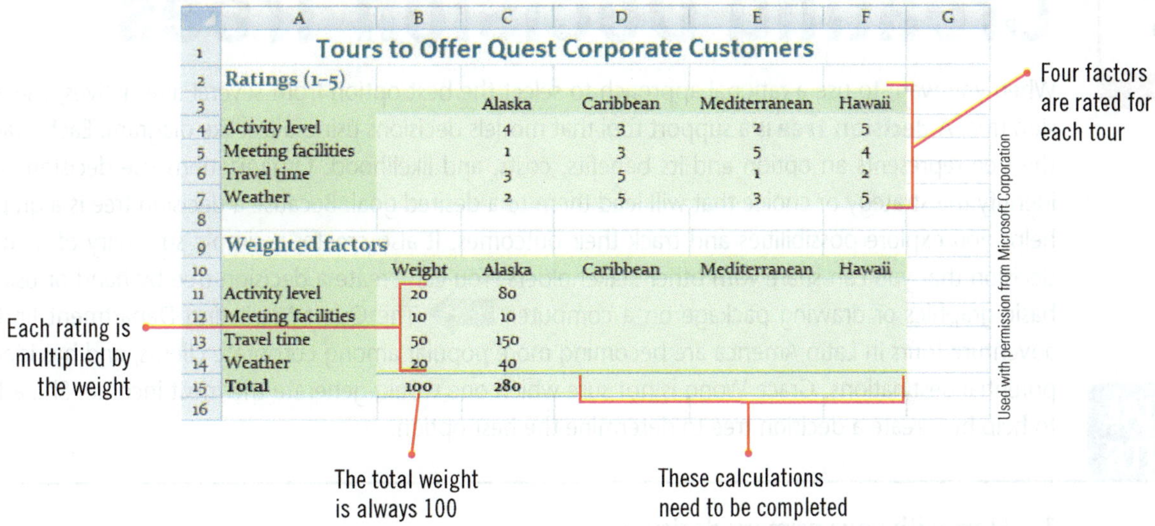

	A	B	C	D	E	F	G
1	Tours to Offer Quest Corporate Customers						
2	Ratings (1–5)						
3			Alaska	Caribbean	Mediterranean	Hawaii	
4	Activity level		4	3	2	5	
5	Meeting facilities		1	3	5	4	
6	Travel time		3	5	1	2	
7	Weather		2	5	3	5	
8							
9	Weighted factors						
10		Weight	Alaska	Caribbean	Mediterranean	Hawaii	
11	Activity level	20	80				
12	Meeting facilities	10	10				
13	Travel time	50	150				
14	Weather	20	40				
15	Total	100	280				
16							

FIGURE 5-12: Normalizing variables

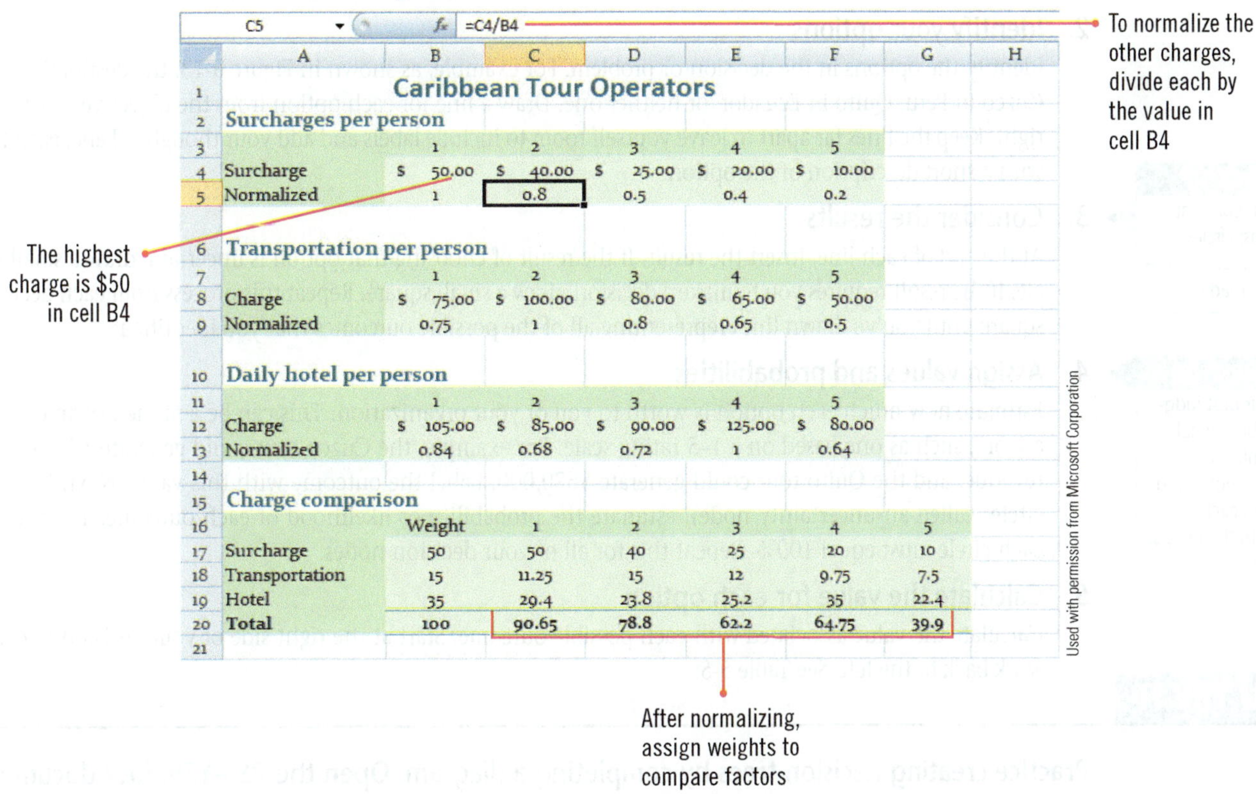

C5 =C4/B4

	A	B	C	D	E	F	G	H
1	Caribbean Tour Operators							
2	Surcharges per person							
3		1	2	3	4	5		
4	Surcharge	$ 50.00	$ 40.00	$ 25.00	$ 20.00	$ 10.00		
5	Normalized	1	0.8	0.5	0.4	0.2		
6	Transportation per person							
7		1	2	3	4	5		
8	Charge	$ 75.00	$ 100.00	$ 80.00	$ 65.00	$ 50.00		
9	Normalized	0.75	1	0.8	0.65	0.5		
10	Daily hotel per person							
11		1	2	3	4	5		
12	Charge	$ 105.00	$ 85.00	$ 90.00	$ 125.00	$ 80.00		
13	Normalized	0.84	0.68	0.72	1	0.64		
14								
15	Charge comparison							
16		Weight	1	2	3	4	5	
17	Surcharge	50	50	40	25	20	10	
18	Transportation	15	11.25	15	12	9.75	7.5	
19	Hotel	35	29.4	23.8	25.2	35	22.4	
20	Total	100	90.65	78.8	62.2	64.75	39.9	
21								

TABLE 5-4: Weighing factors do's and don'ts

guidelines	do	don't
Decision variables	• Identify the decision variables that have the most effect on the decision	• **Don't** include minor decision variables
Weights	• Assign a weight to each important decision variable	• **Don't** assign weights to all decision variables
Normalization	• Account for differences in variables by normalizing them	• **Don't** compare values without normalizing them first

Objective 39
Part 5

Creating Decision Trees

When you want to use a rational approach to select the best option from several alternatives, use a decision tree. A **decision tree** is a support tool that models decisions using a treelike diagram. Each branch of the tree represents an option and its benefits, costs, and likelihood. Organizations use decision trees to identify the strategy or choice that will lead them to a desired goal. Because a decision tree is a graphic, it helps you explore possibilities and track their outcomes. It also creates a simple summary of a complex decision that you can share with other stakeholders. You can create a decision tree by hand or using any basic graphics or drawing package on a computer. case The Quest Marketing Department finds that adventure tours in Latin America are becoming more popular among corporate clients, and has identified potential destinations. Grace Wong is not sure which one would generate the most income. She asks you to help her create a decision tree to determine the best option.

ESSENTIAL ELEMENTS

1. **Start with your primary decision**

   Begin by determining the primary decision to make or problem to solve. This becomes your goal, such as to identify a new destination in Latin America for an adventure tour. Draw a small box on the left side of a piece of paper or on your computer screen. Label this objective box with a description of the problem.

2. **Identify your options**

   Identify the options in the decision or problem. For example, as shown in Figure 5-13, the destinations are Cuzco in Peru, Quito in Ecuador, or neither one. Draw a line for each option from the objective box to the right. Keep the lines far apart to leave yourself room to include labels and add your thoughts. Label each line with a short description of the option.

> **QUICK TIP**
> Squares represent decisions; circles indicate that a choice must be made.

3. **Consider the results**

   At the end of each line, insert the result. If the result of choosing that option is uncertain, draw a small circle. If the result requires you to make a decision, draw a small square. Repeat this process from each decision square until you've drawn lines representing all of the possible outcomes that you identified.

> **QUICK TIP**
> Use your best judgment about what you think each option is worth and compare each option to the others.

4. **Assign values and probabilities**

   Estimate how much each option is worth to you or your organization. This can be a monetary amount or a score, such as one based on a 1–5 rating scale. For example, the Cuzco tour could generate $730,000 in revenue, and the Quito tour could generate $670,000. Label the outcome with this value. Next, for each circle (called an uncertainty node), estimate the probability or likelihood of each outcome. The total at each circle must equal 100%. Repeat this for all of your decision nodes.

5. **Calculate the value for each option**

   Calculate the value associated with each possible outcome. Start at the right side of your decision tree and work back to the left. See Table 5-5.

YOU TRY IT

Practice creating decision trees by completing a diagram. Open the PS5-Y39.docx document and follow the steps in the worksheet. When you are finished, submit the document to your instructor as requested.

FIGURE 5-13: Decision tree

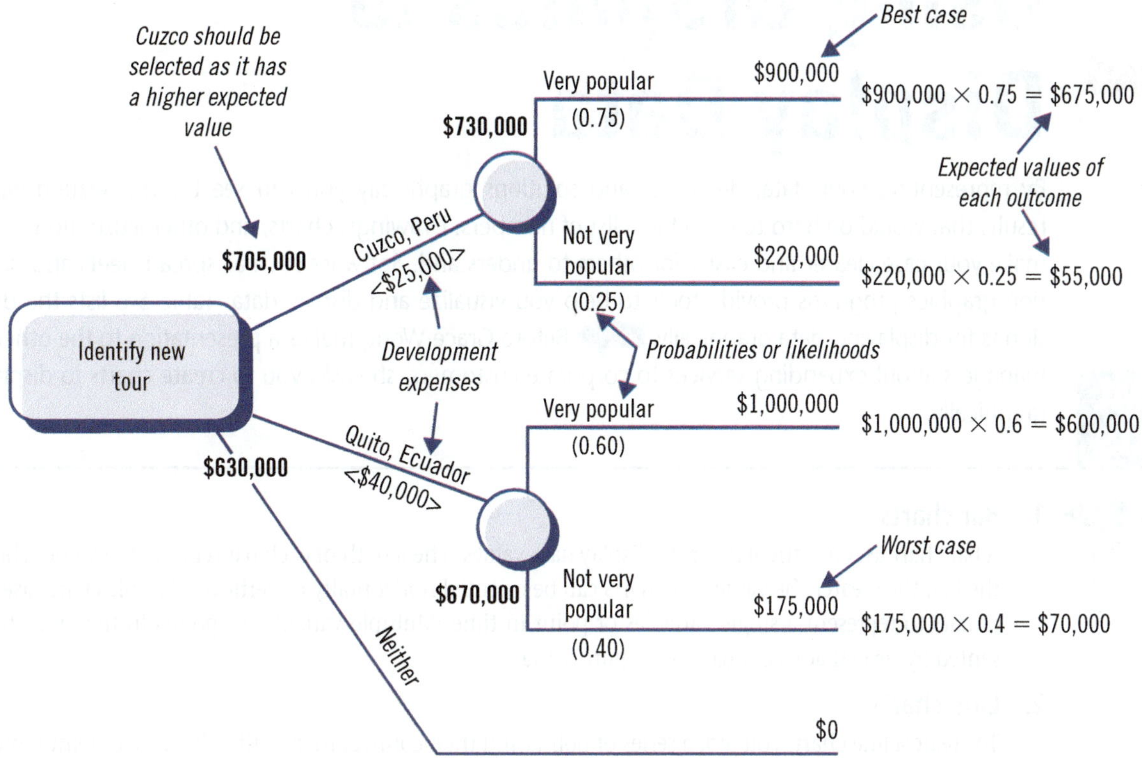

For the new Quest tour, Quito in Ecuador and Cuzco in Peru are two potential destinations. The cost to develop each tour is shown in the decision tree. These expenses are for setting up a tour, promoting it, identifying contractors, and so on. You estimate the revenue of each tour as best- and worst-case scenarios.

TABLE 5-5: Calculating the value for each option

element	shape	description
Uncertainties	Circle	• Multiply each outcome by its probability • Insert this value in the decision tree • Repeat this for each uncertainty
Decisions	Square	• Estimate the costs associated with each option • Subtract cost of the outcome value you calculated to find the benefit of that decision • Repeat this for each decision
Results	Line	• When you have calculated all of the decision benefits (value–cost), choose the option that has the largest benefit. This is the optimal decision.

The art of information graphics

Edward Tufte, author of four influential books on information design, is passionate about graphics, the simpler, clearer, and more meaningful, the better. During his popular presentations to Web designers, economists, business owners, and others, Tufte shows one example after another of poor, confusing, and cluttered diagrams, charts, and graphics and compares them to his translations, which are elegantly simple and easy to understand at a glance. In a recent issue of *BusinessWeek*, Adam Aston described one effective comparison that Tufte makes using a diagram drawn by Galileo to explain the solar system by positioning the sun at its center. "Tufte points to a page from Galileo's *Dialogue Concerning the Two Chief World Systems* to contrast the two views of the solar system. Copernicus' earth-centered rendering is a tangled knot. Galileo's sun-centered solar model is elegantly simple. Then as now, clean design reflects clear thinking, and has a way of wiping away junky analysis and poor presentation." Tufte recommends the same approach to anyone who needs to present visual information, from corporate executives to students.

Source: Aston, Adam, "Tufte's Invisible Yet Ubiquitous Influence," *BusinessWeek*, June 10, 2009.

Objective 40

Part 5

Using Graphics to Display Data

By representing your data, decisions, and solutions graphically you can see trends, relationships, and results that would be hard to detect in a list of numbers. Drawings, charts, and other illustrations also help make your case clearer and easier for others to understand. Software such as spreadsheets and presentation graphics programs provide tools to help you visualize and display data. Table 5-6 lists the do's and don'ts for displaying data graphically. case Before Grace Wong makes a presentation to the other Quest managers about expanding services to corporate customers, she asks you to create charts to display data graphically.

ESSENTIAL ELEMENTS

QUICK TIP
Bar charts with vertical bars are called column charts.

1. **Bar charts**

   A bar chart uses rectangular bars to display data values. The length of each bar represents a value. The longer the bar, the greater the value. Bar charts can be oriented horizontally or vertically. Simple charts use one set of bars to represent a single variables or point in time. Multiple variables or points in time may be represented by several adjacent bars. See Figure 5-14a.

2. **Line charts**

   To create a line chart, you plot a series of points and then connect them with a line. Each point represents a measurement or value. The line shows directions or trends in the data over time. See Figure 5-14b.

3. **Area charts**

   An area chart is similar to a line chart because it compares two or more variables over time. However, it displays the values for each variable as cumulative totals using numbers or percentages. This means that each variable is layered one on top of another. A color or fill pattern highlights each variable.

4. **Pie charts**

   Pie charts are circles divided into sectors, with each sector resembling a slice of a pie. See Figure 5-14c. The size of the slice represents the relative size or frequency of the corresponding variable. Because the entire chart forms a complete circle, it shows the percentage of the whole that each variable represents. Use pie charts to compare data at one point in time, usually to the whole. Pie charts are easiest to interpret when the largest slice represents at least 25–30% of the data. Ideally, a pie chart should emphasize a single variable and compare that slice with the rest of the pie.

QUICK TIP
Most software tools can display 3D scatter plots with up to four dimensions.

5. **Scatter plots**

   Scatter plots display two variables for a set of data. You plot the data for one variable along the horizontal axis and the other variable on the vertical axis. A scatter plot shows correlations between variables, especially nonlinear ones. If the points appear random and unordered, the two variables do not have a strong relationship. See Figure 5-14d.

YOU TRY IT

Practice using graphics to display data by creating a chart. Open the PS5-Y40.docx document and follow the steps in the worksheet. When you are finished, submit the document to your instructor as requested.

FIGURE 5-14: Types of charts

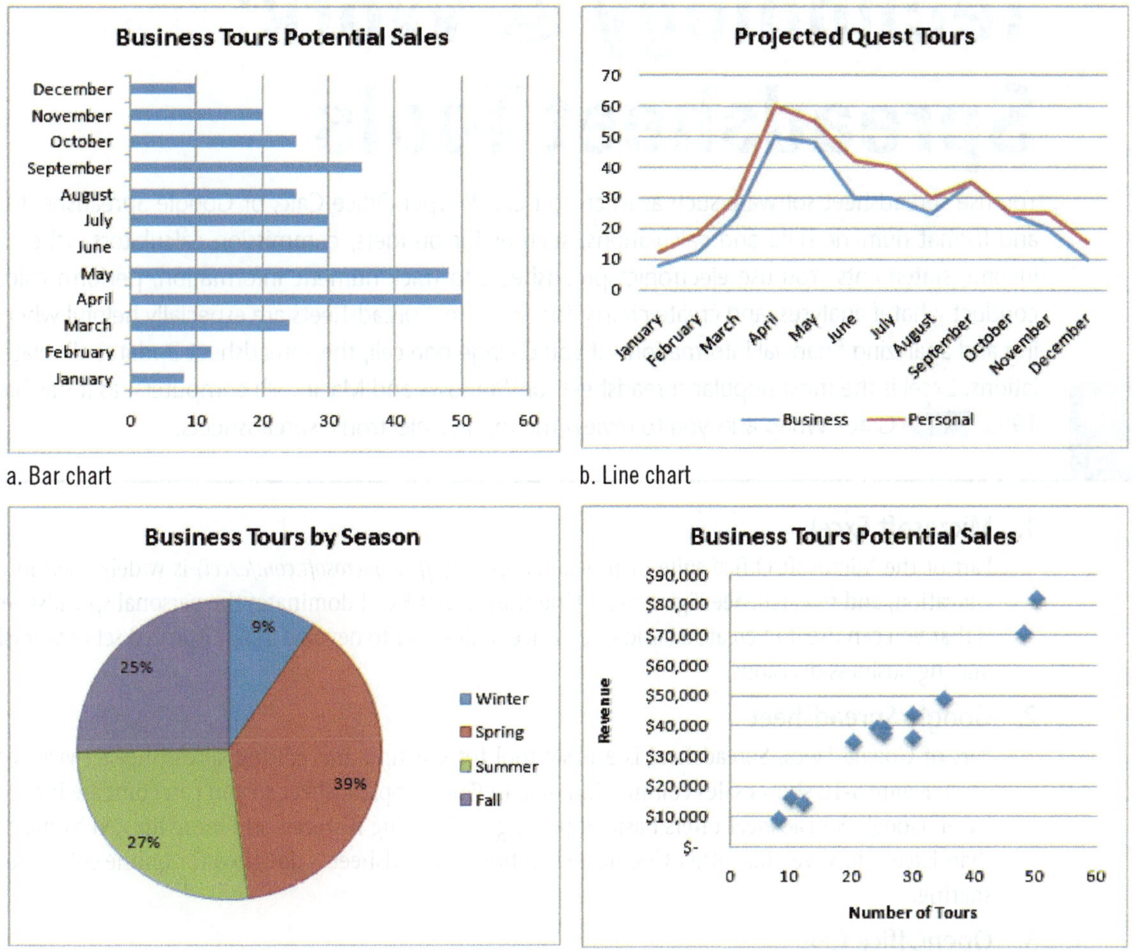

a. Bar chart

b. Line chart

c. Pie chart

d. Scatter chart

TABLE 5-6: Using graphics do's and don'ts

guidelines	do	don't
Bar chart	• Use bars to represent data, with the length of the bar corresponding to the size of the data	• Don't use long text on the horizontal axis
Line chart	• Plot a series of points and then connect them with a line to show directions or trends in the data over time	• Don't plot too many points or you might not be able to see the pattern
Area chart	• Display values for each variable as cumulative totals using numbers or percentages • Use different colors or fill patterns to differentiate each layer • Choose an area chart to represent the volume of data	• Don't hide the area you want to emphasize in the middle of the chart—place it along the baseline • Don't use if you are making a comparison between multiple series—consider using a bar chart instead • Don't use if you are analyzing trends over a period time—consider using a line chart instead
Pie chart	• Compare the percentage of an element with the whole • Use pie charts to compare data at one point in time	• Don't use pie charts to show changes over time • Don't compare sectors across multiple pie charts • Don't create pie charts with many small slices, which are hard to understand
Scatter plot	• Display two variables for a set of data • Show correlations among variables, especially nonlinear ones	• Don't plot more than two variables • Don't interpret a scatter plot the same way as a line chart because a scatter plot combines two values in one point

Technology @ Work: Spreadsheet Tools

You use spreadsheet software such as Microsoft Excel, OpenOffice Calc, or Google Spreadsheet to create and format numeric data and calculations, such as for budgets, commission calculators, schedules, and income statements. You use electronic spreadsheets to track numeric information, perform calculations, conduct what-if analyses, and create charts, for example. Spreadsheets are especially helpful when recording and analyzing financial information—if you change one cell, the spreadsheet updates all related calculations. Excel is the most popular spreadsheet for Windows and Macintosh computers, as it has been since 1993. case Grace Wong asks you to review the top five electronic spreadsheets.

ESSENTIAL ELEMENTS

1. **Microsoft Excel**

   Part of the Microsoft Office suite of programs, Excel (*office.microsoft.com/excel*) is widely used in business, education, and research. See Figure 5-15. One reason that Excel dominates the personal spreadsheet market is that you can use it to create a basic spreadsheet quickly or to develop a sophisticated set of worksheets for making business decisions.

2. **Google Spreadsheet**

   Part of Google Docs, Spreadsheet is a basic tool for creating and editing spreadsheets (*www.google.com/docs*). Figure 5-16 shows sales commission data in Google Spreadsheet so you can compare it to Microsoft Excel. Google Spreadsheet offers basic importing and editing features, and more limited formatting tools than Excel. However, like other Google applications, Spreadsheet is designed for online collaboration and sharing.

3. **OpenOffice Calc**

   A free open source spreadsheet tool, OpenOffice Calc (*www.openoffice.org/product/calc.html*) is an all-purpose spreadsheet modeled after Microsoft Excel, and is freely available on the OpenOffice Web site. It opens and saves files in the XLS format (the Microsoft Excel 2003 format). Unlike Excel, Calc can define series for creating charts based on the layout of your data. It can also save spreadsheets as Portable Document Format (PDF) files, which makes them easy to share with non-Calc users.

4. **Gnumeric**

   Like OpenOffice Calc, Gnumeric is a free, open-source spreadsheet program that is part of the GNOME desktop for computers running the Linux operating system (*www.gnumeric.org*). It is designed to be similar to Excel, though it lacks features such as conditional formatting and PivotTables. Professionals performing statistical analysis consider it a reliable spreadsheet tool.

5. **Apple Numbers**

   If you use a Macintosh computer, you can use Apple Numbers, which is part of the iWork suite of programs (*www.apple.com/iwork/numbers*). Numbers is designed to be easy to use and can create visually rich charts and tables. It lacks the more sophisticated features of Excel, such as PivotTables, PivotCharts, and a programming language for customizing spreadsheets.

YOU TRY IT

Learn more about spreadsheet tools. Open the PS5-TechWork.docx document and follow the steps in the worksheet. When you are finished, submit the document to your instructor as requested.

FIGURE 5-15: Microsoft Excel

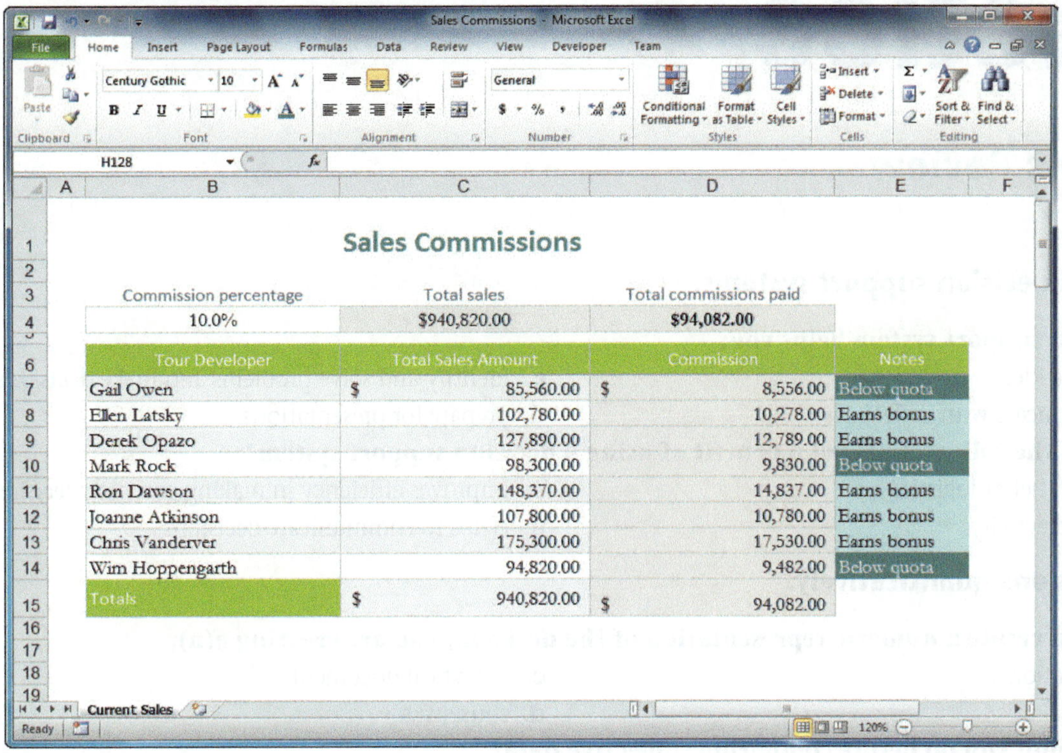

Commission percentage	Total sales	Total commissions paid	
10.0%	$940,820.00	$94,082.00	
Tour Developer	Total Sales Amount	Commission	Notes
Gail Owen	$ 85,560.00	$ 8,556.00	Below quota
Ellen Latsky	102,780.00	10,278.00	Earns bonus
Derek Opazo	127,890.00	12,789.00	Earns bonus
Mark Rock	98,300.00	9,830.00	Below quota
Ron Dawson	148,370.00	14,837.00	Earns bonus
Joanne Atkinson	107,800.00	10,780.00	Earns bonus
Chris Vanderver	175,300.00	17,530.00	Earns bonus
Wim Hoppengarth	94,820.00	9,482.00	Below quota
Totals	$ 940,820.00	$ 94,082.00	

FIGURE 5-16: Google Spreadsheet

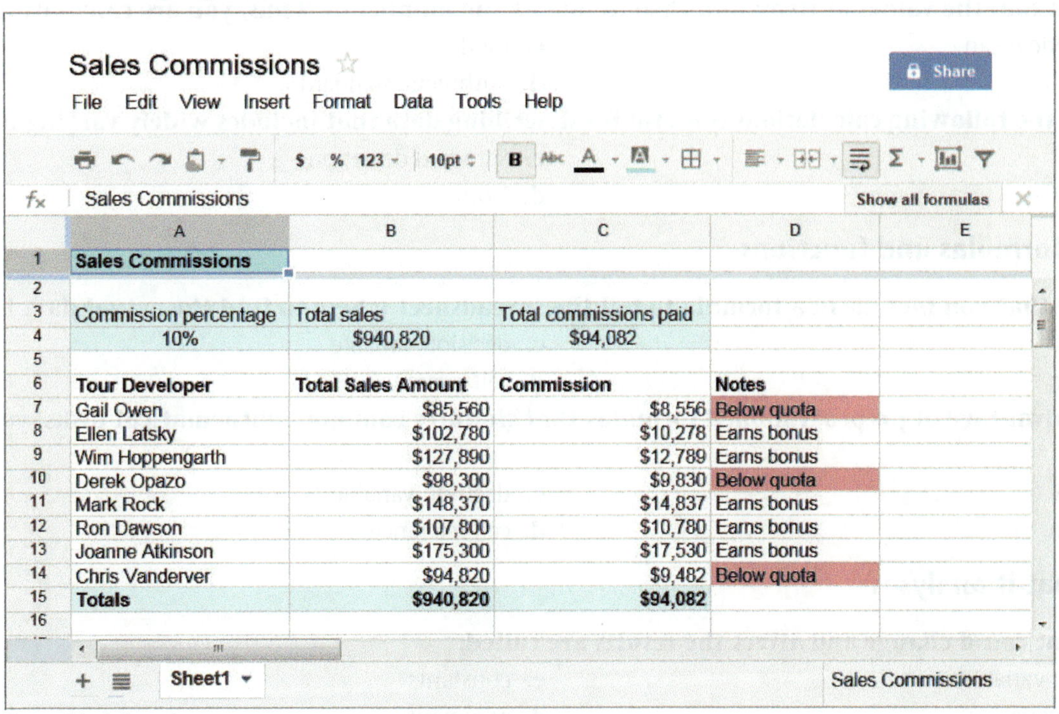

Sales Commissions			
Commission percentage	Total sales	Total commissions paid	
10%	$940,820	$94,082	
Tour Developer	Total Sales Amount	Commission	Notes
Gail Owen	$85,560	$8,556	Below quota
Ellen Latsky	$102,780	$10,278	Earns bonus
Wim Hoppengarth	$127,890	$12,789	Earns bonus
Derek Opazo	$98,300	$9,830	Below quota
Mark Rock	$148,370	$14,837	Earns bonus
Ron Dawson	$107,800	$10,780	Earns bonus
Joanne Atkinson	$175,300	$17,530	Earns bonus
Chris Vanderver	$94,820	$9,482	Below quota
Totals	$940,820	$94,082	

Practice

Soft Skills Review

Understand decision support systems.

1. **A decision support system helps you:**
   - **a.** generate ideas
   - **b.** communicate with colleagues
   - **c.** identify and solve problems and make decisions
   - **d.** prepare for presentations
2. **Which of the following is *not* a benefit of using a decision support system?**
   - **a.** Provides better logistics
   - **b.** Adds objectivity
   - **c.** Improves efficiency in making complex decisions
   - **d.** Helps to communicate decisions

Model decisions quantitatively.

1. **When you create a numeric representation of the decision, you are creating a(n):**
   - **a.** presentation
   - **b.** model
   - **c.** analytical document
   - **d.** consensus
2. **What should you do before comparing subjective data?**
   - **a.** Plot the data
   - **b.** Find the mean
   - **c.** Create a model
   - **d.** Rate it on a response scale

Describe data objectively.

1. **When you sum the values of items and then divide by the number of items, you are calculating the:**
   - **a.** arithmetic mean
   - **b.** median
   - **c.** mode
   - **d.** arithmetic standard
2. **Which of the following calculations is useful for describing data that includes widely varying numbers?**
   - **a.** Median
   - **b.** Mode
   - **c.** Standard deviation
   - **d.** Norm

Work with formulas and functions.

1. **A pointer that you include in a formula to tell the spreadsheet where to find the actual data is called a:**
   - **a.** formula
   - **b.** function
   - **c.** decision variable
   - **d.** cell reference
2. **To take advantage of preprogrammed formulas that simplify common mathematical tasks, you can use a:**
   - **a.** formula
   - **b.** function
   - **c.** decision variable
   - **d.** cell reference

Perform what-if analyses.

1. **Values that could change and affect the results are called:**
   - **a.** decision variables
   - **b.** output variables
   - **c.** constants
   - **d.** arguments
2. **The values that you study with a what-if analysis are the:**
   - **a.** decision variables
   - **b.** output variables
   - **c.** constants
   - **d.** arguments

Weigh factors.

1. **How can you indicate the significance of each variable in a decision?**
   - **a.** Assign an appropriate weight
   - **b.** Convert the values to the same format
   - **c.** Use one as a constant in the model
   - **d.** Normalize the variables
2. **How can you account for differences in variables?**
   - **a.** Create a decision tree
   - **b.** Normalize them
   - **c.** Play what-if
   - **d.** Find the standard deviation

Create decision trees.

1. **In a decision tree, what does each branch of the tree represent?**
   - **a.** An assignment to a member of the group
   - **b.** An option that is unlikely to work
   - **c.** A new idea
   - **d.** An option and its benefits, costs, and likelihood
2. **What shapes do you use in a decision tree?**
   - **a.** Circles, squares, and lines
   - **b.** Circles and diamonds
   - **c.** Rectangles only
   - **d.** Tree shapes

Use graphics to display data.

1. **In a line chart, what does the line show?**
   - **a.** The relation of parts to the whole
   - **b.** Directions or trends in the data over time
   - **c.** Accumulated values
   - **d.** Where data is not related
2. **Circular charts divided into sectors are called:**
   - **a.** circle charts
   - **b.** area charts
   - **c.** pie charts
   - **d.** slice charts

Technology @ work: Spreadsheet tools.

1. **Which of the following is *not* an example of spreadsheet software?**
   - **a.** Microsoft Excel
   - **b.** OpenOffice Calc
   - **c.** Apple Spreadsheets
   - **d.** Google Spreadsheet
2. **Which of the following is an advantage of using Gnumeric?**
   - **a.** It a free, open-source spreadsheet program
   - **b.** It is designed for online collaboration
   - **c.** It is popular with Macintosh users
   - **d.** It is creates elegant PivotTables

Critical Thinking Questions

1. **Decision support tools are widely used in the business world and are becoming increasingly complex and specialized. What do you think are the dangers of developing and using sophisticated decision support tools?**
2. **What are the advantages of using mathematical decision tools such as decision trees and weighted factors?**
3. **Suppose that you are about to make a major decision, such as returning to school full time (or ending your academic career to work full time). How could you use a tool discussed in this Part to help you as you make your decision?**
4. **If you collect too much information for analyzing a decision, you can suffer from analysis paralysis, where you spend too much time thinking about a decision rather than making one. Recall a major financial decision you made recently, such as of a car or housing purchase or rental. Describe your process for making the decision. How could analysis paralysis have affected this process?**
5. **Decision support tools rely on objective, mathematical data. What part do ethics play in using decision support software?**

Independent Challenge 1

Lawrence Media in Nashville, Tennessee, specializes in promotional products for businesses, such as corporate apparel, executive gifts, and product giveaways. You work as an assistant to Ken Lawrence, the founder of the company, and are a member of a group examining sales of the corporate apparel line. First, you analyze monthly sales of shirts, which include t-shirts and polo shirts, including personalized polo shirts. Ken asks you to help him analyze the spreadsheet shown in Figure 5-17.

a. Open the **PS5-IC1.docx** document and follow the steps in the document.
b. Proofread the document carefully to fix any grammar or formatting errors.
c. Submit the document to your instructor as requested.

FIGURE 5-17

	A	B	C	D	E
1					
2	Lawrence Media				
3					
4	T-shirt price	$ 10.00		Total Revenue	$ 18,125
5	Number of t-shirts to sell:	500			
6	Subtotal:	$ 5,000.00		T-shirts	500
7				Polo shirts	1,000
8	Polo shirt price	$ 12.50		Total shirts	1,500
9	Number of shirts to sell:	750			
10	Subtotal:	$ 9,375.00		Maximums	
11				Total shirts	1500
12	Personalized polo shirt price	$ 15.00		T-shirts	1000
13	Number of shirts to sell:	250		Personalized polo shirts	250
14	Subtotal:	$ 3,750.00			

Independent Challenge 2

You work with Carla Marcus, the owner of Sage Realty Services in Winnetka, Illinois. As a member of a team working on the problem of slumping real estate sales, you have been offering Carla suggestions on selling more houses and office space. To improve customer service, Carla wants to use decision support tools to show potential home buyers what they gain when buying a home compared to renting. Part of the spreadsheet she wants to use is shown in Figure 5-18. Carla asks you to help her analyze the spreadsheet and rehearse a what-if scenario.

In the spreadsheet, you enter the amount of appreciation you expect from the house in cell D4. This is the percentage the property should increase in value. The spreadsheet then calculates the net annual cost of home ownership in cell D31. This shows the amount the house is actually costing you when you consider your payments and the increase in value.

a. Open the **PS5-IC2.docx** document and follow the steps in the worksheet.
b. Proofread the document carefully to fix any grammar or formatting errors.
c. Submit the document to your instructor as requested.

FIGURE 5-18

	A	B	C	D	E	F	G
1		Buy or Rent a Home?					
3		Initial Assumption					
4		Estimated annual appreciation in value of home				Decision variables:	
5		Down payment on home		$20,000		Constants:	
6		Estimated closing costs		4,000		Output variables:	
7		Estimated purchase price of home		$285,000			
8		Monthly rent		$1,250			

Real Life Independent Challenge

You can apply the problem-solving techniques you learned in this Part to the decisions you need to make in other parts of your life. Suppose you need to purchase a new computer for your academic or professional work. Complete the following steps to make the purchase decision.

a. In a document or spreadsheet for personal use, list any money you have saved to buy a new computer.
b. List the factors that are important to you, such as computer type (laptop or desktop), monitor type (flat panel, wide screen, or high definition, for example), amount of memory, and so on. These are your decision criteria.
c. Rank how important each factor is in your decision.
d. Assign weights to each factor according to your rankings.
e. Gather information about available computers using online resources or catalogs, for example. List the factors each computer has and compare them to your weighted rankings. In other words, compare each computer against the criteria you selected.
f. The computer with the highest score is the one you should purchase.

Team Challenge

You are working for Colorado Green Builders, a company in Boulder, Colorado, specializing in sustainable building. Overall, the company is committed to solving environmental problems through green building practices. It wants to promote one technique it uses to solve environmental problems in its next ad campaign. Work with your team to identify the specific types of problems green building can solve and to recommend one problem and solution for the ad campaign.

a. Meet as a team to create a list of the types of problems green building practices can solve. Use techniques such as brainstorming or mind mapping.
b. Select one problem to research, and then learn as much as you can about the solution. For example, green building usually involves water conservation and uses techniques such as water harvesting, pond formation, and rain gardens.
c. Meet again as a team to discuss your findings. Using the techniques discussed in this Part, select one problem and solution for Colorado Green Builders to promote.

Be the Critic

You are working for Community Wheels, a company in Berkeley, California that provides hybrid and electric vehicles for short-term rental in the Berkeley and San Francisco area. Community Wheels is analyzing its expenses and deciding which ones to reduce. To compare alternatives, they have created the chart shown in Figure 5-19. Analyze the chart, noting its weaknesses, and send a list of the weaknesses to your instructor.

FIGURE 5-19

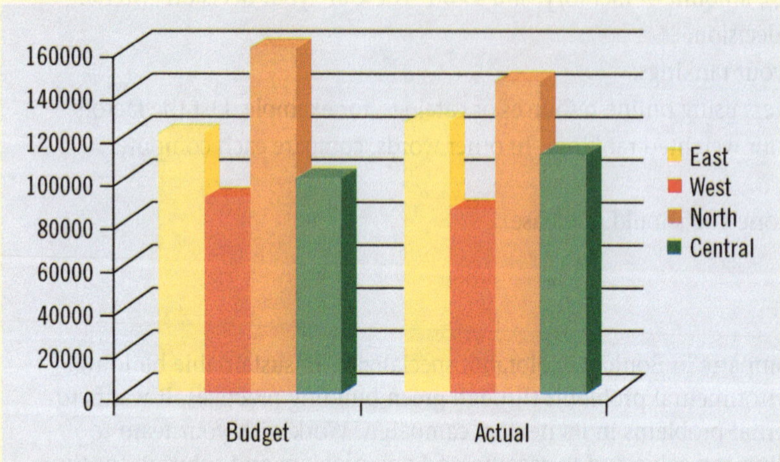

Glossary

5 Whys A problem-solving approach that involves looking at a problem and asking "why?" or "what was the cause of this situation?" at least five times.

Action plan A plan that summarizes the activities the group and other members of the organization agree to perform to make sure the project succeeds.

Adaptive techniques Alternative methods for solving problems. Instead of gathering data, analyzing it, and exploring alternatives systematically, most adaptive techniques involve a combination of intuition, logic, and common sense.

Air time The amount of time available for someone to speak to the group.

Argument (1) A set of one or more claims that support a particular conclusion. (2) A value or cell reference that a function uses in its calculations.

Arithmetic mean The value of a set of data that is usually referred to as the average. The mean is a single value and describes the data in general by showing its central tendency.

Assertion A simple statement that does not include any supporting evidence.

Assumption A proposition or claim that is taken for granted as though it were known to be valid.

Background knowledge The collection of beliefs, facts, experiences, and observations you have amassed during your life.

Bandwagon effect Following the popular opinions and expectations of others, even if you do not share them.

Brainstorming A creativity tool for generating ideas and alternatives. A brainstorming session usually starts by defining a problem, and then listing possible solutions as they occur to you, whether they are obvious, impractical, or far-fetched. The goal is quantity, not quality.

Cause The reason for or the origin (root) of a change, such as customers being unable to afford travel vacations.

Cause-and-effect diagram A popular way to visualize a complex problem. This diagram displays the main problem with lines radiating from the problem like the spine of a fish. These lines show factors that contribute to the problem.

Cell reference A pointer that you include in a formula to tell the spreadsheet where to find the actual data.

Claim A statement that someone says or writes about a topic.

Collective wisdom The shared knowledge and experience a group of people can apply to a problem.

Constant An element of your decision model that is not likely to change much over time.

Convergent thinking Thought processes or methods that narrow options to a manageable set.

Critical thinking The thoughtful, deliberate process of deciding whether you should accept, reject, or reserve judgment about a particular idea. The goal of critical thinking is often to improve choices and reduce the risk of adopting or acting on a flawed assumption.

Crowdsourcing A way of using groups to solve problems. The groups are usually online communities, such as members of a blog or visitors to a Web site, called a crowd. An organization broadcasts a problem to the crowd as an open call for solutions. The crowd submits solutions, and then sorts through them, finding the best ones. The organization selects and owns the ultimate solution, and sometimes rewards members of the crowd.

Dashboard A window that graphically summarizes information about how a business is operating.

Decision A choice you make when faced with a set of options or alternatives.

Decision balance sheet A formal way of organizing an idea's costs and benefits.

Decision model One or more formulas that includes all of the relevant variables and calculates a result.

Decision support system (DSS) Interactive software designed to help you compile useful information from raw data, documents, and business knowledge.

Decision tree A support tool that models decisions using a tree-like diagram. Each branch of the tree represents a different option and its associated benefits, costs, and likelihood.

Decision variable A value that could change and affect the results.

Deductive reasoning Reasoning that takes an argument from general observations or premises to a specific conclusion. If the premises are true, then you assume the conclusion is valid.

Divergent thinking Thought processes or methods used to generate ideas.

Equivocation Using ambiguous or vague words in an argument.

Evaluation criteria The variables that drive your decisions.

Fact A claim that is considered to be true.

Factual matter A claim about which you can collect and analyze data. This term suggests that you are not certain the claim is a fact, but could prove or disprove if necessary.

Fallacy An invalid argument that is presented so that it appears valid.

Fatal flaw An aspect of an idea that would make it unacceptable for some reason.

Group Two or more people who interact with each other, share expectations and obligations, and develop a common identity as a group.

Group dynamics The way that people work and interact with each other.

Groupthink When groups become so cohesive that the members minimize conflict and support consensus without critically considering the merits of ideas and decisions.

Impact analysis A way of evaluating the effects of an idea or alternative.

Indicators Words that signal the speaker is stating a premise or a conclusion.

Inductive reasoning Reasoning that attempts to draw a broad conclusion from specific examples or premises.

Intuition Your knowledge of something without having to discover or learn it; typically your first reaction to a problem or question. When you solve a problem intuitively, you react immediately and instinctively, without following a particular procedure.

Issue Any controversial subject that you discuss, dispute, or review. An issue is different from a simple topic of conversation because it raises questions or concerns.

Logistics How resources such as information and people are provided where they are needed.

Mashup A Web application that combines features or information from more than one source.

Median The value of a set of data that separates the higher values from the lower values.

Mode The value in a set of data that occurs most frequently. The mode does not have to be a unique number.

Model To create a numeric representation of the situation.

Normalization A way to make all of the data consistent with your decision model.

Opinion A claim that someone believes is true.

Organizational memory The history and culture that a group must function in, including the various processes, personalities, and subtleties of how the organization operates.

Outlier A value that is extremely high or low, or an experience that is extremely good or bad.

Output variable A value in the results that could change if the decision variables change.

Pecking order A hierarchy; the organization of people at different ranks in an administrative body.

Premise What you claim or contend.

Problem In an organization, an obstacle that stands in the way of achieving a desired goal. In short, a problem is the difference between the current state and where you want to be.

Problem owner The person who has a problem that needs to be solved.

Problem statement A clear, concise description of the problem and the effect you expect from the solution.

Risk An exposure to a chance of loss or damage.

Root-cause analysis A study that determines the real basis for the problems that you solve.

Self-serving bias Persuading yourself to see data as you most want it to appear.

Social conditioning Conditioning that encourages you to accept the beliefs, traditions, and values of your social group. Social conditioning helps you feel part of the greater whole, but it can also prevent you from considering unpopular alternatives.

Sound argument A valid argument with true premises.

Stakeholder A person who is affected by a problem or decision or whose involvement you need to resolve the matter.

Standard deviation A measure of the variability of a set of data.

Superman complex When a person or group develops a sense of invulnerability.

Symptom Evidence of a change, such as a decrease in revenue.

Synergy When two or more people work together to produce something greater than the sum of their individual efforts.

Systematic Doing something such as solving a problem in a methodical and organized manner. Systematic problem solving takes a reasoned, rational approach and is appropriate for larger, more complicated problems or situations that involve a lot of risk.

Team A group of people who organize themselves to work cooperatively on a common objective.

Three Pile method A technique for reducing ideas to a manageable number.

Valid argument An argument with a conclusion that logically follows from the premises.

What-if analysis A method of analyzing data that allows you to study how changing one or more of the input variables would affect the output.

Worst-case scenario A situation or conclusion that could not be any worse; the worst possible outcome.

Index

5 Whys, **Problem-Solving 10**

A

action plans, **Problem-Solving 88**, Problem-Solving 89

Adam, John A., Problem-Solving 65

adaptive techniques, Problem-Solving 38–39

agreements, building sustainable, Problem-Solving 88–89

air time, **Problem-Solving 86**

alternatives, developing, Problem-Solving 28–29

alternatives, rating, Problem-Solving 30–31

Amazon Kindle, Problem-Solving 66–67

analytical hierarchy matrix, Problem-Solving 30–31

analyzing
- data, Problem-Solving 26–27
- problems, Problem-Solving 4–5

Apple Numbers, Problem-Solving 114

area charts, Problem-Solving 112

arguments, **Problem-Solving 50**, **Problem-Solving 104**
- assessing credibility of, Problem-Solving 54–55
- exploring weaknesses in, Problem-Solving 56–57
- identifying, Problem-Solving 52–53
- slippery-slope, Problem-Solving 60–61
- valid, sound, Problem-Solving 54

arithmetic mean, **Problem-Solving 102**

assertions, **Problem-Solving 52**

assessing argument credibility, Problem-Solving 54–55

assumptions, **Problem-Solving 56**

Aston, Adam, Problem-Solving 111

B

background knowledge, **Problem-Solving 54**

bandwagon effect
- avoiding, Problem-Solving 17
- described, **Problem-Solving 16**

bar charts, Problem-Solving 112, Problem-Solving 113

biases, avoiding, Problem-Solving 16–17

Blink, the Power of Thinking Without Thinking **(Gladwell)**, **Problem-Solving 39**

books, electronic, Problem-Solving 66–67

botnets, Problem-Solving 33

brainstorming
- described, **Problem-Solving 28**, Problem-Solving 29
- reverse, Problem-Solving 80

Bubbl.us, Problem-Solving 79

business mashups, Problem-Solving 42

C

cause-and-effect diagrams, **Problem-Solving 10**, Problem-Solving 11

causes, **Problem-Solving 10**
- determining, Problem-Solving 10–11
- separating from effects, Problem-Solving 62–63

cell reference, **Problem-Solving 104**

Challenge.gov, Problem-Solving 18–19

charts
- types, Problem-Solving 112
- using to display data, Problem-Solving 113
- viewing data in different ways, Problem-Solving 27

circular reasoning, Problem-Solving 60–61

claims, **Problem-Solving 50**

closure, reaching, Problem-Solving 82–83

collaboration through crowdsourcing, Problem-Solving 18–19

collective wisdom, **Problem-Solving 28**

command style, Problem-Solving 82–83

communicating with large groups, Problem-Solving 86–87

composition errors, Problem-Solving 62–63

consensus, building, Problem-Solving 86

consensus decisions, Problem-Solving 77, Problem-Solving 82

constants, **Problem-Solving 106**, Problem-Solving 107

consultative approach, Problem-Solving 82

consumer mashups, Problem-Solving 42

convergent thinking
- described, **Problem-Solving 80**
- using, Problem-Solving 80–81

cost-benefit analyses, Problem-Solving 80

costs
- vs. benefits, Problem-Solving 40–41, Problem-Solving 80
- of problems, Problem-Solving 10

creating
- decision trees, Problem-Solving 110–111
- effective problem statements, Problem-Solving 8–9
- ethical solutions, Problem-Solving 40–41

mashups, Problem-Solving 42–43
mind maps, Problem-Solving 28–29
sustainable agreements, Problem-Solving 88–89
creative, and critical thinking, Problem-Solving 58–59
credibility, assessing argument, Problem-Solving 54–55
crisis management, Problem-Solving 15
criteria, evaluation, Problem-Solving 30
critical thinking, **Problem-Solving 50**
becoming critical thinker, Problem-Solving 64–65
and feeling, Problem-Solving 59
overcoming obstacles to, Problem-Solving 58–59
steps in (fig.), Problem-Solving 51
critics, and cynics, Problem-Solving 64
Crocker, Stephen, Problem-Solving 77
crowdsourcing, **Problem-Solving 18**
cynics, and critics, Problem-Solving 64

D

Damasio, Antonio, Problem-Solving 59
dashboards, **Problem-Solving 42**
data
assigning numeric values to, Problem-Solving 100–101
describing objectively, Problem-Solving 102–103
gathering, analyzing, Problem-Solving 26–27
types to collect (table), Problem-Solving 27
using graphics to display, Problem-Solving 112–113
viewing in different ways, Problem-Solving 27
decision balance sheet, **Problem-Solving 80**, Problem-Solving 81
decision model, **Problem-Solving 100**, Problem-Solving 101
decision support system (DSS)
described, **Problem-Solving 98**
understanding, Problem-Solving 98–99
decision tree
creating, Problem-Solving 110–111
described, **Problem-Solving 110**
decision variable, **Problem-Solving 106**, Problem-Solving 107, Problem-Solving 108
decisions, **Problem-Solving 2**
decision support system (DSS), Problem-Solving 98–99
modeling quantitatively, Problem-Solving 100–101
questions to ask before making (fig.), Problem-Solving 41
staggering, Problem-Solving 38
weighing factors, Problem-Solving 108–109
working with formulas, functions, Problem-Solving 104–105
deductive reasoning
avoiding fallacies, Problem-Solving 60–61
described, **Problem-Solving 52**, Problem-Solving 53
defining
problems, Problem-Solving 3
success, Problem-Solving 36
departments, creating new, Problem-Solving 98–99
describing data objectively, Problem-Solving 102–103
diagrams
cause-and-effect, Problem-Solving 10–11
decision, Problem-Solving 99
displaying data using graphics, Problem-Solving 112–113
divergent thinking, **Problem-Solving 78**
diversity, Problem-Solving 74
documenting data, information sources, Problem-Solving 26
Doodle scheduling tool, Problem-Solving 90–91
DSS. *See* decision support system (DSS)
dubious assumptions, Problem-Solving 56

E

e-books, Problem-Solving 66–67
Edison, Thomas, Problem-Solving 64
effects, separating from causes, Problem-Solving 62–63
egocentric thinking, avoiding, Problem-Solving 58
electronic books, Problem-Solving 66–67
Eli Lilly, Problem-Solving 13
e-mail spam, and unintended consequences, Problem-Solving 33
equivocations, **Problem-Solving 60**
error detection and group dynamics, Problem-Solving 74
ethical solutions, developing, Problem-Solving 40–41
evaluating
argument weaknesses, Problem-Solving 56–57
options, Problem-Solving 30–31
evaluation criteria, **Problem-Solving 30**
Exploratree thinking guides, Problem-Solving 79

F

facts
described, **Problem-Solving 50**
vs. opinions (fig.), Problem-Solving 51
factual matters, **Problem-Solving 50**
fallacies, **Problem-Solving 60**
avoiding deductive, Problem-Solving 60–61
avoiding inductive, Problem-Solving 62–63
false causes, Problem-Solving 62
feeling, and critical thinking, Problem-Solving 59
formatting formulas, Problem-Solving 104

formulas
entering in spreadsheets, Problem-Solving 105
working with, Problem-Solving 104–105
free writing, Problem-Solving 78
functions, working with, Problem-Solving 104–105

G

Galileo, Problem-Solving 111
Gates, Robert, Problem-Solving 77
gathering data, Problem-Solving 26–27
Gladwell, Malcolm, Problem-Solving 39
Gnumeric spreadsheet program, Problem-Solving 114
Google Calendar, Problem-Solving 90–91
Google spreadsheet, Problem-Solving 114–115
GoToMeeting, Problem-Solving 86
graphics
information, Problem-Solving 111
using to display data, Problem-Solving 112–113
group decision methods (table), Problem-Solving 83
group dynamics, **Problem-Solving 74**
avoiding group traps, Problem-Solving 84–85
building sustainable agreements, Problem-Solving 88–89
reaching closure, Problem-Solving 82–83
understanding, Problem-Solving 74–75
working with large groups, Problem-Solving 86–87
group traps, avoiding, Problem-Solving 84–85
groups, **Problem-Solving 74**
evolving to teams, Problem-Solving 76–77
solving problems (crowdsourcing), Problem-Solving 18
working with large, Problem-Solving 86–87
groupthink
described, Problem-Solving 77, **Problem-Solving 84**
looking out for, Problem-Solving 84–85
guesstimating, Problem-Solving 65
Guesstimation (Weinstein & Adam), Problem-Solving 65

H

Haidt, Jonathan, Problem-Solving 59
hasty generalizations, Problem-Solving 62
Howe, Jeff, Problem-Solving 18
humility, intellectual, Problem-Solving 64

I

identifying
arguments, Problem-Solving 52–53
key variables, Problem-Solving 34
problem symptoms, Problem-Solving 8–9, Problem-Solving 12
risks, Problem-Solving 14–15
impact analysis, **Problem-Solving 80**, Problem-Solving 81
implementing solutions, Problem-Solving 32–33
indicators, **Problem-Solving 52**
inductive reasoning
avoiding fallacies, Problem-Solving 62–63
described, **Problem-Solving 52**, Problem-Solving 53
information
gathering, Problem-Solving 5
graphics, Problem-Solving 111
InnoCentive, Problem-Solving 13
intellectual humility, Problem-Solving 64
interdependencies, identifying, Problem-Solving 12
interrelationships, Problem-Solving 26
intuition, **Problem-Solving 2**
issues, **Problem-Solving 50**

J

Joblighted, Problem-Solving 43
Johnson & Johnson crisis management, Problem-Solving 15
journaling, Problem-Solving 78
junk e-mail, Problem-Solving 33

K

Kindle, Problem-Solving 66–67
Kinicki, Angelo, Problem-Solving 75

L

Lakhani, Karim, Problem-Solving 13
leadership, star power vs. team effectiveness, Problem-Solving 75
Lehrer, Jonah, Problem-Solving 59
line charts, Problem-Solving 112, Problem-Solving 113
logistics
described, **Problem-Solving 86**
managing, Problem-Solving 86–87

M

majority rule, Problem-Solving 83
managing
crises, Problem-Solving 15
logistics, Problem-Solving 86–87
risks, Problem-Solving 14–15
solutions, Problem-Solving 34–35
Mann, Tony, Problem-Solving 65
Masher tool, Problem-Solving 43
mashups
creating, Problem-Solving 42–43
described, **Problem-Solving 42**
median, **Problem-Solving 102**
meetings
online, Problem-Solving 86, Problem-Solving 87
scheduling, Problem-Solving 90–91

memory, organizational, **Problem-Solving 74**, Problem-Solving 75
Microsoft Excel, Problem-Solving 114–115
mind mapping, Problem-Solving 78, Problem-Solving 79
mind maps, developing, Problem-Solving 28–29
MindMeister, Problem-Solving 79
Mitroff, Ian, Problem-Solving 15
mode, **Problem-Solving 102**
modeling
decisions (do's and don'ts), Problem-Solving 103
decisions quantitatively, Problem-Solving 100–101
monitoring solutions, Problem-Solving 34–35

N

NASA's Stardust@Home, Problem-Solving 18–19
National Science Foundation (NSF), Problem-Solving 13
normalization, Problem-Solving 58, **Problem-Solving 108**, Problem-Solving 109
"not invented here," avoiding, Problem-Solving 16
numeric values, assigning to data, Problem-Solving 100–101

O

online
meetings, Problem-Solving 86, Problem-Solving 87
scheduling tools, Problem-Solving 90–91
open source science, Problem-Solving 13
OpenOffice Calc spreadsheet tool, Problem-Solving 114
opinions
described, **Problem-Solving 50**
vs. facts (fig.), Problem-Solving 51
order of operations, Problem-Solving 104, Problem-Solving 105
organizational memory, **Problem-Solving 74**, Problem-Solving 75
outliers, **Problem-Solving 58**
output variable, **Problem-Solving 106**
overhead, organizing, Problem-Solving 84
owners. *See* problem owners

P

pace, managing, Problem-Solving 88
pecking order
and assumed roles, Problem-Solving 77
described, **Problem-Solving 76**
Phelps, Elizabeth, Problem-Solving 59
Phoenix Suns, Problem-Solving 75
pie charts, Problem-Solving 112, Problem-Solving 113
plans
action, **Problem-Solving 88**
developing, Problem-Solving 32
plurality, Problem-Solving 83
positive outcome bias, Problem-Solving 16–17
premises, **Problem-Solving 52**
priorities, and pecking order, Problem-Solving 76
probabilities, estimating, Problem-Solving 110
problem owners, **Problem-Solving 6**
problem solving
adaptive techniques, Problem-Solving 38–39
in a blink, Problem-Solving 39
developing alternatives, Problem-Solving 28–29
ethical solutions, developing, Problem-Solving 40–41
evaluating options, Problem-Solving 30–31
solutions, implementing, Problem-Solving 32–33
solutions, verifying, Problem-Solving 36–37
traps, avoiding, Problem-Solving 16–17
understanding, Problem-Solving 2–3
problem statements
described, **Problem-Solving 8**
developing effective, Problem-Solving 8–9
problems, **Problem-Solving 2**
analyzing, Problem-Solving 4–5
defining, Problem-Solving 3
determining causes, Problem-Solving 10–11
simplifying complex, Problem-Solving 12–13
working with owners, stakeholders, Problem-Solving 6–7
promoting your solution to problem, Problem-Solving 6, Problem-Solving 7

R

range voting, Problem-Solving 83
ranking subproblems, Problem-Solving 12
rating
alternatives, Problem-Solving 30–31
subjective data, Problem-Solving 100–101
reaching closure, Problem-Solving 82–83
reasoning, deductive and inductive, Problem-Solving 52
reminders, sending, Problem-Solving 90
reverse brainstorming, Problem-Solving 80
risk/reward ratio, Problem-Solving 14–15
risks
described, **Problem-Solving 14**
identifying and managing, Problem-Solving 14–15

roles, pecking order and assumed, Problem-Solving 77

root-cause analysis, **Problem-Solving 10**

S

scatter charts, Problem-Solving 112, Problem-Solving 113

scenarios, testing, Problem-Solving 106–107

scheduling tools, online, Problem-Solving 90–91

self-serving bias, **Problem-Solving 16**

simplifying complex problems, Problem-Solving 12–13

Skype, Problem-Solving 86

slippery-slope fallacies, Problem-Solving 60–61

social conditioning, **Problem-Solving 58**

software, mind mapping, Problem-Solving 79

solutions
- delaying, deferring, Problem-Solving 38
- developing ethical, Problem-Solving 40–41
- implementing, Problem-Solving 32–33
- monitoring, managing, Problem-Solving 34–35
- verifying, Problem-Solving 36–37

sound arguments, **Problem-Solving 54**, Problem-Solving 55

spam, Problem-Solving 33

Spradlin, Dwayne, Problem-Solving 13

spreadsheet tools, Problem-Solving 114–115

spreadsheets, entering formulas in, Problem-Solving 105

staggering decisions, Problem-Solving 38

stakeholders
- described, **Problem-Solving 6**
- notifying of solution, Problem-Solving 32–33

standard deviation, **Problem-Solving 102**

star power vs. team effectiveness, Problem-Solving 75

stress, avoiding, Problem-Solving 84

success, defining, Problem-Solving 36

SUM function, Problem-Solving 104

Superman complex, **Problem-Solving 84**

SWOT (strengths, weaknesses, opportunities, and threat) analysis, Problem-Solving 84–85

symptoms
- described, **Problem-Solving 10**
- identifying, Problem-Solving 12

synergy, **Problem-Solving 76**

systematic, **Problem-Solving 2**

T

team effectiveness vs. star power, Problem-Solving 75

teams
- described, **Problem-Solving 76**
- evolving from groups to, Problem-Solving 76–77

TechCrunch, Problem-Solving 66

testing to reduce risks, Problem-Solving 14

thinkers, becoming critical, Problem-Solving 64–65

thinking
- convergent, Problem-Solving 80–81
- divergent, Problem-Solving 78
- groupthink, Problem-Solving 77

"thin-slicing", Problem-Solving 39

three-pile method, **Problem-Solving 80**

tools
- decision support, Problem-Solving 98–99
- spreadsheet, Problem-Solving 114–115

Tufte, Edward, Problem-Solving 111

Tylenol crisis, Johnson & Johnson, Problem-Solving 15

U

unintended consequences, Problem-Solving 33

V

valid arguments, **Problem-Solving 54**, Problem-Solving 55

variables
- decision, **Problem-Solving 106**, Problem-Solving 107, Problem-Solving 108
- identifying key, Problem-Solving 34
- normalizing, Problem-Solving 107–108
- output, Problem-Solving 106
- rating subjective, Problem-Solving 100

verifying solutions, Problem-Solving 36–37

voting methods, Problem-Solving 82

W

Web applications, mashups, **Problem-Solving 42**

Weinstein, Lawrence, Problem-Solving 65

what-if analyses
- described, **Problem-Solving 106**
- performing, Problem-Solving 106–107

worst-case scenarios, **Problem-Solving 36**

X

XMind, Problem-Solving 79